The Creative Curriculum for Early Childhood

Third Edition

Diane Trister Dodge
Laura J. Colker

Contributing Writers

Marilyn Goldhammer
Judy Jablon
Carol Copple

Illustrated by
Jennifer Barrett

TEACHING STRATEGIES INC.

Washington, DC

Cover design and layout
Elisabeth Glover Hudgins

Illustrations on pp. 251-254
Julie Headland

Published by

Teaching Strategies, Inc.
P.O. Box 42243
Washington, DC 20015

Distributed by

Gryphon House, Inc.
P.O. Box 275
Mt. Rainier, MD 20712

ISBN 1-879537-06-0

Library of Congress Catalog Card Number: 91-67416

Preface

The Creative Curriculum for Early Childhood evolved over many years as I worked with teachers in a variety of early childhood settings. It did not begin as a purposeful effort to write an early childhood curriculum. Rather, in my role as an education specialist and trainer, I worked with teachers to assess what was happening in their classrooms and to enhance their teaching skills. I met with many creative and innovative teachers from whom I learned a great deal. But too often I saw tired and discouraged teachers who were struggling to provide the best for young children.

There were many reasons for the problems I observed. In classrooms where teachers were using a content-oriented curriculum, I noted a tendency to emphasize teacher-directed activities and to allocate less time for free choice and child-initiated play. Teachers worked hard at "teaching" and focused less on facilitating children's learning. To individualize the program, some teachers tested children and then built their curriculum around preparing children for these tests. They focused on skills and deficits and failed to see the whole child.

I was also distressed by the paperwork requirements many teachers were obliged to meet. Elaborate lesson plans outlined everything they did on a given day, leaving little room to be creative and to respond to children's immediate interests. Often plans were unchanged from one year to the next, regardless of their effectiveness.

In response to pressures from parents and administrators to "prepare children for first grade," some teachers were using worksheets and teaching the calendar, letters, and numbers, whether or not the children were interested or actually learning meaningful concepts. Although aware that it was difficult to get children to stick to these tasks and to listen, they persevered even when faced with inattentive children. Many of these teachers were not enjoying their work; their innate creativity was stifled. As a result, they were failing to promote self-esteem, creativity, and a desire to learn in children.

Many teachers I worked with wanted to allow more time in the daily program for self-selected activities. They understood that children learn most effectively when they can explore and make discoveries using concrete materials that are of interest to them. These teachers were not always successful when they tried to make changes in their program. They complained that children didn't use the materials as they were intended to be used and that they often wandered from one activity to another, unable to sustain their play. Some teachers found that children had difficulty making choices and didn't take care of materials or return them to their appropriate places. These experiences were discouraging to teachers who wanted to make changes in their program.

An Environmental Focus

My first strategy for addressing these problems was to help teachers look at the classroom environment and how it was failing to support them. Classroom organization was often working against the teacher's goals for children. The dramatic changes in children's behavior each time we rearranged a classroom convinced many teachers with whom I worked that room arrangement is a powerful teaching tool—one that can support teachers and free them to engage in more positive interactions with children.

Once the environment was organized and arranged to support free choice and active learning, we began to focus on the learning potential in each area of the room and outdoors. By stressing interest areas instead of content or skills, we kept the focus on the environment where learning takes place. The workshops I developed during this time stressed how to set up interest areas, how children can learn in each area, and the teacher's role in promoting learning and growth. Documenting the workshops led to the idea of developing a set of curriculum modules, each focusing on a distinct area of the preschool classroom.

Development of the *Creative Curriculum*

The Creative Curriculum for Early Childhood emerged from this focus on the environment as a set of modules and trainers' guides. Originally published in 1979, it included four interest areas: Blocks, Table Toys, Art, and the House Corner. In 1986 and 1987, teachers in three Head Start programs received training on the curriculum and field-tested it in their classrooms. They provided us with suggestions for enhancing and expanding the content. In 1988, the second edition of the *Creative Curriculum* was published. The original four books were revised and merged into one volume with a module on Setting the Stage and three additional interest area modules: Sand and Water, Library, and Outdoors.

Since 1988, the *Creative Curriculum* has been implemented in a wide range of early childhood programs and public schools across the United States, Canada, and in Australia. Teachers and trainers respond positively to the practical approach that clearly explains how to organize the environment to support children's social development and active learning. For many teachers the curriculum validates what they have always believed about appropriate practice. No matter what other curriculum models teachers use, the *Creative Curriculum* can serve as the foundation for any program based on child development theory. Because we know that young children learn best through interactions with the physical and social environment, the curriculum keeps the focus on the environment. By continually changing and enriching the environment, teachers can support learning and creativity in children. The approach defined in the *Creative Curriculum* frees teachers to respond to children's interests and explorations. It emphasizes establishing a partnership with parents and offers practical ideas for explaining the curriculum to parents.

The Third Edition

Good early childhood teachers continually adapt and expand the curriculum they are using in order to respond to the individual needs and interests of the children they teach. So too does a curriculum need to be dynamic in nature, responding to changing priorities and evolving concerns. In this latest edition of the curriculum, we have attempted to address these needs.

Since the previous edition was completed in 1988, much attention in the professional literature has been focused on emerging literacy, developmentally appropriate assessment, and the role of technology in the early childhood classroom. This revised version addresses these topics.

In addition, through my work with teachers in using the *Creative Curriculum*, my own views have expanded over time. Thus in this version, I have sought to incorporate some of these ideas, such as the importance of dramatic play in children's lives and how children with disabilities can be included in the classroom.

The third edition, therefore, is an attempt to make the *Creative Curriculum* timely as well as relevant for the preschool and kindergarten teacher. The *Curriculum* is divided into two parts. Part I, Setting the Stage, has two new chapters. "Meeting the Needs of Individual Children" addresses screening and appropriate assessment and suggests ways that the program can be modified to include children with disabilities. "Organizing Children's Learning" explains the relationship of play to academic learning and shows how teachers can promote emergent literacy, math, science and social studies in each of the interest areas. Part II, Interest Areas, now includes three new modules: Music and Movement, Cooking, and Computers. A final addition is the Child Development and Learning Checklist designed to assist teachers in assessing each child's growth based on the goals and objectives of the *Creative Curriculum*, in order to plan appropriate learning experiences for every child in the program.

It is my hope that this latest edition will serve you, the children you teach, and their parents as well.

Diane Trister Dodge
December 1991

Acknowledgments

The list of individuals and organizations that have contributed to the development of this curriculum has grown since the first and second editions were published. Because *The Creative Curriculum for Early Childhood* describes the practices of many skilled early childhood educators, I want to begin by acknowledging the important work of the thousands of teachers and trainers I have met over almost three decades—people who have helped me grow professionally and enabled me to continually expand this curriculum.

Two government grants made it possible for me to document my work with teachers and make revisions to the *Creative Curriculum*. I am indebted to Dr. Pamela Coughlin, Clennie H. Murphy, and E. Dollie Wolverton of the National Head Start Bureau, who believed strongly that Head Start programs should be offered a choice in selecting a developmentally appropriate curriculum. They enabled me to field-test the curriculum in three Head Start programs from 1986 to 1987. Two skilled trainers, Peter Pizzolongo and Ruth Uhlmann, provided training and support to staff at the Franklin-Vance-Warren program in Henderson, North Carolina; Operation Breakthrough in Durham, North Carolina; and Fauquier County Community Action Program in Warrenton, Virginia. Their experiences and feedback were invaluable in expanding the curriculum.

In 1990, through a Discretionary Grant from the U.S. Department of Health and Human Services, Administration for Children, Youth, and Families, I began a three-year project focused on extending the curriculum into the early grades. In the initial phase of the project, we have been working with Head Start, pre-kindergarten, and kindergarten teachers. This project would not be possible without the support of three individuals representing the agencies that are collaborating with Teaching Strategies: Helen Taylor, Executive Director of the National Child Day Care Association, Inc., which is the lead grantee on the project; Beverly Langford-Thomas, Executive Director of the District of Columbia Public Schools Head Start Program; and Maurice Sykes, Director of Early Childhood, District of Columbia Public Schools.

Several individuals have been invaluable in the development of the *Creative Curriculum* and they deserve special recognition. Dr. Laura J. Colker is listed as a co-author because of the substantial contributions she has made to the second and third editions of the curriculum. She drafted the new modules on Cooking and Computers and helped refine many of the interest-area modules. Marilyn Goldhammer was a contributing writer on the second edition, and her ideas and expertise remain an important part of the curriculum. Judy Jablon has been my co-trainer and colleague in extending the curriculum into the early grades. She worked with me to develop the chapter on Organizing Children's Learning and provided input on the entire curriculum. Carol Copple drafted the module on Music and Movement and was instrumental in designing the *Creative Curriculum* Child Development and Learning Checklist. Kris Hansen and Melissa Morrison contributed to the content of the Outdoors module, and Doris Ablard helped us show how the curriculum could be adapted for children with disabilities.

We refined the curriculum after receiving input from several educators who reviewed and critiqued our drafts. I am especially indebted to Dr. Jenni Klein, whose wise counsel has guided my thinking since I first met her in 1975, and to Dr. Sara Smilansky whose research on dramatic play inspired my thinking about the true value of the house corner. Dr. Judith Rothchild-Stolberg and Dr. Mary Lewis generously shared their perspectives and encouraged my work. Elaine Robey reviewed several drafts of the Computer module and Sherrie Rudick gave equal attention to the Cooking module. Dr. Herman Axelrod and Kris Hansen critiqued the sections on adapting the curriculum for children with special needs. The work of Dr. Samuel Meisels was invaluable to us in designing our own Child Development and Learning Checklist. And I owe a special note of thanks to Austine Fowler, Early Childhood Education Supervisor in the District of Columbia Public Schools and the pre-kindergarten and kindergarten teachers at Marie Reed and Katie C. Lewis Elementary Schools who reviewed the final drafts and implemented the curriculum in their classrooms.

The format and design of this third edition of the *Creative Curriculum* are substantially improved because of the involvement of several talented individuals: Jennifer Barrett, who illustrated the curriculum; Elisabeth Glover Hudgins, who designed the layout and cover; David Riley, who helped us conceptualize a new organization for the book; Martha Cooley, who edited the manuscript; Debra Foulks, who coordinated production; and Frank Harvey, for word processing.

To all these people and the many others who helped make the *Creative Curriculum* a reality, I remain forever grateful.

CONTENTS

Introduction

What is an early childhood curriculum? Ask this question and you'll hear many different answers. Some people will refer to a book of activities that precisely outlines what, when, and how children should be taught. Others will say more broadly that "curriculum is everything": an early childhood teacher simply needs to follow children's interests and build on what happens each day.

Teaching young children is a creative process, one that lies somewhere between these two extremes. Early childhood teachers do not need to follow a prescribed course of study as might someone teaching adults a class in biology or history. Nor can teachers simply react to what happens each day, without any goals or plans in mind. Rather, early childhood teachers depend on a curriculum framework that sets forth the program's philosophy, goals, and objectives for children as well as guidelines for teaching that address all aspects of a child's development: socio-emotional, cognitive, and physical. An early childhood curriculum provides the framework for what actually happens in a planned environment where children interact with materials, their peers, and adults. The primary teaching goal is to help young children use the environment productively and see themselves as capable learners—as individuals who are developing the skills and understandings that will enable them to make sense of the world and to succeed in it.

Teaching young children in the context just described requires spontaneity—the ability to see and use everyday opportunities to help children solve problems, explore new materials, and find answers to questions. It also requires constant thinking and decision making on the part of the teacher:

- Should I intervene or should I step back and let the child try to solve a problem?

- What questions can I ask to help the child think through a solution?

- Is the child ready for these materials, or will they prove frustrating?

- Is the room arrangement working, or do I need to modify it?

There is general agreement among experts that a good curriculum for young children must be developmentally appropriate.* This means that the quality of the program will be defined in large measure by the extent to which the environment, activities, and interactions are rooted in the teacher's understanding of developmental stages and knowledge of each child. The decisions teachers make in planning the curriculum and in reacting spontaneously to what happens each day are therefore based on a knowledge of normal child development and what is known about each child's interests, abilities, needs, and background.

To plan appropriately, teachers must find answers to questions such as these:

- What can I expect of children at this stage of development?

- How do children learn best?

- What do I know and what do I need to find out about each child that will help me individualize the program?

---

* See Sue Bredekamp (ed.), *Developmentally Appropriate Practice in Programs Serving Children Birth Through Age 8* (Washington, DC: National Association for the Education of Young Children, 1986).

- What activities and learning materials are appropriate for each child?
- How can I adapt the environment and materials for children with disabilities?
- What role will each child's parents play in the program?

An effective early childhood curriculum offers teachers answers to these questions. It serves as the basic framework, enabling teachers to make appropriate decisions. Inherent in this framework are the following:

- *A statement of philosophy*—the beliefs and theories that guide curriculum development and implementation, including an understanding of how children develop socio-emotionally, cognitively, and physically.
- *Goals and objectives*—the skills, attitudes, and understandings we want children to develop.
- *The physical environment*—specific guidance on the importance of room arrangement and how to select and display materials to support the development of trust, independence, and initiative.
- *The teacher's role*—a clear definition of teaching strategies that promote learning and growth.
- *The parent's role*—a commitment to the joint partnership of parents and teachers in promoting each child's growth and development.

The *Creative Curriculum* offers teachers the guidance, support, and freedom to be creative and responsive to children. Because children learn from their daily interactions with the environment, a carefully organized and rich environment is the foundation for the *Creative Curriculum*. Central to the use of the environment is an understanding of the potential of various materials to enhance learning and teaching, and a knowledge of how these materials meet the developmental needs of young children. By focusing on the developmental progress of each child, the *Creative Curriculum* offers an ideal setting for all children, including those with disabilities.

The *Creative Curriculum* focuses on interest areas. It describes in detail what and how children learn and the teacher's role in using each of the following interest areas to support children's development:

- Blocks
- House Corner
- Table Toys
- Art
- Sand and Water
- Library
- Music and Movement
- Cooking
- Computers
- Outdoors

The *Creative Curriculum* fosters creativity in both children and teachers. Being creative means thinking of new ideas, obtaining information by asking questions, learning through trial and error, and benefiting from mistakes. Children's creativity is supported by an environment that encourages them to try out ideas and to risk making mistakes. Teachers' creativity is supported by a curriculum framework that encourages them to be innovative and responsive to children. By focusing on both teacher and child, the *Creative Curriculum* provides a blueprint for developing an educational setting in which young children can thrive.

Part I
SETTING THE STAGE

I. Philosophy and Theory of the *Creative Curriculum*

The *Creative Curriculum* is rooted in educational philosophy and theory as well as practice. It relies heavily on Erik Erikson's stages of socio-emotional development, Jean Piaget's theories of how children think and learn, and on principles of physical development.

How Children Develop Socially and Emotionally

The theories of Erik Erikson provide a helpful framework for understanding children's socio-emotional development. Erikson defined eight stages of socio-emotional growth from infancy to old age. At each stage people confront particular socio-emotional circumstances that must be addressed. How these situations are handled determines how a person's character and personality develop.

To illustrate, at the first stage of development, children learn to either trust or mistrust their environment. Infants who receive consistent and loving care learn that their environment can be trusted. They trust that they will be fed when they are hungry, changed when they are soiled, and comforted when they are upset. They also learn that when parents go away, they will return. This sense of trust gives children the security to venture out on their own. Independence is an outgrowth of trust.

During the early childhood years children deal with three of the eight stages of socio-emotional growth. They learn:

- to trust others outside their families;
- to gain independence and self-control; and
- to take initiative and assert themselves in socially acceptable ways.

How the Curriculum Supports Trust, Autonomy, and Initiative

The *Creative Curriculum* shows teachers how to foster positive responses to these three stages. The type of environment described in the *Creative Curriculum* helps children develop a sense of trust and belonging. Children can feel safe and encouraged to explore not only materials but also their relationships with peers and adults. They feel important and valued when others listen to them, seek out their ideas, and allow them to express themselves.

The environment encourages both autonomy and self-control. Children learn to handle their feelings in acceptable, socially appropriate ways. When they are encouraged to make decisions for themselves, children experience a sense of control over their lives. They learn that what they say and do is important and has an effect on others.

Competence and initiative are fostered in this type of environment. By setting clear, age-appropriate expectations for behavior and by letting children know what is expected of them, teachers can engender success and minimize frustration. Children's concerns about doing things "right" diminish because they are encouraged to learn from their mistakes, to explore, and to take risks.

Through the *Creative Curriculum*, children's socio-emotional development is enhanced in the ways outlined below.

- *Children develop a sense of trust when teachers:*

  follow a consistent schedule;
  carry through on announced plans and/or promises;
  make contact with each child during the day; and
  make positive comments about children's play activities.

- *Children develop a sense of competence when teachers:*

  reinforce and value their play activities;
  give them developmentally appropriate materials to play with;
  provide them with materials that support and challenge their abilities;
  praise their efforts;
  help channel their frustrations; and
  encourage them to see tasks through to completion.

- *Children develop a sense of initiative when teachers:*

  provide them with ample opportunities for creative expression;
  allow them to explore the environment freely;
  permit them to get messy during sand, water, or art activities;
  encourage make-believe play;
  allow them to work independently; and
  promote problem solving and risk taking.

In sum, the *Creative Curriculum* encourages teachers to recognize the interplay between socio-emotional, cognitive, and physical growth.

How Children Learn to Think

Children learn by doing. Through active involvement with their environment, children attempt to make sense of the world around them. They learn by observing what happens when they interact with materials and other people. They spontaneously engage in activities such as block building, painting, or dramatic play, adding pieces of information to what they already know and thereby generating new understandings. Children learn simple concepts and then use these concepts to grasp more complex ideas.

Concrete and Literal Thinking

Young children view the world concretely, and as they mature, their view changes. What they know at any given point will depend on the first-hand experiences they have had. By interacting with their physical environment (indoor and outdoor) and their social environment (other children and adults), they continually broaden their frame of reference.

For the young child everything is concrete and literal:

- Three-year-old child to parent: "We went on a walk at school today. We were looking for signs of winter, but I only saw one STOP sign."

- Parent reading to a four-year-old: "...and then he bawled him out." Child, incredulously: "You mean he took away all his hair?"

Conclusions about cause and effect also have concrete origins for the young child:

- A three-year-old observes: "Today we are having fish because the teacher is late. Whenever the teacher is late we have fish."

- A four-year-old notices that a friend doesn't want ice cream one night. Later that night, the friend becomes sick. The next day when offered ice cream, the child says, "Yes, because if I don't have ice cream, I'll get sick like Laurie did."

In each case the child has noted certain events and interpreted them in an effort to make sense of the world.

Learning from the Environment

The *Creative Curriculum* builds on Piaget's theories of development in young children. Piaget believed that all children learn through active exploration of their environment, beginning in infancy. By grasping, rolling, pounding, smelling, sucking, and crawling around and over everything they come in contact with, infants and toddlers discover that objects have weight, volume, color, and texture.

During the preschool and kindergarten years, children add to what they have learned in these early explorations. As children's learning expands, the environment plays a critical role. The richer the environment, the more concrete opportunities there are for children to learn by interacting with materials and people. The teacher's role is to create an environment that invites children to observe, to be active, to make choices, and to experiment.

Development of Language

Language development begins during the first few months of life. Infants respond to the language in their world. They listen to the sounds they hear around them and notice differences in timing, rhythm, and pitch. Infants need to hear lots of speech before they develop their own. By three or four months, infants begin to produce their own sounds. They coo and babble. At around 9 to 12 months, babbling peaks. At 10 to 15 months, most infants can understand and respond to a number of words. They start using words to name objects and people in their world: "Dada," "car." They may say "doggy" for every animal with four legs. Children begin to make sentences by putting two words together to describe an action ("me go," "my ball"). They soon learn to add adjectives ("my big ball") and negatives ("no go outside"). By listening to how adults and older children use words, young children gradually expand their vocabularies.

Preschool children supplement what they have learned through these early experiences. They use words as symbols for people, things, movements, feelings, and ideas. They develop the ability to talk about their observations and experiences as they explore their world. Their environment becomes larger and richer as they learn to understand others and express their ideas more effectively.

However, the world they learn about through language makes sense only if the words are tied to real life experiences. Young children must have first-hand contact with the world they hear about if they are to understand what is being said.

Learning to Classify

During the early childhood years, children also begin to think in terms of classes, numbers, and relationships. They group things on the basis of one or more classifying schemes:

- descriptive classifications (size, color, shape, or other attributes);

- generic classifications (general categories, such as animals, transportation vehicles, shells, or plants); and

- relational classifications (function or association, such as cup and saucer or firefighter and firetruck).

These groupings are made as children physically manipulate real objects and discuss their actions. The ability to classify and organize information is a critical thinking skill that enables children to make sense of their experiences. Their early efforts to understand how things are related may not always be correct, but their ideas provide evidence of their thinking processes. For example, when a child says to the father of a friend, "You can't be a policeman, you're a daddy," she is letting us know that she thinks that people who are classified as "daddies" can't also belong to another group labeled "policemen."

Developing Abstract Thinking Skills

Through the development of language and the ability to think in terms of classes, numbers, and relationships, children acquire the foundation for such abstract skills as reading, writing, and computing. Young children need many opportunities to play with real objects as they use language, symbolize, and classify. The *Creative Curriculum* emphasizes children's direct manipulation of materials so they can build repertoires of experience. The curriculum gives teachers an approach to helping children learn to solve problems by providing each child with information-gathering and questioning strategies. Children who are good problem solvers are better prepared for our increasingly complex world. They are more likely to be flexible in their thinking and able to use a variety of problem-solving techniques.

How Children Develop Physically

Physical development is sometimes taken for granted in early childhood education. We assume children will progress through a predictable sequence of stages and acquire predictable skills. To a certain extent this is true; however, a number of factors can promote or slow down physical development.

Normal physical development relies on good health, proper nutrition, and a safe environment. Proper nutrition, beginning during the prenatal months, is crucial to both mental and physical development. During these years children need well-balanced meals and snacks that are high in nutrients and low in fats, salt, and sugar.

Many health problems can be identified through a screening process. Disabilities or developmental lags, chronic conditions such as allergies, poor posture, or abnormal fatigue will affect development and should therefore be diagnosed and treated to ensure optimal growth. Finally, a safe environment is a prerequisite for promoting physical development. Children need an indoor and outdoor space where they can try out all their newly acquired skills without danger of injury.

As young children grow physically, their muscles develop and mature. Children are able to perform more complex and refined actions. Both gross and fine motor development are important, although gross motor development usually comes before fine motor development.

Gross Motor Development

Gross motor skills involve the large muscles of the body. Most young children enjoy activities such as running, skipping, throwing, catching, jumping, climbing, pulling, carrying, and balancing. These activities allow children to use and refine their gross motor skills in a natural way. When children are physically ready to develop a new skill, they need many opportunities to try these new skills over and over again.

In the *Creative Curriculum*, teachers enhance gross motor skill development by providing a safe space, equipment, and plenty of time for children to practice skills. By offering encouragement, guidance, and reinforcement for efforts and accomplishments, teachers establish an environment in which children are inspired to participate in activities requiring physical skills.

Fine Motor Development

Fine motor activities involve the use of small muscles such as those in the wrist and hand. Refinement and coordination of these muscles are critical for writing. Appropriate activities for developing fine motor skills include building block towers, molding clay or playdough, using scissors or tongs, stringing beads, placing pegs in holes, drawing with crayons or markers, and painting.

As children gain control over their small muscles and learn to coordinate movements, their drawings usually reflect their increasing skills. From making scribbles and marks on a page, they start to draw circles, curves, and lines and then begin to combine these shapes. Gradually, these shapes remind them of something, and they will name what they draw. Their drawings begin to look more and more like real objects and people, and they may experiment with letters. By the time they are five, most children can write their names.

The *Creative Curriculum* shows how teachers can set up an environment and plan activities that allow children to develop and practice their fine motor skills as they become developmentally ready and interested.

Importance of Physical Development

The *Creative Curriculum* offers guidance for teachers on how to help children develop physical skills that are important for future learning tasks. For example, when children string beads, line up shells in a sandbox, or use the zipper on a self-help frame, they are refining their eye-hand coordination, their small muscle skills, and their sense of directionality. Developing these physical skills lays the foundation for cognitive abilities in reading, writing, and math.

Physical development also affects children's socio-emotional development. As children learn what their bodies can do, they gain self-confidence. The more they can do, the more willingly they try new and increasingly challenging tasks. This positive attitude means that children are more willing to try out new physical skills without fear of failure. It also gives them a positive attitude toward growing and learning in other areas of development.

The theories that define how children learn and develop socio-emotionally, cognitively, and physically are essential to designing and implementing a developmentally appropriate curriculum. Teachers who understand developmental theory are equipped to make appropriate decisions as they plan for young children.

II. Goals and Objectives

In an early childhood curriculum, well-thought-out goals and objectives are important planning tools for teachers in defining and implementing the curriculum. Goals and objectives state what children can be expected to achieve and provide a way of assessing each child's growth during the year. They provide a measure for assessing the effectiveness of the curriculum itself.

Clear goals and objectives that stem from a comprehensive philosophy and theory help you as a teacher know where you are heading with each activity and how to carry it out. For example, one goal of socio-emotional development is to acquire and demonstrate cooperative, pro-social behaviors. With this goal in mind, you might do the following:

- set up the physical environment so children can work successfully in small groups;
- help children learn to share and take turns by first providing duplicates of materials and then using waiting lists or timers so children have a concrete way of knowing when they will have a turn;
- post a job chart so each child has responsibilities for maintaining the room; and
- help children work through disputes so they learn skills in negotiating and problem solving.

Listed below are specific goals and objectives for children between three and five years of age who participate in a program using the *Creative Curriculum*. All children should not be expected to reach every objective listed here during their preschool and kindergarten years. There are large differences in development that are perfectly normal. These goals and objectives are offered as guideposts for teachers implementing the *Creative Curriculum*. They can be modified, or others may be added as appropriate.

Socio-Emotional Development

- *To experience a sense of self-esteem:*
  identify oneself as a member of a specific family and cultural group
  feel proud of one's heritage and background
  demonstrate confidence in one's growing abilities
  demonstrate increasing independence
  stand up for one's rights
- *To exhibit a positive attitude toward life:*
  demonstrate trust in adults
  be able to separate from parents
  demonstrate interest and participate in classroom activities
  participate in routine activities easily
- *To demonstrate cooperative, pro-social behavior:*
  seek out children and adults
  understand and respect differences

accept responsibility for maintaining the classroom environment
help others in need
respect the rights of others
share toys and materials
work cooperatively with others on completing a task
resolve conflicts constructively

Cognitive Development

- *To acquire learning and problem-solving skills:*

    demonstrate an interest in exploring
    ask and respond to questions
    show curiosity and a desire to learn
    use planning skills
    observe and make discoveries
    find more than one solution to a problem
    apply information and experience to a new context
    use creativity and imagination
    persist in tasks

- *To expand logical thinking skills:*

    classify objects by similarities and differences
    put together objects that belong together
    recall a sequence of events (e.g., first, second, last)
    arrange objects in a series (e.g., smallest to largest)
    recognize patterns and be able to repeat them
    increase awareness of cause-and-effect relationships

- *To acquire concepts and information leading to a fuller understanding of the immediate world:*

    demonstrate an awareness of time concepts (e.g., yesterday, today)
    identify names of objects and events
    make comparisons (e.g., more/less, larger/smaller, taller/shorter)
    use words to describe the characteristics of objects (e.g., colors, shapes)
    identify the roles people play in society
    identify relationships of objects in space (below, inside, under)
    count in correct sequence and match one-to-one

- *To demonstrate skills in make-believe play:*

    assume a pretend role
    make-believe with objects
    make-believe about situations
    sustain play
    interact with other children

- *To expand verbal communication skills:*

    recall words in a song or finger play
    follow simple directions

use words to explain ideas and feelings
talk with other children during daily activities
make up stories
participate in group discussions

- *To develop beginning reading skills:*

    acquire a love of books
    listen to a story and explain what happened
    demonstrate knowledge of how to use books (e.g., turning pages)
    recognize pictures and text on a page

- *To acquire beginning writing skills:*

    make increasingly representational drawings
    imitate recognizable letters and numbers
    recognize written names
    label pictures
    demonstrate an interest in using writing for a purpose (e.g.,
    making signs, sending letters)

Physical Development

- *To enhance gross motor skills:*

    use gross motor skills with confidence
    walk up and down steps
    run with increasing control over direction and speed
    jump over or from objects without falling
    use large muscles for balance (e.g., walk on tiptoe, balance on one foot)
    catch a ball or bean bag
    throw an object in the intended direction
    ride and steer a tricycle
    climb up or down equipment without falling

- *To enhance and refine fine motor skills:*

    coordinate eye and hand movements (e.g., completing puzzles, chopping)
    use small muscles to complete tasks (e.g., building, stringing)
    use small muscles for self-help skills (e.g., pouring, zipping)
    use writing and drawing tools with increasing control and intention

- *To use all senses in learning:*

    demonstrate skill in discriminating sounds
    demonstrate visual discrimination skills
    discriminate by taste and smell
    discriminate differences in texture

Taken together, the goals and objectives within these three areas of development form the foundation for the *Creative Curriculum*. By focusing on children's socio-emotional, cognitive, and physical growth, the *Creative Curriculum* promotes an integrated and effective developmental approach to learning.

III. The Physical Environment

We are all affected by our environment. Our physical surroundings affect how we feel, how comfortable we are, how we relate to others, and how successfully we accomplish what we set out to do.

For young children the environment is particularly important. The size of the classroom and outdoor play areas, the colors of the walls, the type of furniture and flooring, the amount of light, and the number of windows all influence how children learn. You can do many things to create a supportive and interesting environment for young children. Thoughtful arrangement of the indoor and outdoor environments will support your goals for children.

Establishing Interest Areas

A classroom for young children benefits from having clearly defined, well-equipped interest areas that are arranged to promote independence, foster decision making, and encourage involvement. When the room is divided into interest areas, children are offered clear choices. An area set aside for books, art, or table toys provides opportunities for quiet play. Areas set aside for dramatic play, block building, woodworking, or large muscle experiences give children options for active play.

The following guidelines should be considered in arranging your interest areas:

- Separate noisy areas from quiet ones (e.g., blocks and house corner together, library and tables toys on another side of the room).
- Clearly define each area using shelves, and furniture.
- Display materials at a height accessible to children so they can see what choices are available.
- Separate children's materials from teachers' supplies.
- Logically place interest areas near needed resources (e.g., art area near water).
- Ensure that teachers can see all the areas without obstruction.
- Incorporate a traffic pattern that keeps children from constantly interrupting each other.

In the *Creative Curriculum*, the environment typically includes space for the following activities:

- Blocks
- House Corner
- Table Toys
- Art
- Sand and Water
- Library
- Music and Movement
- Outdoors

To further enrich the program, especially for older preschoolers and kindergarten children, we suggest adding space for Cooking and Computers.

Based on the foregoing criteria for arrangement of interest areas, the following floor plan illustrates what a *Creative Curriculum* classroom might look like:

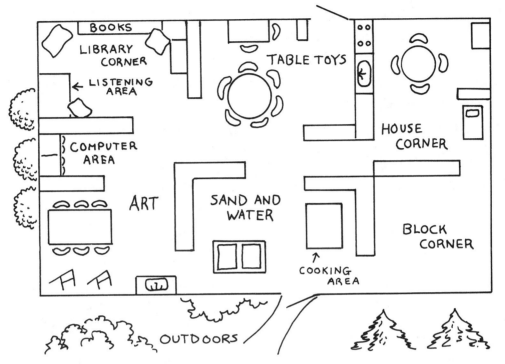

Assessing the Effectiveness of Interest Areas

To ensure that the interest areas are effective as settings for learning, you will need to observe and assess how children are using these areas. You can do these observations during work time, when children select their own activities. Your ongoing, informal observations will enable you to learn what materials children typically select, how children use these materials, and how children relate to their peers. With access to such information, you can make the appropriate changes to the learning environment.

Here are some questions to consider:

How Children Select Interest Areas and Materials

- Which areas are rarely used during work time?
- Which interest areas and materials are selected most often?
- Does the traffic pattern permit children to play safely?
- Do children select the same, similar, or different materials daily?
- Are children able to find and return materials independently?
- Do children show gender-related preferences for materials or toys?

How Children Use Materials

- What do children actually do with the selected materials?
- Do children have the skills to use materials successfully?
- Do children use materials appropriately and creatively?

- Which types of materials seem to stimulate dramatic play? Group play?
- Do different children play differently with the same materials?
- Which materials hold children's interest the longest?
- How does the selection of materials change over the course of the year?
- Are there enough materials to keep children meaningfully involved?
- Do children help care for materials and return them where they belong?

How Children Interact with Peers and Adults

- How do children socialize? Do they approach others or wait to be invited?
- Which children play together most often?
- How do children ask for help from adults? From peers?
- Which play experiences seem to foster cooperative play? Solitary play?

You will know that your interest areas are effective if children are able to: make choices and select activities on their own; use materials appropriately and creatively once they enter an area; stick with an activity and stay involved for a designated period of time; experience success when they play in an interest area; and help care for materials.

In each of the interest-area modules in the *Creative Curriculum*, you will find specific questions to consider as you observe children's use of that area. Also included are suggestions for continually enhancing the environment so that children are challenged and motivated to learn.

Messages in the Environment

The types of materials in a classroom and the way in which they are organized convey important messages to children. A room that is attractive, cheerful, orderly, and filled with interesting objects conveys the message: "This is a comfortable place where you can explore, feel safe, and learn." Teachers who are aware of the power of the environment are able to arrange indoor and outdoor spaces to convey the messages they want children to receive. Listed below are specific suggestions for conveying positive messages to children through your environment.

This Is a Good Place to Be

- Neutral colors (gray, off-white, beige) are used on the walls, and bright colors are used selectively to highlight interest areas or mark storage areas on shelves.
- Furniture is clean and well-maintained.
- Wall decorations are largely made up of children's art displayed attractively at their eye level and with large spaces of blank wall so that children are not overwhelmed.
- Decorations such as (non-poisonous) plants, fabric-covered pillows, and colorful tablecloths are used in the classroom.

You Belong Here

- There is a cubby or basket where each child can keep personal things and with each child's name and/or picture inside.
- Furniture is child-sized and in good condition.
- Pictures on the wall, in books, and in learning materials include people of different ethnic backgrounds and economic means and people with disabilities.
- Children's artwork is displayed and protected.
- Materials, equipment, and furniture are adapted so children with disabilities can be involved in all areas of the classroom.

This Is a Place You Can Trust

- A well-defined schedule is provided so children learn the order of events that occur each day.
- Pictures illustrate the schedule so children can "read" it.
- Consistency is provided in routines such as eating, napping, and toileting.
- Shelves are neat and uncluttered so children can see what materials and toys are available.
- Furniture and materials are arranged consistently and labeled so children know where to find the things they need.

You Can Do Many Things on Your Own and Be Independent

- Materials are stored on low shelves, encouraging children to select and use materials on their own.
- Materials are logically organized (drawing paper is near the markers and crayons, pegs are near the pegboards) and located in areas where they are to be used (table toys on a shelf near low tables, blocks and props in the block corner).
- Shelves are labeled with pictures that show children where toys and materials belong.
- An illustrated job chart shows what each child's responsibilities are.
- Open spaces outdoors encourage children to use their bodies freely.

You Can Get Away and Be by Yourself When You Need To

- Small, quiet areas of the room accommodate one or two children.
- There is a large pillow or stuffed chair in a quiet corner of the classroom.
- There are headphones for a phonograph or tape recorder for individual listening.

This Is a Safe Place to Explore and Try Out Your Ideas

- There are protected and defined quiet areas for small group activities (e.g., a table with three to four chairs enclosed by low shelves containing table toys).
- Smocks are available for art activities and water play so that children can express themselves without fear of getting soiled.

- Protected floor space is clearly defined and out of the line of traffic so that children can build with blocks.

- The outdoor area is fenced in and protected.

- Attractive displays of materials invite children to use them.

- Toys are rotated so there is frequently something new to interest children.

Identifying Problems Related to the Room Arrangement

Even if you have carefully organized the physical environment, things don't always go according to plan. There are times when no matter what you do, children seem restless. They may fight over toys, wander about, become easily distracted, or use materials roughly. Although there are many possible reasons for such behaviors, the room arrangement may be one contributing factor.

The following chart presents possible environmental causes for children's restless or disruptive behavior and identifies strategies for rearranging the space to correct and prevent further recurrences of the problem.

PROBLEM BEHAVIOR	POSSIBLE CAUSES	HOW TO CHANGE THE ENVIRONMENT
Running in the classroom.	Too much open space; room not divided into smaller areas.	Use shelves and furniture to divide the space.
Fighting over toys.	Few duplicate toys; children asked to share too often.	Provide duplicates of toys; show children when it will be their turn (e.g., use a timer with a bell, a sand timer, or a list with names of children waiting for their turn).
Wandering around; unable to choose activities.	Room too cluttered; choices not clear; not enough to do.	Get rid of clutter. Simplify the layout of the room and materials. Add more activity choices.
Easily distracted; trouble staying with a task and completing it.	Areas undefined and open; children can see everything going on in the room.	Use shelves to define areas so children are not distracted by other activities.
Materials used roughly; children resist cleaning up materials.	Materials on shelves are messy; no order to display of materials.	Make a place for everything. Use picture labels to show where materials go.

When children's behavior is troublesome, consider the suggestions in this chart. Your room arrangement may be working against your goals, and a few changes can make a dramatic difference. Because the physical environment provides the setting in which children can thrive and learn, thoughtful arrangement of indoor and outdoor spaces is a basic element of the *Creative Curriculum*. Effective use of the physical environment will give you more time to interact with children and to promote learning.

IV. Meeting the Needs of Individual Children

The children you teach are individuals—each one has unique interests, experiences, abilities, and needs. To teach effectively, early childhood educators must always keep in mind the dynamics and needs of the group of children as well as the individual characteristics and needs of each child in the group.

An understanding of child development is a good place to start. When the curriculum is based on a knowledge of how children grow and develop—socially, emotionally, cognitively, and physically—then the activities, environment, schedule, and expectations for children's behavior and learning are likely to be appropropriate for the children in the group. When the curriculum encourages teachers to respect and value differences among children—cultural, ethnic, ability, and gender—and provides a way to assess each child's individual strengths, interests, and needs, then the program is more likely to be responsive to and appropriate for each child. This focus on each child is called *individualizing*. It is the practical application of a philosophy that recognizes, values, and plans for differences in how children develop, the rate at which growth occurs, and the individual life experiences that children bring to the program.

Understanding Children's Basic Needs

In planning a program that meets the needs of individual children, teachers must consider where children are in their development when they arrive at the program. Abraham Maslow's "Hierarchy of Needs" provides a helpful framework for assessing children's basic needs.

MASLOW'S HIERARCHY OF NEEDS

As this hierarchy shows, "cognitive" needs (the drive to know, to understand, to explore) are high on the list. Before a child can be receptive to and interested in learning and exploring, four other basic needs must be met. These first four needs and their relevance to early childhood educators are described below.

Physiological needs are the most basic needs of all living creatures. Children who come to school hungry are focused on hunger. Efforts to teach a hungry child are destined to fail until this need is satisfied. This is why many early childhood programs and schools provide breakfast, snacks, and lunch for children who otherwise might not receive a balanced meal before coming to school.

Safety is the need to feel secure, safe, and out of danger. Children coming into a strange environment need to know that it is a safe place. As a teacher, you prove to these children that they will be protected and that no harm will come to them while they are at school. The feeling of safety enables children to reach out to others and to explore.

Belongingness—feeling accepted and loved—comes after safety. You may have children in your class who do not believe that they are worthy of being loved or accepted. In an effort to seek acceptance and love from adults, these children often exhibit behavior that tests acceptance—acting out and attacking others because they are angry or hurt. They expect to be rejected and therefore behave in ways that prove to everyone around them that they are worthy of the rejection they have experienced. These children need adults who are consistent and caring, not harsh and judgmental. They need to hear messages like this:

> "I can't let you kick anyone. Kicking hurts. I won't let anyone hurt you, and I can't let you hurt other people."

Rather than this:

> "You're a bad girl. Only bad girls kick."

Self-esteem—a sense of one's own worth—is the fourth basic need. Self-esteem comes from daily experiences that confirm who we are and what we are capable of doing. When children have positive experiences, their self-esteem grows and they see themselves as people who can do things successfully. If children's experiences are predominantly negative, their sense of self suffers. Perhaps the important adults in their lives constantly shame and belittle them in an effort to make them conform and behave. As a result, these children may have learned the following messages:

> "I am a failure."
> "I can't do it right."
> "I will never be able to do it."

Such children are discouraged. They give up easily or don't even try to complete a task.

Children's sense of identity and self-esteem is rooted in their culture and ethnic background. We live in a world of many different cultures. Messages that society gives to individuals from a particular culture affect children's self-esteem.

Children from different cultures may experience school in different ways. There may be differences in learning styles or ways of communicating. Teachers must value and respect cultural differences in order to promote self-esteem in children. By learning even a few words of a child's primary language or including songs or recipes from each child's family in the day's activities, teachers can

convey the message that differences are valuable and interesting. By including dress-up clothes and cooking utensils from different cultures in your house corner, children learn that differences are valued.

Maslow has presented human needs in a hierarchy to indicate that basic needs must be met first. As an early childhood educator, you consider all these needs as you work with each child. A comprehensive early childhood program addresses all areas of development—social, emotional, cognitive, and physical—because each area is related to the others. To understand each child's development and to plan appropriately for each child, you will need strategies for assessing individual needs and abilities. This process begins with screening.

Screening in Early Childhood

Good teachers are continually observing children and screening for any signs of problems. Some early childhood programs, such as Head Start, require that all children be screened at the beginning of the year. The purpose of screening is to identify any children who might be in need of special services because of a developmental lag or a health problem. Developmental screening is only a preliminary identification of those children who should be evaluated in greater depth. By identifying a child's problem early, teachers can design corrective measures so that the child will be more likely to succeed in school.

The screening process begins when a child is first enrolled in a program. Parents come in for an interview with staff and often complete a parent questionnaire. Specific questions can elicit important information on the child's development. Topics covered in the interview form may include the following:

- the child's birth history;
- the child's health (e.g., eyesight, hearing, any history of headaches or fainting spells);
- self-help skills (e.g., eating, sleeping, washing, dressing);
- temperament (e.g., active, quiet, cries easily);
- ability to use language and to follow directions; and
- skills such as drawing, the ability to catch and throw ball, play preferences, and so on.

Parental input is the first essential piece of information in the screening process. As the child's teacher, you provide additional information as you observe the child's daily interactions with peers, adults, or materials. Because you see each child in relation to others, you can often pick out differences that may be important indicators of developmental lags or potential problems.

Some programs use a screening instrument (test) as part of the screening process. Screening instruments are particularly useful in identifying children whose problem is not immediately evident and who therefore may be overlooked. A typical screening instrument assesses four major areas of development:

- *Personal/Social:* self-help skills, capacity to enjoy playing with materials and other children.
- *Visual and Fine Motor Adaptive:* small-muscle control, eye-hand coordination, ability to remember visual sequences and to reproduce objects on paper.

21

- *Gross Motor/Body Awareness:* balance, ability to imitate body positions, and large motor coordination.

- *Language and Cognition:* speech and language, ability to reason, count, solve problems, and remember and repeat auditory sequences.

If your program uses a screening instrument, it should be one with established reliability and validity. *Reliability* means that the instrument consistently gives similar results. *Validity* means that the results are accurate: the instrument tests what it is supposed to test. It is also important to find out if the instrument you are considering is designed for the age group of your children, whether it has been standardized with a population similar to yours, and whether it is available in the child's primary language. All these factors affect whether the results you obtain are reliable and valid.[1]

Children who are identified as "at risk" in the screening process should be referred to specialists for an in-depth diagnostic evaluation. The child's parents are informed and fully involved in the diagnostic process. Evaluation results can be invaluable to both you and the child's parents, who together with experts will determine a course of action to best meet the child's needs.

Ongoing Assessment

Ongoing assessment is the process of observing and recording children's work and developmental progress. Teachers need a system that enables them to document each child's growing abilities, interests, and skills in order to plan appropriate experiences and activities that will enhance development and learning for every child in the classroom.

Ongoing assessment enables teachers to plan and implement the curriculum in ways that will best suit the needs and interests of a particular group of children. Because the *Creative Curriculum* addresses all areas of development, observations should focus on the identified goals and objectives in each developmental area. We recommend two methods for assessing children's progress: a checklist and a portfolio of children's work.

Checklist for Documenting Children's Progress

A checklist outlines behaviors and skills that can be observed during regular classroom activities. These behaviors and skills should reflect the goals and objectives of the curriculum. Many teachers find it helpful to have this kind of framework to guide their observations.

In Appendix A you will find the *Creative Curriculum* Child Development and Learning Checklist for documenting children's progress. The checklist should be completed for each child at least twice during the year: about one month after the child has entered the program and again before the end of the year. For some children you may want to use the checklist more often, perhaps focusing on specific areas of concern. The information you gather will enable you to determine each child's progress and to plan for each child's growth. It can be kept in the child's folder and shared with parents.

---

[1] See Samuel J. Meisels, *Developmental Screening in Early Childhood: A Guide* (3rd ed.) (Washington, DC: National Association for the Education of Young Children, 1989), for information on screening instruments.

Portfolios of Children's Work

The portfolio—a collection of a child's work—documents the child's progress and facilitates planning for each child. The portfolio should be large enough to accommodate a growing sample of items such as drawings and writing samples, photographs of block structures, stories the child has dictated and/or illustrated, and even tape recordings of a child reading or telling a story. The portfolio can also include teacher observations that seem significant, such as a dramatic play episode or the child's handling of a difficult social interaction.

Selecting the items for a portfolio can be especially meaningful if you involve children in the process. Periodically, you might invite children to review samples of their work and choose what items they want to preserve in their portfolios. Questions to guide this selection process are helpful: "What are you most proud of?" or "What was most difficult for you to do?" Portfolio items should all be dated and labeled.

Portfolio items are more useful when they are organized in a logical way so you can refer to them when you are planning for each child. The categories used in the developmental checklist are one way of organizing portfolio items. The following samples of children's work might be included in their portfolios:

- *Socio-emotional development:*

    A chart of the activity choices the child has made over a one-week period
    Notes from parent conferences
    Observations of the child's interactions with other children
    Observations of the child's dramatic play

- *Cognitive development:*

    Artwork reflecting an understanding of relative sizes
    Tape recordings of a child telling a story
    Samples of invented spelling
    Drawings with captions
    Charts the child has made to track information (e.g., the growth of a plant)
    Teacher observations of how the child responds to stories

- *Physical development:*

    Photographs of block structures or pattern block designs
    A collage that involved cutting and pasting
    Drawings
    Notes on games the child has successfully mastered
    Photographs of a child on a climber

Items in the portfolio can be shared with parents at conferences to illustrate the child's progress in the program.

Using Information Gathered to Individualize

Individualizing means recognizing and allowing for differences in development and interests when planning activities and changes to the environment so that there is sufficient variety to meet the needs and interests of each child.

Careful assessment of each child reveals that in any group of children, there are individual differences in development. These differences are quite normal and to be expected. In any group, some children will be able to use scissors and some won't; some will be very verbal and some will have a limited vocabulary; some will scribble and others will be making representational drawings; some will use the props in the house corner to role-play experiences they have had and others will use the props as toys to manipulate and explore.

Children not only have unique patterns of development but also enter the program with their own interests, experiences, and learning styles. Some children are enamored of cars or dolls; others express their ideas through art materials. Some are fascinated by fire engines and all sorts of large vehicles; others may not have one major interest but will be responsive to whatever new materials and experiences are offered. Individualizing means that teachers know each child's preferences and interests and use this information to create a learning environment appropriate for each child. Individualization requires that teachers plan daily activities that promote individual growth by building on each child's interests.

How Individualizing Works

To illustrate how information gathered about a child helps teachers individualize, consider the example of Kim. An observational record reveals that Kim rarely selects an activity on her own. She wanders around the room and watches what other children are doing. She doesn't get involved in an activity unless a teacher intervenes. Kim's teachers might try several strategies to help Kim make choices on her own:

- talking with Kim quietly each morning to discuss the various choices of activities and helping her select one she'd like to try;

- setting up a system to help Kim and other children select an activity by placing a card with their name or picture on a planning board located in each interest area; and

- planning an activity Kim would enjoy and encouraging her to ask one or two other children to join in.

In another example, a teacher might find that several children are having trouble using scissors. The teacher could plan activities to help strengthen small muscles, such as picking up objects with tongs, molding clay, and playing with manipulative toys such as pegboards and tinker toys.

One of the easiest ways to individualize the program is to provide a variety of developmentally appropriate activities for children every day. In this way children learn to make choices. They decide which interest areas and activities they like best and select materials that appeal to them. They also determine how long to spend in an interest area and who they want to play with in that area. Allowing children to make choices is also one of the best strategies for promoting positive behavior. Children who are interested in the activities offered and who are appropriately challenged are more likely to feel good about themselves and get along well with others.

Helping Children Get Along with Others

The development of social competence—getting along with others—is an underlying goal of early childhood education. Social competence includes the ability to initiate and maintain relationships with others. A child must learn how to approach other children, how to negotiate issues that come up, how to take turns, and how to communicate effectively.[2] Children who are able to develop and maintain friendships are more likely to lead successful and productive lives as adults.

Children's social development is strengthened when they have secure relationships with their parents and teachers and many opportunities to play with other children. When the important relationships in their lives are unreliable and children have few opportunities to play with others, they are less likely to develop effective social skills. Some children appear to develop social skills with ease. They instinctively know how to make friends and find their place in a group. They get pleasure from being with other children and relating to adults. Other children, however, may need more time and help to feel comfortable in a group. Once they feel comfortable, they too can join in and make friends.

Children who are unable to make friends and who tend to feel rejected a great deal of the time often have serious problems later in life. Such children may have low self-esteem and lack the social skills they need to develop friendships. Because they aren't accepted by their peers, they have fewer opportunities to develop social skills. They have difficulty breaking the cycle of rejection.

Children present different challenges to teachers. Those who are especially shy or overly aggressive often have difficulty getting along with others. You can help these children by first identifying the nature of the problem. By building on their strengths and helping them gain acceptance, you will be helping these children acquire social competence.

Shy Children

In almost every group there is a shy child. You may feel empathy for these children and want to help them become part of the group. Before offering assistance, however, it's important to observe to see if a shy child actually needs your assistance. The child may need to experience success with solitary play—for example, completing a new puzzle—before progressing to group play. A shy child may need to observe other children at play to learn how to be part of the group. Beginning with a small group and then moving into a larger group, the shy child can move at his or her own pace.

There are some children, however, who will need your intervention and support. You can offer this help in indirect ways without making it obvious to anyone else that the help is being offered. Comments such as "be nice to Billy" or "can you let Shantelle play, too?" are not helpful. They tend to make a shy child feel self-conscious or embarrassed. The other children may go along with your suggestions for a time, but you won't have accomplished the goal of helping the child learn social skills.

What Teachers Can Do

The following are suggestions for helping shy children gain acceptance:

- *Observe the child* at play so you know what interests and skills are most evident.

---

[2] Lilian G. Katz and Sylvia C. Chard. *Engaging Children's Minds: The Project Approach* (Norwood, NJ: Ablex Publishing Co., 1989).

- *Help the child feel accepted.* Use the child's primary language. Read stories about how shy children learn to get along with others. (See the Library module for suggestions.) Talk about how you think the child feels: "It feels a little strange when you don't know the other children. You'll get to know them soon and feel much better."

- *Describe the child's actions.* "How did you build so high without letting the blocks fall? You must have placed them very carefully."

- *Plan an activity for a small group* that you know will interest the child. For example, if playdough is a favorite activity, invite the child and one or two other children to help you make a batch.

- *Interpret what the child is observing.* When you see the child watching other children, make a connection. "You've been watching Jessie and Pammy at the water table." If the child responds positively, you can ask a question to extend the conversation. "Do you think Jessie can make the water go up the tube? Let's go over to the water table and find out."

- *Help the child find a friend.* Try inviting the child and one of the more social and sensitive children to help you do a task. "Our garden looks very dry. I bet the plants are thirsty. Joseph, can you and Teresita help me carry this water to our garden?"

Aggressive Children

Some children's behavior will challenge even the most patient adult. They might kick, bite, hit, spit, and use other means of aggression to express their unhappiness or inability to relate positively to others. In their unhappiness, such children cannot take turns, negotiate, or cooperate with others. Their behavior causes other children to not want to include them in their play.

Finding the Reasons for the Behavior

It is natural for you to feel impatient with a child who frequently hurts other children or uses force to make others let him or her into the group. But because you are a professional, you must learn to overcome angry and negative feelings about an aggressive child. It may help to remember that the children who hit or bully other children are troubled or in pain, emotionally. They feel unhappy or insecure, and they need adults to help them learn positive ways of relating to other children. These children must feel safe and cared for before they can develop self-esteem and the social skills to make friends and play with other children. Part of your job is to try to discover the underlying causes of the child's behavior—the source of the troubled response he or she is making to the world.

Punishment Versus Discipline

One of the most important tasks in growing up is learning what behaviors are appropriate and which ones are not permissible. If our only goal is to make children behave, the task is simple. Adults are bigger than children and can force them to behave. But children who are forced, provoked, or shamed into behaving are likely to learn the following:

"I am a bad person."
"I need to watch out for adults."
"I had better not get caught."

These children tend to behave well only when someone is watching because they don't want to be punished. They do not learn for themselves what behaviors are acceptable and why certain behaviors are not tolerated. Punishment may stop children's negative behavior temporarily, but it doesn't help them develop self-discipline. Instead, it may reinforce their bad feelings about themselves.

Although the words "discipline" and "punishment" are often used to mean the same thing, they are actually very different. Discipline means guiding and directing children toward acceptable behavior. The most important goal of discipline is to help children gain inner controls. Teachers discipline children to help them learn the consequence of their actions.

What Teachers Can Do

To develop self-discipline, children need to be offered choices and opportunities to make decisions, knowing what the logical consequences will be. Teachers must clearly state in advance the choices and the consequences. For example, you might say, "Sanchez, if you keep knocking down Tyler's blocks, you will have to leave the block area. You can make your own buildings and knock them down if you want. Or you can find something else to do." This type of guidance helps a child develop self-discipline because it sets limits and offers a choice. It results in less anger and fewer power struggles than does punishment.

You can use a variety of approaches to guide children's behavior. No one approach works for every child or every situation. The approach used should be based on your knowledge of the child and the particular problem. Positive guidance approaches include the following:

- *Anticipate and plan ahead* so that you can head off problems. "This new table toy is going to be very popular. I'd better set up a system for taking turns before I introduce it."

- *Look for reasons why a child is misbehaving.* Discuss the situation with a colleague. "Tyesha's mother is in the hospital. She is probably worried about her."

- *Focus on the child's behavior,* not the child's value as a person. "I like the way you wiped the table, Marguerite" (rather than "you're a good girl for wiping the table").

- *Help children understand the consequences of their actions.* "Shantaye and Annie, the doll broke when you were both pulling its arms. You will have to wait until it's fixed before you can play with it again."

- *Explain the choices available.* "If you want to drive your truck, Susan, you must drive on the rug, not under the easels."

- *Help children use problem-solving skills* to develop solutions. "I can see it is hard for you to share your bear, Carlos. Where can you put it until you go home?"

- *Help children refrain from dwelling on mistakes* so that they learn to move on. "Your paint cup spilled. Let's go find a sponge to clean up."

- *Watch for restlessness.* Give children room to release their energies and frustrations physically. "Kathy, you seem fidgety this afternoon. Why don't you and Leroy try out the climber for a little while? I'll watch you climb."

In guiding children's behavior, it is important to be clear, positive, and firm. Establish simple but clear rules and limits for your classroom and enforce them consistently. Too many rules confuse children. They are more likely to respect rules when they understand the reasons behind them and when they help make up the rules. For example, to help children understand why it's important to keep the water in the water table, you might ask: "What might happen if we squirt water on the floor?" As children come up with answers, (when the water spills, the floor gets slippery; someone might fall and get hurt), they might also think of a rule: "Keep the water in the water table." Children might also make suggestions such as keeping sponges and towels near the table so that everyone can help clean up any spills.

State rules positively and firmly rather than harshly and judgmentally. The following chart offers some alternatives.

SAY OR DO THIS	INSTEAD OF THIS
"Use quiet voices inside, save your loud voices for outside."	"Will you stop screaming!" or "You're giving me a headache."
"You're angry, but hitting hurts. Let's talk about what's bothering you."	"Haven't I told you not to hit other children?"
"Use the shovel to dig with; if you want to throw something, you can throw the ball."	"If you don't put that shovel down right now, I'm going to take it away."
"It's dangerous to push people on the slide. They may get hurt."	"If you don't stop pushing other children on the slide, they'll start pushing you."
"Careful drivers put on their brakes or sound their horns."	"Stop running those trucks into the walls!"
"Throw the stick over the fence so no one will get hurt."	"Put that stick down. Don't you know someone might get hurt?"
"Keep the puzzle on the table so the pieces don't get lost."	"Did you dump the puzzle pieces on the floor again? I told you not to do that."
"Wipe your brush on the jar, so it won't drip."	"You're dripping paint all over the floor! Why don't you find another activity?"

Helping Children Learn to Share

As every early childhood teacher knows, learning to share materials is often difficult for children, especially for younger children and those who are new to the program. It is very hard for them to have to wait for their favorite puzzle or truck.

Children who have not had their own toys or space are often reluctant to share. By allowing them to have sole possession of a toy or book, they will find it easier to let go and share. As children begin to feel part of the group and develop friendships, they see the value of sharing. When children play

together successfully and work cooperatively on a joint project, they learn the benefits of sharing. Encouraging children to play together is one way to promote sharing.

Making It Easier for Children to Wait for a Turn

Part of sharing is learning to wait for a turn. You might say, "In five minutes it will be your turn," but for young children five minutes can seem an eternity. It isn't just that children are impatient; they really have no concept of how long one minute is. The following strategies help children learn about time in concrete terms:

- Bring a *kitchen timer* with a bell to the classroom. The sound can be used to alert children to when their time is up.

- Have children use an *egg timer* with sand in it to determine their turns. (A homemade timer is described in the module on Sand and Water.)

- Post a *waiting list* in popular interest areas, and list the children waiting for a turn. Older children might be able to write their own names on the list. Children can then see for themselves how many children will have a turn before it is their own. After they have finished their turn, they can cross their names off the waiting list.

- Use a *clock* to show children how to track the time. Point out that "when the big hand gets to the three, it will be your turn."

When children are given the tools with which to solve their own disputes, they learn to take responsibility for their behavior. Children can be taught to "use their words," as the following example illustrates:

Peter:	"She hit me!"
Teacher:	"Tell Jean you don't like it when she hits you."
Jean:	"Well, I had the police hat and he took it."
Teacher:	"The next time anyone takes something from you, tell them that you are using it and that they can have it when you are done. Hitting hurts and doesn't solve the problem."
Peter:	"But I need the police hat."
Teacher:	"What else could you use while you're waiting?"
Peter:	"There's another hat, but it doesn't have a badge."
Teacher:	"How could we make it look more like a police hat?"
Peter:	"I could make a badge and tape it on. But I still want to use the police hat tomorrow."
Teacher:	"You make the badge for today. I'll make a sign so that we can remember that you have the police hat on Thursday."

With practice, children learn an important rule: no one hits in the classroom. They also learn a better way of dealing with disagreement: talking about it. Problem-solving skills can be enhanced by writing signs to confirm the agreed-upon solution. Signs are powerful messages for children. Children ask each other what their signs mean. Some children even want to wear their signs; others simply post their signs on the walls. Children who can't read will be proud of their signs and

29

memorize its content. Signs used in this way promote social development and cooperation as well as emergent literacy.

Including Children with Disabilities in Your Program

Inclusion of children with disabilities in the classroom (or mainstreaming) can be a very rewarding experience for everyone involved. Children with disabilities are children first. They can thrive in an environment that is accepting of differences and where adults strive to meet each child's individual needs.

For the teacher, including children with disabilities in the program means helping these children live, learn, play, and make friends in the least restrictive environment. This environment provides opportunities for each child to become as independent as possible. By working with parents, specialists, and staff members to adapt the facilities and program structure to meet the individual needs of children with disabilities, you can help these children to perform as much as possible like typically developing children.

The Creative Curriculum for Early Childhood is appropriate for all three- to five-year-old children, including children with disabilities. Because the curriculum is developmentally based, it provides a useful framework for assessing where children are in a continuum and for meeting their individual needs. Its emphasis on organizing the physical environment to promote learning is especially important for children who need more structure and predictability in their lives.

Planning for children with disabilities requires careful thought and often the assistance of specialists. It is very important to know the child's learning style, likes and dislikes, and how the specific disability may or may not affect the child's learning and activities. Task analysis—a process of breaking down tasks into sequential and manageable steps so the child is successful at each step— is one method that may be helpful.

Sometimes adjustments in the daily schedule are recommended because these children may need to have their day paced differently. For example, they may need extra quiet time or an opportunity to get up and move around more during circle time. Transition times are often difficult for children with emotional or attention problems. You will need to help these children develop coping strategies for these times. Explaining ahead of time that a transition is coming may assist a child to get ready for it. Having a teacher or friend with the child during a transition time may help to make the transition easier and smoother.

Children with behavior problems may need extra help controlling their behavior. Some children need very concrete demonstrations of how to share toys or play cooperatively with other children. Many children with disabilities, including language-delayed children, benefit from demonstrations along with verbal directions.

Extra support for staff is an important element of addressing the needs of children with disabilities in the classroom. A short time during each day should be set aside for the staff to discuss management and curriculum concerns regarding the entire class, especially children experiencing difficulties with various aspects of the overall program. It is also helpful to secure assistance from appropriate outside professionals, such as speech and language pathologist, clinical psychologist, or occupational therapist. These specialists can often provide insights about the child's needs and strengths and strategies for working with the child. Opportunities to participate in training sessions, and frequent contact and communication with parents are also useful for the classroom teacher.

Guidelines for Teaching Children with Disabilities

The strategies suggested for working with children who have one or more disabilities are good teaching practices for all children. However, they are especially important in working with children who have special needs.

- *Consult with the parents.* A child who comes with a diagnosed disability has probably already been evaluated by a specialist. The parents can provide valuable information on how to work with their child.

- *Consult with a specialist.* While the strategies for working with different disabilities may overlap, it is essential for teachers to have specific guidance on each disability. Advice should be sought from specialists to learn the most up-to-date instructional approaches.

- *Focus on integrating the child into daily activities.* Children with disabilities benefit from the opportunity to operate in the least restrictive environment. They can make tremendous strides in their development being with other children who will themselves benefit.

- *Set goals.* Establish realistic goals for each child based on observation and actual performance. These goals should be reviewed frequently and revised as needed.

- *Modify the physical environment.* Modification of the physical space may be needed to ensure access. Providing a quiet place may be important for some children. Others may need additional space cues, such as tape on the floor or a special rug during circle time.

- *Break down tasks.* Carefully analyze classroom activities to determine just what skills are needed. Ranking these skills sequentially for various activities will make it easier to determine why a child may be having difficulty completing a simple task and what aspects of that task are most difficult. Task analysis will also help determine the level of difficulty or complexity of a series of activities.

- *Pace activities.* Children with special needs may need more time to complete tasks. Extra quiet time may be needed for one child, while another may need to be able to move around during circle time or rest period.

- *Teach to each child's strengths.* Based on observations, conversations with parents, as well as the results of formal test information, determine each child's most effective mode of learning.

- *Promote cooperative learning.* Encouraging children to work in pairs on a task in a cooperative learning setting benefits both the helper and the child who is helped. It also builds social skills and an appreciation of individual differences.

- *Plan for transition times.* Arrival and departure times, as well as changes of activities during the day, are difficult for some children. Both the arrival time in the morning and the departure time in the afternoon may need to be highly structured and predictable. During the day, giving advance notice that a shift in activities is taking place may help. A "buddy" system can also ease transition times.

- *Encourage independence.* Some children may need extra support at various times to develop skills as well as self-confidence. Gaining independence is important for all children and it is especially important for the self-esteem of children with disabilities.

- *Allow time for practice and repetition.* As children are introduced to new skills, they need opportunities to practice and repeat them until they demonstrate mastery.

- *Involve parents.* Be sensitive to the fact that parents of children with disabilities may need extra consideration, support, and time. Close communication, use of a short written report and/or checklist, and parent visits are very helpful for promoting a partnership.

Language Considerations

It is not unusual for children with learning problems and developmental delays also to experience delays in language development; they may have trouble finding the exact words for what they want to say. Children with mental retardation tend to have difficulty in comprehension as well as receptive and expressive language skills. The language of hearing-impaired children may be characteristic of much younger children and may not be an accurate reflection of their actual intelligence. Children with cerebral palsy may have articulation problems that make it difficult for them to be understood.

Early childhood teachers need to be attuned to the developmental milestones in language acquisition and alert to the level of language development of children in order to make needed adaptations. Here are some suggestions which could be incorporated into regular classroom activities:

- *Be a good listener.* It may be difficult to understand children with language delays or articulation problems. Try to be patient and understanding in order to affirm the importance of what these children are saying.

- *Talk about what you are doing.* Verbal explanations along with actions help reinforce language for young children.

- *Look and listen.* Ensure that you have a child's attention through a verbal reminder or a gentle touch. Be alert to nonverbal clues exhibited by the child.

- *Give directions simply.* Some children may need to have directions repeated or rephrased. Make sure they are listening when you start to speak and that they understand the task at hand.

- *Be patient.* Allow enough time for a response; don't rush the child.

- *Give a choice of words.* If a child is having difficulty finding the right word, offer three words from which he or she can make a choice.

- *Be responsive.* Respond to what a child is telling you and if possible expand by rephrasing and elaborating on the statement.

- *Model appropriate language.* Rather than correcting grammar or pronunciation, simply repeat the phrase correctly.

Accommodating Children with Disabilities in the *Creative Curriculum*

As stated earlier, the approach outlined in the *Creative Curriculum* allows you to accommodate children with disabilities into your program. On the next page is a chart outlining various strategies to assist you in meeting the specific needs of children with identified disabilities. These are general guidelines, not specific recommendations. Each child is an individual and there are great differences among all children regardless of whether or not they have a disability. These differences depend on the severity of the handicap, level of intelligence, the child's temperament, the family situation, and the type of experiences the child has had.

It is also important to recognize that a child may have more than one disability. A child with a physical disability, for instance, may also have a language delay. A learning-disabled child may also have an attention deficit disorder (ADD) and language delay, as well as perceptual problems. The advice of specialists should always be sought when addressing needs that may be beyond your experience and expertise.

Working with Children Prenatally Exposed to Drugs or Alcohol

Early childhood programs, particularly those in urban areas, are enrolling an increasing number of children whose disability was caused by prenatal exposure to drugs and alcohol. Since the onset of the crack cocaine epidemic in the mid-1980's, an alarming number of pregnant women have taken drugs and given birth to infants who may show the following effects: abnormal motor development, tremors in their arms and hands when they reach for objects, unusual muscle tone and movement patterns, and difficulty in relating to or accepting comfort from others. Not all infants whose mothers used drugs or alcohol exhibit these symptoms. The severity of the problem may vary depending on a wide range of factors, including the extent, duration, and type of drugs the mother used.

As these children begin entering school, their teachers may be confronted by a wide range of behaviors that cause them concern. We are just beginning to learn about the effects of prenatal exposure to drugs and to design approaches that will help these children succeed. Many of the strategies offered in this curriculum will be appropriate and effective in meeting their needs. You will also want to seek the advice of experts if you need additional help.

ACCOMMODATING CHILDREN WITH DISABILITIES

Language Delay	Expand on what child says; talk about what you are doing; model the correct usage and pronunciation instead of correcting. Provide frequent visual or concrete reinforcement. Keep directions simple; encourage child to repeat them for reinforcement. Explain new concepts or vocabulary.
Attention problems	Start with short group sessions and activities. Provide visual clues (e.g., define floor space with tape). Offer a limited number of choices. Provide positive reinforcement for sustained attention. Help child quiet down after vigorous play. Plan for transition times, including arrival and departure.
Developmental delays and learning disabilities	Allow for extra demonstrations and practice sessions. Keep all directions simple, sequenced, and organized. Offer extra help in developing fine and gross motor skills, if needed.
Emotional/social problems	Provide extra structure by limiting toys and defining physical space for activities. Allow shy child to observe group activities until ready to participate. Help aggressive child control behavior through consistent enforcement of rules. Observe dramatic play for important clues about feelings and concerns. Help child learn how to express feelings in appropriate ways.
Mental retardation	Establish realistic goals for each child. Provide frequent positive feedback. Sequence learning activities into small steps. Allow adequate time for performance and learning. Encourage cooperative play and help the child move from independent to parallel to group interaction.
Impaired hearing	Obtain child's attention when speaking; seat child close to voice or music. Repeat, rephrase as needed; alert other children to use same technique. Learn some sign language and teach signing to the entire class. Provide visual clues (e.g., pictures or . . — . . — to represent rhythm). Demonstrate new activities or tasks.
Impaired vision	Ensure child's safety at all times without being overprotective. Provide verbal clues for activities. Introduce child to equipment and space verbally and through touch. Use a "buddy" system.
Physical disability or poor coordination	*Accessibility* Organize physical space to accommodate child in wheelchair. Use tables that accommodate wheelchairs or provide trays on wheelchairs. Use bolsters or other supports for floor activities. Provide adaptive equipment for standing. Learn about the availability of assistive technology and devices. *Manual dexterity* Use magnetic toys to facilitate small muscle activities. Attach bells to wrist or ankles for musical activities. Use adaptive scissors or spoons as needed.

V. Schedules and Routines

The daily schedule and routines form the basic structure for each day. If planned to suit the developmental and individual needs of the children in your group, the daily schedule and routines will make the day go more smoothly and enjoyably for everyone.

The Daily Schedule

A good schedule for young children offers a balance between the following types of activities:

- active and quiet times;
- large group activities, small group activities, and time to play alone or with others;
- indoor and outdoor play times; and
- time for children to select their own activities and time for teacher-directed activities.

Including routines and transition times in the daily schedule acknowledges their importance and ensures that adequate time will be provided for them. Depending on the length of your program day, you will want to allow time for some or all of the following routines:

- arrival and departure;
- meals and snacks;
- sleeping/resting;
- self-help skills such as toileting, dressing, and washing hands;
- clean-up; and
- transitions from one activity to another.

The Importance of Consistency

Consistency is an important characteristic of the daily schedule. Young children feel more secure when they can predict the sequence of events and have some control over their day. They delight in reminding the teacher that "snack comes next" or telling a visitor that "now we go outside." In addition, predictability provides children with a rudimentary sense of time, as they begin to learn what comes first in the day, second, next, and last. A consistent schedule also helps build trust.

Consistency does not, however, preclude flexibility or spontaneity. A special occurrence can be reason enough to alter the daily routine. For example, the sight of a snowfall can alter class plans. Similarly, on a day when an activity is especially successful or when children are engrossed in a group project, extra time can be allotted by eliminating or shortening another activity. Children can be told, "You are so busy working today that we'll extend the work time a while longer."

As with all aspects of the *Creative Curriculum*, the schedule should be developmentally appropriate. Waiting times should be kept to a minimum and adequate time allotted for putting on coats and hats, eating meals and snacks, and cleaning up. Work periods should be long enough to give children time to select materials and activities, plan what they want to do, and clean up afterward without feeling rushed.

SAMPLE DAILY SCHEDULE

Early Morning Schedule

7:30 - 8:30   **ARRIVAL:** Children participate in quiet activities and prepare for breakfast.

8:30 - 9:00   **BREAKFAST and CLEAN-UP:** As children finish breakfast, they read books or listen to music until all are ready for the next activity.

Daily Schedule for Full Day Programs

8:45 - 9:00   **ARRIVAL:** Children select quiet activities set out on tables, such as puzzles, books, or drawing.

9:00 - 9:15   **MORNING MEETING:** Teacher brings the group together for songs, discussion of day's activities, planning work time, and sharing.

9:15 - 10:30   **WORK TIME:** Children choose from activities in the interest areas.

10:30 - 10:45   **CLEAN-UP:** Children put away toys and materials, use the bathroom, and help set tables for a snack.

10:45 - 11:00   **SNACK**

11:00 - 11:15   **CIRCLE TIME:** Teacher brings the group together to discuss the work time or for a music and movement activity or a story.

11:15 - 11:50   **OUTDOOR PLAY:** Children select from a variety of activities in interest areas outdoors.

11:50 - Noon   **PREPARATION FOR LUNCH OR GOING HOME:** Children wash hands and help set the tables. In half-day programs, children prepare to leave.

Noon - 12:30   **LUNCH AND CLEAN-UP**

12:30 - 12:45   **STORY TIME:** Teachers read to children in one or more groups.

12:45 - 1:45   **REST TIME**

1:45 - 2:15   **QUIET WORK TIME:** Children select from a variety of choices requiring minimal clean-up, such as table toys, drawing, and writing, books, and the listening center. (In child care programs, children may sleep through this period.)

2:15 - 2:30   **CLEAN-UP:** As children finish putting materials away, teachers gather them for circle time.

2:30 - 3:00   **STORY TIME AND DISMISSAL**

Late-Afternoon Schedule

3:00 - 3:15   **SNACK AND PREPARATION TO GO OUTDOORS**

3:15 - 4:15   **OUTDOOR PLAY**

4:15 - 5:15   **SELF-SELECTED ACTIVITIES:** Children select from a variety of activity choices.

5:15 - 6:00   **CLEAN-UP AND SMALL-GROUP QUIET TIME:** Teachers read to children and may involve them in helping prepare for the next day's activities.

This sample schedule may vary from the one you establish for your group of children. You will need to make changes to suit the requirements of your program and the needs of your children. For example, some all-day programs that offer breakfast and lunch set up a "snack bar" during the work time rather than having a formal time for snack. Children take their own snack when and if they wish without interrupting their play.

To help children learn the schedule, you can illustrate each time period in pictures and post it in the room where children can see it easily.

Circle Time

Circle time provides an opportunity for children to develop a sense of belonging to a group. Social skills are enhanced when children learn to share ideas and listen to the ideas of others. Circle times are most successful when the activities planned are age-appropriate and the amount of time allotted considers the children's attention spans, interests, and abilities. Children most enjoy group activities they can participate in directly, such as storytelling, finger plays, music/movement activities, exercises, and games.

To plan an effective circle time, consider the following suggestions:

- Whenever possible, divide a large group into two smaller groups; this allows for more participation.

- Schedule circle times for 10- to 15-minute periods; if an activity is especially successful, it can always be continued or repeated later on.

- Use smooth, orderly transitions to ease children in and out of circle time. Use the activity itself to help gather the children together; for instance, begin singing a song to bring the children to the area.

- Avoid activities such as demonstrations or lengthy discussions where the children sit for long periods listening to the teacher without interacting.

- Give children clear, simple directions about the activity and what they are expected to do.

- Be prepared to change, shorten, or eliminate a group activity that just isn't working or to extend an activity that is highly successful.

How children behave during circle time is a good indicator of its success. If they all seem restless, circle time may be too long. If several children are not paying attention or annoying their neighbors, the activity may not be holding their interest. Such observations tell a teacher that it's time to change or end the activity.

Transition Times

Attention to transition times is essential for effective classroom management. Transition times can be chaotic; they can also be relaxed and can afford opportunities for learning and reinforcing concepts and skills.

If transition times are a problem, ask yourself the following questions:

- Do the children have sufficient notice that a transition is coming?

- Are transitions treated as an important activity, or are they rushed? Are they too long?

- Do children know what is expected of them during transitions?

- Is everyone expected to do things at the same time, or are allowances made for individual differences?

Here are several ways to make transitions go smoothly:

- *Individualize the process.* Try to avoid having all children move from one activity to another as a group. For example, as individual children finish their snack, they can get a book to read until everyone is ready to go outside. Or, as children finish in the bathroom, they can return to the classroom to put on their coats.

- *Give children notice.* Five to ten minutes before clean-up time, talk to the children in each interest area: "You have time for one more puzzle" or "There is just enough time to finish that painting but not to start a new one."

- *Allow sufficient time.* Treat clean-up time as an experience that is valuable in and of itself, and allow enough time for clean-up so children won't feel rushed.

- *Assign children tasks.* Involve children in setting up for a snack or lunch, cleaning up after art, and collecting trash after a meal. This not only smooths the transition but also teaches children responsibility.

- *Be clear and consistent.* Provide clear directions to children during transition times and be sure that the expectations are age-appropriate. Keep the same routine each day so that children know what to do on their own.

- *Be flexible.* When possible, allow children extra time to complete special projects or activities in which they are particularly involved. For example, if several of the children have spent all of free play building a "city" and need time to complete it, allow them this extra time. Other children can be asked to help clean up the art area or house corner.

Mealtimes

Mealtimes, like other scheduled activities, are exceptionally good learning times. Children can learn to serve themselves, to eat with a group, and to try new foods. Good experiences at mealtimes can help children develop positive attitudes toward food and nutrition.

There are many ways in which teachers can make mealtimes enjoyable and foster positive attitudes. First, it is important to remember that children—like adults—have individual eating patterns, likes and dislikes, and home experiences with mealtimes that need to be respected. Emphasize eating and relaxing with the group rather than forcing children to try particular foods. Table manners, too, are secondary with this age group. Children will learn to use utensils and napkins as their skills develop. They will also learn by watching others, which is one reason why it is valuable for teachers to sit with children during mealtimes.

The following suggestions will help you turn mealtimes into pleasant settings for children's learning and growth.

Make Mealtimes Sociable

- Establish a calm and pleasant atmosphere. A quiet activity, such as a story before lunch, helps set a quiet tone.

- Encourage children to talk about what they are eating, how the food is prepared, or something of a purely social nature. Pleasant conversation will create a comfortable atmosphere.

- Organize mealtimes so that you don't have to keep jumping up from the table. This behavior is disruptive and causes children to do the same. To minimize the need for you to leave the table, keep extra foods on a cart near the table and have extra napkins, sponges, and paper cups nearby.

- Allow children enough time to eat. Some children are slow eaters. Mealtime should not be rushed. Ample time should be allotted for setting up, eating, and cleaning up.

Encourage Children to Help

- Children can assist by setting the table, sponging the table after eating, and passing a trash can around.

- Provide small plastic pitchers, baskets, and sturdy serving utensils that children can use to pour their own milk or juice and serve their own food. Give children time to practice with the pitchers during water play, and be tolerant of spills and accidents.

Don't Use Food as a Reward or Punishment

- Food becomes a means of manipulation when it is used to reward or punish behavior. Avoid promises or threats involving food. It is especially important that children not be threatened with having a snack or meal taken away. If a child acts out during a meal, the best response is to deal with the inappropriate behavior and sit near the child or separate the child from the group.

- Talk with parents about their child's eating habits, food preferences, and what mealtime is like at home. Share your goals for mealtime with parents and ask for suggestions of foods they know their child enjoys.

Rest Time

The length of the rest time will vary depending on how long children spend in your program each day. For children who spend six hours or more at school, rest time provides rejuvenation for the afternoon program. Because naps are often associated with home, many children have a difficult time settling down. This is normal and to be expected.

It's also important to remember that children have different sleep patterns and different ways of falling asleep: some drop off right away, some need to suck their thumb to relax, and others keep their eyes open until the very last minute. You may find that each child in the group needs something different to help them rest. Here are some suggestions for making rest time go smoothly.

Preparing for Rest Time

- Plan a quiet activity for the group right before rest time, such as a story, finger play, quiet song, or listening to music.

- Assign a cot and a specific area for each child.

- Allow children to bring sleep toys or special blankets from home to use at rest time. These objects can be stored in the child's cubby and brought out by the child at rest time. Children should not be teased about needing these things; they will give them up when they are ready.

During Rest Time

- Allow children to settle down at their own pace. Avoid trying to force children to sleep. If you encourage them to relax, sleep usually follows. It often helps to circulate around the room, rub a child's back, or just sit on a cot near a restless child.

- Supervise rest time. An adult should be with the children at all times.

- Have a plan for children who wake up before rest time is over and for children who do not sleep. For example, provide books to look at or quiet table toys.

- Let children wake up at their own pace, without the expectation that they will wake up quickly or cheerfully from a deep sleep.

If you are having a particular problem with a child during rest time, you may want to consult the child's parents. They could offer important insights that will help you meet the child's needs.

VI. Organizing Children's Learning

Are children really learning in a program where the curriculum emphasizes child-initiated activities and play? This is an important question to address. Visitors to an early childhood classroom may see children and teachers involved in so many different activities that they may not understand what learning is taking place and how these different activities relate to one curriculum. To a casual observer, the children are "just playing." Parents, administrators, and many teachers worry that children may not be learning what they need to know to succeed academically if "all they do is play."

Ensuring Children's Academic Success

Many parents and administrators are familiar with the statement that "play is children's work," but they still make a distinction between work and play. For some, work is defined as structured tasks such as worksheets that children complete in order to learn the alphabet and numbers. Drilling children on phonics or numbers is viewed as a way of preparing them for reading and math. This type of work is often seen as having more value and relevance to school success. It is easier to measure children's progress and to see the relationship of such activities to academic learning than it is to see the relationship of play to learning. To try to ensure that children succeed, some schools focus more attention on this type of learning, pushing an "academic" program earlier and earlier. The theory is that "earlier is better": the sooner children start academic learning, the more likely they will be to succeed.

Why, then, are so many children failing kindergarten and first grade in schools that stress academic skills and rote learning at an early age? Why are many of the children who master these skills later requiring remedial help, repeating grades, and dropping out of school?[3] The reason is that this type of abstract, rote learning is not appropriate for young children. They *can* learn these skills if we teach them, but this doesn't mean that children really *understand* what they are learning. If they are not ready to understand what we are teaching them and are not motivated to learn it, then they won't be able or motivated to use their new skills.

How We Measure Success

Success in school is highly valued and important. Therefore, we must have both a clear definition of success and agreement on what educational approaches will help us achieve our goals for children. One way to define success is to ask ourselves this question: "Will the children we teach today grow up to be competent students who can succeed academically, and competent adults who can relate well to others and contribute to their families and society?" If we want children to be successful learners now and in the future, we have to teach them to think for themselves, to solve problems, and to get along with others. These abilities are acquired when children are encouraged to explore their environment actively, to solve real problems that have meaning for them, and to work cooperatively with others to complete tasks. This is what children are doing when they are "playing." These goals underlie the educational approach defined in the *Creative Curriculum*.

---

[3] L.J. Schweinhart, D.P. Weikart, and M.B. Lerner. "Consequences of Three Preschool Curriculum Models Through Age 15," *Early Childhood Research Quarterly* 1(1) 1986, 15-35.

To implement this type of curriculum effectively, teachers, administrators, and parents must appreciate the value of play and its role in helping children learn the skills, understandings, and attitudes that will ensure their academic success.

The Role of Play in the *Creative Curriculum*

While all children play, their play is not all the same. There are different kinds of play; each one contributes something different to a child's development and academic success. Dr. Sara Smilansky identifies four types of play: functional play, constructive play, games with rules, and dramatic play.[4] As children engage in these different types of play, teachers shape children's learning by participating in their play and asking questions that encourage them to think.

Functional Play

Functional play is typical of children from six months to six years of age. In functional play, children explore and examine the functions and properties of objects and materials in their environment. They examine how things feel, taste, smell, and sound, and what they do. Functional play helps children understand their environment better. When children are encouraged to explore and discover, their curiosity is heightened and they are motivated to learn more.

To promote functional play, teachers create an interesting and challenging environment filled with materials and objects that attract children and inspire their explorations. They talk with children about what they are doing to help them label and organize their world and to challenge their thinking. For example, teachers make statements and ask children to describe what they are discovering:

- "You found out that it's easier to make the sand go through the funnel when it's dry."

- "Is it hard or soft?"

- "What kind of noise does it make?"

---

[4] Sara Smilansky and Leah Shefatya. *Facilitating Play: A Medium for Promoting Cognitive, Socio-Emotional and Academic Development in Young Children* (Gaithersburg, MD: Psychosocial and Educational Publications, 1990), pp. 1-3.

- "What does it do?"
- "What did you learn about the shells in our collection?"
- "You added yellow paint to the red paint and got orange. What do you think will happen if you add yellow to the blue paint?"
- "What are some ways we can use this collection of bottle caps?"

Descriptive statements and requests for information make children aware of what they are doing and encourage them to use words to describe their actions and discoveries. By talking with children, you help them acquire and use language for labeling and organizing.

Constructive Play

The materials children explore in functional play are often used to construct something else. For example, when children have explored the functions of blocks—how they feel, their weight and size, how they can be used—they begin to use blocks to construct something purposeful, such as a road or a house. Similarly, after exploring the properties of sand, children may begin using the sand to make a castle, a tunnel, or a birthday cake.

The teacher's role in promoting constructive play is to take cues from children and extend their ideas. It's important to avoid guessing or assuming that you know what the child intends—because you may be wrong. Rather, the idea is to validate and reinforce children's constructive play and to ask questions such as the following:

- "You've been working in the block corner a long time today. Tell me about your building."
- "How did you decide to shape the clay that way?"
- "Would you like to tell me about your drawing?"
- "What different things can we make with the sand today?"

Such statements and questions invite children to talk about what they are doing without feeling pressured or judged.

Games with Rules

This type of play is guided by rules that everyone involved must understand and agree to in order for the play to succeed. Examples of games with rules are Hide and Seek, Hopscotch, Red Light-Green Light, and Simon Says. Board games and card games are governed by rules and many are appropriate for young children.

Games with rules help children concentrate, understand rules, and control their behavior in order to conform to the rules. They also teach children to compete and to deal with success and failure. In the *Creative Curriculum*, games with rules are often played outdoors or during music and movement activities.

Dramatic Play

The fourth type of play is dramatic play or, when it involves several children interacting in a pretend episode, socio-dramatic play. In this type of play, children take on a role, pretend to be someone else,

and use real or pretend objects to play out the role. Children can't pretend unless they have experienced something that they can reenact. This recreating of experiences is a cognitive task requiring that they remember past experiences, select the aspects that are relevant, and use gestures and words that will convince others that they are playing the role correctly.

The Relationship of Dramatic Play to Academic Success

Research findings indicate that there is a direct relationship between the ability to pretend and children's academic success.[5] To think abstractly means to create mental pictures or symbols that stand for real objects or events. When children engage in dramatic play, they develop the ability to substitute symbols for real objects and events. When they are older and learning about history, literature, science, and math, they will need to construct mental images in order to succeed as learners. For example, to understand history, they have to be able to visualize in their minds what life was like in the past and how events are related. To solve a simple math problem, they have to create a mental picture of the problem so they know whether to add, subtract, divide, or multiply. Many learning tasks require the ability to visualize what we are thinking about or reading and to come up with alternative ways of considering an issue or question. This is what children learn when they engage in dramatic play.

All children are born with the tendency to engage in dramatic play, but not all children have acquired the skills to play pretend. If no one encouraged their pretend play, these skills need to be taught at school. Although pretend play can take place in all areas of the classroom, the house corner is the central place where children engage in dramatic play. When teachers take an active role in the activities in the house corner, they help children develop the high level of skills that advances their overall development and learning. The elements of dramatic play and socio-dramatic play and the teacher's role in promoting children's play are discussed in detail in the House Corner module.

How Children Learn Academic Subjects through Play

Children begin learning "academic subjects"—reading, math, science, and social studies—almost from the time they are born. Their understanding of the world emerges and evolves every day as children spontaneously work at making sense of the world by interacting with their environment, with materials, and with other people. In this way they gain new skills and concepts as well as more complex ways of thinking. For example, the crying infant picked up by a caregiver gradually learns that her actions elicit a response (cause and effect). The toddler pushing a chair back and forth across the room is experimenting with area and distance (spatial relationships). The preschooler first scribbling on paper and then proudly "reading" the story to his teacher explores writing (print as a means of communication). These examples illustrate how children discover concepts in science, math, literacy, and social studies through active, concrete, everyday experiences as they play.

Implementing the *Creative Curriculum* helps you create an environment that supports children's natural desire and ability to learn. Talking to children, asking open-ended questions, and providing materials and activities that reflect and build on children's interests and experiences are some of the

[5] J.E. Johnson. "The Role of Play in Cognitive Development." In E. Klugman & S. Smilansky (Eds.), *Children's Play and Learning: Perspectives and Policy Implications* (New York: Teachers College Press, 1990).

A. Pellegrini. "The Relationship Between Kindergartners' Play and Achievement in Pre-reading, Language and Writing." *Psychology in the Schools*, 17(4), 1980, 530-535.

ways you can support children's learning. When you plan activities that emphasize rote learning or the memorization of skills, children feel frustrated because they are unable to build on their prior experiences and have difficulty constructing meaning.

Children learn most effectively when the learning opportunities you provide build on their knowledge and experience. All children come to preschool and kindergarten programs with some conception of literacy, math, and science. For example, most young children can recognize a "McDonald's" sign whether or not they can read; can sort bottle caps into groups of different colors whether or not they know the colors' names; or can stand in front of a fan to cool off even though they don't know how the fan works. The extent of children's knowledge prior to school depends to some degree on the quality and quantity of experiences they have had and the nature of their interactions with adults.

The following chart summarizes goals for preschool and kindergarten children's learning of literacy, mathematics, science, and social studies. These goals can be achieved as children play in each interest area of the classroom (as illustrated in the chart on pp. 57-58).

Literacy	Mathematics	Science	Social Studies

• Observe real-life settings in which reading and writing are used
 	
• Acquire a love for literature
 	
• Develop oral language skills
  - self-expression
  - questioning
  - vocabulary
 	
• Use a variety of ways to communicate ideas
 	
• Use beginning reading and writing skills
	• Understand mathematical relationships
	  - patterning
	  - sorting and classifying
	  - making graphs (organize, collect, represent, compare, and interpret data)
	  - measuring
	  - geometry
	  - probability
	
	• Use mathematical thinking skills in real life-situations
	
	• Develop understanding of time concepts
	
	• Identify a range of solutions to problems
	
	• Acquire a positive attitude about mathematics
		• Discover relationships of growth and change (matter, plants, animals), and cause and effect, based on concrete experiences
		
		• Observe and make discoveries (using all senses)
		
		• Classify by similarities and differences
		
		• Communicate observations and classifications (describe, draw, graph data)
		
		• Predict events based on observations
			• Recall and recreate experiences with blocks and in dramatic play
			
			• Acquire beginning awareness of how the community works
			
			• Develop an awareness and appreciation for cultural diversity
			
			• Identify roles people play in society
			
			• Identify common characteristics of events
			
			• Use beginning mapping skills

The remainder of this chapter presents an overview of how children's learning emerges in literacy, mathematics, and science, and how children begin to learn about social studies through themes and projects.

Emergent Literacy

Emerging literacy is the growing ability of children to construct meaning from print. Research tells us that the ability to read and write begins when children are very young. As the parents of infants and toddlers talk to them and read stories, a lifelong process of learning to read and write begins. Literacy skills—the ability to speak, read, and write—emerge interdependently in children.

How Young Children Explore Literacy

Children are natural communicators. The infant's first cooing noises and attempts to imitate sounds are the beginnings of meaningful language. As their vocabularies increase and they use more complex sentences, children's literacy skills emerge. Listening to and talking about stories, observing parents reading newspapers or writing notes, and noticing the labels on food packages are just a few of the ways in which children develop an awareness that print is used to communicate messages. Learning to read is not simply a matter of recognizing letters and words; it is the process of constructing meaning from print. Awareness of print is an essential first step in learning to read and write.

Some children come to school having already acquired a number of literacy skills, such as a rich vocabulary, knowing how to hold a book, recognizing words in the environment, or making scribbles on paper and calling them a story. By observing children's interactions with books and print in the environment, you can assess their beginning literacy skills. It is essential to have realistic expectations of children's abilities based on their age and stage of development. (The developmental stages of using books and writing can be found in the Library module.)

What Teachers Can Do

By building on what children already know, you help them feel competent and excited about learning. When young children experience the value of print—by making signs for their buildings, having their words captured on a picture, or experimenting with writing their own stories—they are motivated to learn more about reading and writing. You show children that print is an important means of communication when you engage in activities such as the following:

- making shopping lists with the children for classroom and cooking supplies;
- making lists for morning circle times;
- writing thank-you notes to classroom visitors or people visited on a trip and invite children to do the same, using scribbles or invented spelling;
- pointing out street signs on a walk;
- saying words out loud as they are written on a chart;
- pointing to the words on a page as a story is read aloud;
- encouraging children to "write" notes and messages to you and to other children; and

- using open-ended questions and statements to help children express thoughts and feelings.

Studies show that children learn best when literacy experiences are functional rather than contrived. In a functional literacy event, the experience is initiated by the child to accomplish a meaningful purpose. In a contrived literacy event, the teacher determines what will happen. Here are two examples:

A functional literacy event: A four-year-old makes some lines and shapes on a piece of paper and then tells her teacher, "This is a letter to my mommy. Could you write 'Mommy' for me over here?" She points to the top of the page. Later, the teacher observes the same child attempting to write an uppercase M.

A contrived literacy event: A teacher tells the four-year-olds in her class to make Mother's Day cards and then shows them how to write the word "Mommy." The missing element here is the children's initiative.

Class books can promote literacy in the *Creative Curriculum* classroom. Making books, reading them at story time, and displaying them on open shelves lets children see how print is used to document events as well as how books are made. Here are two suggestions:

- Take photographs of children working in different interest areas of the classroom. Mount the photographs on colored construction paper. Have children dictate brief captions for the pictures. Laminate the pages or cover with clear contact paper. Assemble pages with metal binder rings or yarn.

- Each time the class takes a trip or has a special event, such as a new classroom pet or a visitor to the classroom, create a book using photographs with captions or children's drawings.

Although very important, the library corner is not the only area where literacy skills can be developed. You can support the development of emergent literacy in all areas of the classroom. For example, you might put paper and markers near the block area so children can make block signs such as "Don't Knock Over" or "Gas Station." In the art area, you can help children develop communication skills by asking open-ended questions or making statements such as these: "Tell me about your picture" or "How did you create these shapes? Did your hand go around and around?" In this way you encourage children to put their ideas into words.

When teachers create a "literate environment," all children can explore and experiment with language, reading and writing at their level of readiness and interest.

Emergent Mathematical Thinking

Mathematics is not simply number recognition, just as reading is not simply recognizing letters and sounds. It is easy to think of mathematics as the rote learning of symbols and rules. When children are taught mathematics by rote memorization, they learn the facts but are unable to apply what they have learned in problem-solving situations. They often become bored or intimidated by math.

Mathematics is the ability to think logically, to solve problems, and to perceive relationships. It is one way we use to make sense of the world, because it helps us find order and logic by noticing patterns, making predictions, and solving problems.

How Young Children Explore Mathematics

To become mathematical thinkers, children need to explore, manipulate, and organize concrete materials before they can be expected to use abstract symbols. Through play, children can begin to question, analyze, and discuss their discoveries and see how mathematics is part of everyday life. This helps them become logical thinkers and experience math as both useful and satisfying.

Young children between three and five are naturally engaged in emergent mathematical thinking. For example, a three-year-old will crawl into a small cardboard box looking for a cozy space. A four-year-old will study the blocks on the floor to see which one he needs to make the sides of his building the same height. All preschool and kindergarten children bring some mathematical experiences with them when they come to school. They have seen numerals on clocks, on food packages, on the menu posted in a restaurant. They express mathematical concepts when they make statements such as these: "He has more candy than I do" or "My doll is bigger than yours."

What Teachers Can Do

In the *Creative Curriculum*, teachers help children observe and think about the mathematical relationships they encounter in everyday life as they play with blocks, pour water at the water table, prepare snacks, or use rhythm instruments. In response to a child playing in a cardboard box, a teacher might say, "I see you made yourself fit into a very small space." The child's response might be something like this: "I scrunched myself up" or "I made myself small." Or the teacher could say, "You made your body very small to fit into the little box." In this way the teacher helps the child grasp a concept and learn the mathematical language that goes with it—in this case, "small."

Mathematics is integrated throughout all interest areas in the *Creative Curriculum*. As children play using concrete materials and have opportunities to describe what they are doing, they begin to develop an understanding of mathematical relationships. These experiences include:

- recognizing patterns,
- sorting and classifying,
- graphing,
- estimating,
- measuring, and
- probability.

Recognizing Patterns

Patterns refer to any kind of relationship, sequence, repetition, organization, or cause and effect. Patterns are part of each child's life both at home and at school. In all subject areas—mathematics, science, literature, and the arts—a child can be engaged in identifying, extending, and creating patterns.

Pattern recognition develops important problem-solving skills. To identify, extend, and create patterns, a child must be able to organize information, perceive similarities and differences, and make judgments. Young children benefit from opportunities to play with patterns using all their senses: seeing, hearing, touching, and even tasting and smelling. For example, you can help children notice patterns in the repeating lines on a sidewalk, the veins on leaves, the sounds of a foghorn at the harbor, the texture of the bricks on the school building, and the smells coming from the cafeteria at the same time each day. Or, using color cubes, you may ask a child to continue your pattern of red, blue, red, blue. Children become aware of patterns when they are encouraged to "read" their patterns aloud.

Sorting and Classifying

Sorting and classifying are essential beginning math activities because they help children develop logical thinking skills. Children love to make and use collections. They may begin to sort and make sets without any plan in mind. Then they begin to sort more purposely—for example, by properties such as color, shape, or size. As children develop and refine their sorting skills, they can sort by more than one attribute. By encouraging them to describe their sorting rules, you extend their mathematical thinking. Questions and statements such as "How did you make your group?" or "Tell me how these are alike" or "Where would this one go?" help children verbalize their thinking and provide teachers with an assessment of what children know.

Graphing

Graphing is a direct extension of sorting and classifying. A graph presents information in an organized way. As a visual representation of data, it helps children see relationships. Graphing is a way for children to display many different kinds of information in different forms. A simple graph of the kinds of shoes children are wearing could progress in the following sequence:

- *Concrete:* shoes with ties, velcro, or buckles, and slip-on shoes
- *Pictorial:* pictures representing the types of shoes
- *Symbolic:* abstract symbols representing the types of shoes

After children have learned how to display data in graph form, they can then analyze and interpret the data. This involves comparing, counting, adding and subtracting, and using such terms as greater than, less than, equal and not equal. The graph pictured here was made after the children in one classroom collected leaves on a walk.

To help children interpret this graph, a teacher might ask questions such as the following:

- "Which kind of leaf did we collect the most of? The least?"
- "Which leaves did we collect an equal number of?"
- "What else does this graph tell us?"

OUR LEAVES

| MAPLE | | ELM | DOG-WOOD | | BIRCH | | OAK | PINE |

Estimating

Estimation is the ability to make an intelligent guess about a problem. Because of the advances made in calculator and computer technology, estimating is more important than ever. Estimation and mental computation (which goes along with estimation) help children decide when an answer is reasonable or sensible. For example, while building with blocks, a child may estimate that she needs about four blocks to make the road between two buildings. Or, if a teacher observes a child constructing a road, she might ask, "About how many long blocks would you need to connect your two buildings? Let's see." Early experiences with estimation help children determine whether an estimate is acceptable or an exact calculation is needed.

Measuring

The focus of measurement activities in early childhood is on developing an understanding of the principles and uses of measuring rather than on specific skills. Measurement is a mathematical skill that we use every day. Children benefit from opportunities to use materials and participate in hands-on activities that help them develop an understanding of the concept of measurement.

Including many hands-on activities to measure time, temperature, mass, and capacity helps children become comfortable with measurement. Materials such as clocks, scales, thermometers, measuring cups, and rulers can be introduced and made available for children's explorations. Children can make their own measuring tools. For example, they can trace and cut out paper hands and feet to use for measuring length or area. Blocks and other small materials can be used to measure mass. Guidance from you and encouragement to describe their thinking and actions help children better understand these experiences.

Probability

Probability refers to the likelihood of a specific event. Working with data, thinking about predictions, and asking new questions are all essential critical thinking skills that relate to probability. Young children can begin to explore probability as they toss coins, roll dice, spin spinners, and spill painted beans. Probability-related activities help children develop problem-solving skills and provide practice with numbers. As children explore these activities, you can encourage them to describe, question, and discuss what they are doing.

Emergent Scientific Thinking

In too many early childhood classrooms, science is only a table filled with collections of leaves, shells, acorns, and other natural materials. These collections remain on the table for a while and then the children tend to ignore them. This approach alone does not promote emergent scientific thinking. Science is an active process of inquiry and investigation, not a static table of collections. It is a way of thinking and acting, asking questions, and solving problems.

How Young Children Explore Science

Young children are investigators, curious and full of wonder. They are born scientists. Infants and toddlers do the work of scientists as part of their everyday life as they observe their surroundings, test things out, and make discoveries. Squeezing a banana, examining an earthworm, and pouring sand through a sieve are a few of the ways in which young children experiment with and observe the material world. Using all their senses—touch, sight, smell, taste, and hearing—they discover relationships of change and growth and of cause and effect. This is emergent scientific thinking.

Teachers using the *Creative Curriculum* support children's enthusiasm for exploration by encouraging them to ask questions, make predictions, and discover many different ways to test their hypotheses.

What Teachers Can Do

You can create an environment that promotes emerging scientific thinking by enabling children to explore and experiment in all interest areas of the classroom. You can help children become more deeply engaged in their investigations by asking open-ended questions, providing rich experiences, and extending the "science moments" that naturally arise in the early childhood classroom.

Open-ended questions are especially important for the development of emergent scientific thinking in young children. They provide children with a foundation for critical thinking and problem solving. You encourage children's sense of wonder when you ask questions such as these:

- "What do you think might happen if...?"
- "How do you think we will find out...?"
- "What do you see happening when...?"
- "Why do you think that happened?"
- "How would you describe what you see?"

Here are a few examples of how you can foster scientific thinking during a daily routine or as children play in various interest areas:

- ***During clean-up time:*** As children prepare to wipe up the finger paints from the table, you might ask: "Tenesha, what do you think might happen if you used a wet sponge to wipe up the paint and I used a dry sponge? Shall we try?" Then you might ask, "What do you notice? Why do you think that happens?"

- ***At the sand table:*** As children play, you might ask: "Which kind of sand do you think can make a bigger pile, wet or dry? Would you like to experiment?" And then, "What did you find out? Why do you think that happens?"

- ***In the block area:*** As you observe children building, you might ask: "Which wall is the strongest? Why do you think so?" And then, "How could you test the walls? What did you find out?"

As children make collections, you can encourage them to classify by similarities and differences and describe what they see through drawings, graphs, and discussions. When you invite children to observe something and describe what they see, you let them know that you are interested in what they think. Helping children become careful observers who can describe what they see promotes their confidence and competence as scientific thinkers, as the following example illustrates:

During outdoor play, a teacher suggests to a few children, "Let's lie on the ground and look at the sky. What do you think we'll see?" The children eagerly lie down and point out birds, clouds, a plane, and a nest on a tall tree. The teacher asks, "What do the clouds look like to you?" After listening attentively, she suggests, "Do you want to be like a scientist and record what you see? Let's go inside for some dark paper and chalk. You

can make a picture of how the clouds look today." While they work, the teacher asks, "If you drew a picture of the clouds each day this week, do you think the clouds would look the same?" She encourages them to speculate. As the week progresses other children become involved in the project, and the drawings are displayed and discussed.

When teachers invite children to make predictions, test their ideas, and observe the outcomes, they are engaging children in the scientific method. The scientific method includes:

- identifying problems,
- making predictions,
- experimenting to find solutions,
- observing what happens, and
- thinking and talking about what we do and see.

Teachers using the *Creative Curriculum* nurture children's sense of exploration and expand their thinking when they join them in their spontaneous explorations and offer opportunities for discovery that build on their natural curiosity. This means seeing the possibilities for science everywhere—in the classroom environment and outdoors. Here are some additional examples of things you can do:

- While preparing a snack with children, have children observe a carrot before and after it is grated by handling it and tasting it. Ask them to describe their observations. Many children are interested in how things change.

- Have plants and animals in your classroom. Help children learn how to care for them. Demonstrate observation skills by saying things such as "I noticed Winky (the guinea pig) liked the lettuce we fed him yesterday—he ate it really quickly," you encourage children to pay attention to details. By asking "what else do you think he might like to eat?" you let children form hypotheses and test them out.

- Invite children to bring in clumps of snow from outdoors and put them in the water table. Ask children to think about what might happen to the snow. Or outline puddles with chalk after a rain, and have children speculate the next day about what happened to the water.

- Help children learn about ecology and the importance of caring for the environment by setting up recycling bins and repairing a broken toy rather than throwing it out.

- Set up a "smelling table" on which you can place things you and children bring in. Let them sniff. (You may have to teach them how, as most young children blow instead of sniff.) Ask them to describe the smells. You might ask questions such as these: "Which ones do you like best? Least? How could we group the kinds of smells? Spicy, sweet, rotten?" The same activity can be done with tastes.

- Place a variety of materials on a tray: sandpaper, aluminum foil, velvet, sponge, cork, cotton balls, pebbles, and plastic wrap. As children explore the materials, you might ask, "Can you compare the cotton to something you have felt before?" ("It's as soft as my kitten's coat. It tickles like when my brother tickles me.")

Fostering children's emergent scientific thinking means allowing children to find answers for themselves. When you always give answers to children's questions, it often inhibits their thinking. Instead, by posing new questions or asking children why they think something is the way it is, you help them see that there are interesting things to wonder about, new questions to ask, and endless ways to experiment with materials to find out what they want to know.

In the *Creative Curriculum*, children explore literacy, mathematics, and science in all interest areas. One way to integrate their learning is to develop themes that interest and engage children. Themes also provide opportunities for children to explore social studies.

Themes in the *Creative Curriculum*

Themes help children learn about the world around them (social studies). Themes enable children to acquire information and concepts through meaningful activities that take place in each of the interest areas. The content of the curriculum begins with the "here and now": the environment that children know firsthand.

Teachers using the *Creative Curriculum* select themes on the basis of what they know about the community and the interests of the children, not because a curriculum book dictates that it's time for children to learn about farm animals. This means that curriculum themes used by teachers in Alaska might be quite different from those selected by teachers in rural Virginia or a program in Chicago. In many areas of Alaska, an appropriate theme might be "The Life of a Salmon" because children see salmon swimming upstream every year. This theme would not be appropriate for children in rural Virginia or Chicago. In Virginia, children might study "Apple Orchards"; in Chicago, a theme might be "Stores in Our Neighborhood."

Themes begin with what children know and see every day. An animal theme in an Alaskan program might include seals, whales, walruses, and puffins. The same theme in a rural farming community might include cows, horses, chickens, pigs, and geese. Teachers in each of these locations can select appropriate animals to represent in the pictures they display, the books they read, the props they put in the block corner, and the activities they plan.

Themes can grow from unexpected events that offer rich opportunities for exploration. Suppose, for example, a large construction project is initiated close to your center or school. The children see large machinery brought in to dig the foundation; they see pipes being laid and foundation walls going up. Because of the children's enthusiasm, you decide to incorporate a construction project into the curriculum by making regular visits to the site and encouraging children to talk about the work being done and the changes they notice. You could enrich the classroom environment to extend learning around this theme by:

- displaying pictures of how buildings are constructed;
- adding bulldozers, tubes, backhoes, ramps, derricks, and construction workers to the block corner if possible;
- including hard hats, lunch boxes, carpenter aprons, work boots, and work shirts in the house corner;
- displaying books in the library corner that illustrate construction work;

- including construction materials in the table toy area, such as Legos and table blocks;
- planning a group mural of the building going up so that children can "build" a representation of the building; and
- taking photographs of the construction site to illustrate the changes and have the children develop a story based on the photos.

Steps in Planning a Theme

To use themes most effectively, planning is essential. The following are several steps to help you organize your planning:

Select an appropriate topic. An appropriate topic for a theme matches the developmental abilities of the children and offers rich opportunities for exploration and discovery.

At each stage of development, children have different interests and abilities. Three-year-olds are primarily focused on themselves and their families. Although they are just beginning to show an interest in other people and places, their primary interests are still homebound. Four-year-olds' curiosity extends beyond themselves to include others—they want to know about the other children in their class and their families. They ask questions about the neighborhood they see each day. Five-year-olds ask many questions and want to know about how things are made, how they work, and who makes them.

In considering a possible theme, you can use the following questions to determine whether the topic is a good one:

- Can the topic or theme be explored from a variety of perspectives—the place, the people, the objects used?
- What possibilities for exploration are there in your school's neighborhood? What do the children see each day? What trips can be arranged in the immediate environment?
- What unique experiences and interests do the children bring to school? Think about the children's families. Do they speak different languages? Plan themes of study that give children opportunities to share their experiences, extend their interests, and help them think about similarities and differences in people's cultures.

Become familiar with the subject. Teachers are also learners. Learning about the subject to be studied involves taking trips, locating books and materials, and talking to people. Exploring the environment first helps you anticipate children's questions and interests.

Bring materials related to the theme into the classroom. Interesting materials and props can stimulate discussions and elicit children's investigations. Some materials to collect for a post office theme might be a mailbox, mail carrier's hat, and mailbag for the house corner; books about the post office for the library; and mail trucks and mail carriers for the block corner. Because children have different learning styles and react to materials in different ways, it's important to have a variety of materials. Encourage children and their families to bring in materials that relate to the theme. As you collect books and pictures about the theme, be sure they show respect for different ethnic groups, lifestyles, and gender roles.

Think about what children will learn. When teachers are realistic about what concepts children are developmentally ready to learn from a theme, the experiences will probably be more meaningful. Concepts are the "big ideas" that children learn. A focus on concepts allows children to begin to make generalizations. For example, as four-year-olds study the post office, they learn many facts, such as who carries the mail, where you go to buy stamps, and how mail trucks deliver packages all over the country. Four-year-olds can understand the concept that there are many people who do special jobs.

Develop questions for inquiry. Open-ended questions are an excellent way to begin a discussion during which children can share what they know, express their ideas and opinions, and develop oral skills. It is also a way for you to determine what is confusing to the children. To illustrate, following a trip to the local post office by a class of four year olds, you might ask, "What were some things we saw at the post office?" Listening to the children's responses, you will learn what the children remember seeing, what they understood, and what misunderstandings they acquired.

Plan activities and experiences. Activities and experiences that are concrete and build on what children already know help them learn. Children learn most effectively from first-hand experiences. Therefore, trips are a rich resource for learning. Trips offer children a firsthand opportunity to gather information actively—by asking questions, handling objects, and comparing what they see with what they already know.

Invite parents to participate in the theme. Parents and relatives can be wonderful helpers and resources. Family members can help during trips, come in to talk to the class about their work, assist with cooking projects, or share a special skill.

Think about how the theme will end. Some units and themes last for a week; others might continue for a month or more. The length of time depends on the nature of the theme, the age of the children involved, and the level of interest exhibited by the children. For themes that have extended over several weeks, closure is particularly important. The end of a theme may be a class book with drawings, writing, and photographs; a display of projects and artwork; or a breakfast with parents to share stories and experiences. These closing activities enable children to share what they have learned and experience a sense of pride in their accomplishments.

Assess your work and the work of children. Throughout the study you can observe and record children's comments and questions, their involvement with projects, their successes, and their confusions. Samples of children's work, photographs of their constructions, and photocopies of their writing can be collected and added to children's portfolios.

How Teachers Promote Learning in All Interest Areas

The experiences that children have as they explore literacy, mathematics, science, and social studies take place in all interest areas of the classroom. To illustrate this concept, we have developed a chart that shows how learning can take place in the ten interest areas that form Part II of the *Creative Curriculum.*

Examples of How Early Childhood Teachers Using The *Creative Curriculum* Promote Learning in Literacy, Mathematics, Science, and Social Studies

	LITERACY	MATHEMATICS	SCIENCE	SOCIAL STUDIES
BLOCKS	• Have paper, markers, and tape available for children to make signs for block buildings. • Hang charts and pictures with words at children's eye level.	• Suggest clean-up activities that require children to sort things by shape and size. • Use terms of comparison, such as taller, shorter, the same length.	• Talk with children about size, weight distribution, balance, and stability. • Introduce experiments with momentum using ramps, balls, and marbles.	• Include block people that represent a range of jobs and cultures. • Display (and change) pictures of buildings in the neighborhood.
HOUSE CORNER	• Include books and magazines. • Introduce uses of print (shopping lists, receipts, letter writing, etc.).	• Add telephones, menus, and other items with numbers on them. • Participate in play; talk about prices, addresses, times of day.	• Introduce props such as a stethoscope or binoculars. • Model hygiene skills by washing "babies" or dishes.	• Display props to reflect different themes. • Include props related to different kinds of jobs.
TABLE TOYS	• Invite children to describe what they are making. • Reinforce vocabulary (names of colors, shapes, sizes).	• Provide collections for sorting and classifying. • Have children extend patterns with color cubes, beads, etc.	• Talk about balance and weight as children use table blocks. • Ask children to describe color, shape, size, and texture of table toys.	• Create "flip books" that reflect classroom themes. • Include or rotate puzzles according to themes addressed in the curriculum.
ART	• Invite children to dictate stories to go with artwork. • Share books about famous artists.	• Use terms of comparison (the blue paint is darker than yesterday). • Introduce cookie cutters with playdough.	• Include sensory materials such as paint, playdough, and clay. • Use water and brushes for outdoor painting so children can explore evaporation.	• Display postcards or other reproductions of artwork from various cultures. • Encourage children to paint and draw what they see on a field trip.
SAND AND WATER	• Write letters in the sand. • Encourage children to use words to describe how the sand and water feels.	• Provide measuring cups, spoons and containers of varied sizes. • Ask estimation questions ("how many cups do you think it will take to fill the yellow pitcher").	• Make a bubble solution and provide different kinds of bubble blowing tools. • Put out magnifying glasses so children can examine different kinds of sand.	• Invite children to describe roads and tunnels created in the sand. • Hang pictures (of rivers, oceans, lakes, and beaches) near water table.

	LITERACY	MATHEMATICS	SCIENCE	SOCIAL STUDIES
LIBRARY CORNER	• Encourage children to "read" stories to each other. • Have stuffed animals and puppets available for dramatization of stories.	• Add number stamps to writing center. • Include books about math concepts: size, number, comparisons, shapes.	• Include books about pets, plants, bodies, water, inventions, etc. • Read books that show people making discoveries.	• Include books related to themes. • Include books that reflect diversity of culture and gender.
MUSIC AND MOVEMENT	• Incorporate poetry in music and movement experiences. • Have children use instruments for the sound effects in stories.	• Play percussion games emphasizing patterns, softer, louder, etc. • Use language in movement activities that develops spatial-relationship thinking.	• Encourage children to experiment with what sounds can be made with different parts of the body. • Use a tape recorder to record children's voices; play back for children to identify.	• Show videotapes reflecting songs and dances of many cultures (and languages). • Talk with children about instruments from different cultures.
COOKING	• Use pictures and words on recipe cards. • Post signs that remind children to wash hands.	• Discuss whether ingredients will rise or fall when cooked. • Use measuring cups and spoons.	• Encourage children to taste, smell, touch, listen, and observe at each step of process. • Observe how heating and freezing change substances.	• Encourage parents to bring in recipes reflecting family cultures. • Visit stores that sell foods of different cultures.
COMPUTERS	• Label software boxes. • Use drawing programs to make pages for a book.	• Provide children with programs that focus on patterning. • Have children categorize programs: games, drawing, etc.	• Help children observe cause and effect by hitting a key. • Use software that engages problem-solving skills.	• Invite a visitor who uses computers. • Take a trip to a computer store.
OUTDOORS	• Bring colored chalk and other writing materials outside. • Have children observe street signs in the neighborhood.	• Have children look for patterns in nature. • Invite children to make collections on a walk, and then sort, classify, and graph them.	• Take a "Let's Find" walk in the neighborhood. • Invite children to listen to the sounds of birds.	• Take many trips in the neighborhood. • Invite children to make maps of outdoor environment using chalk on concrete.

Planning in the *Creative Curriculum*

Planning in the *Creative Curriculum* means thinking through how you will translate your goals for children into developmentally appropriate learning experiences. Effective planning will enable you to keep track of what is going on in the classroom, and see where progress is made and where change may be necessary.

Teamwork is essential for effective planning. By working together, teachers, assistants, and volunteers can exchange ideas, share observations of children, and discuss new strategies. Written plans provide a record of the curriculum over a period of time. Such plans help teachers chart the

progress of individual children and the group as a whole. This in turn helps determine if program goals and objectives are being met.

Three types of planning are important: long-range planning, trip planning, and weekly plans. Each is discussed below.

Long-Range Planning

Long-range planning encourages you to think about several months at a time. This is necessary if you want to organize a logical sequence of themes. For example, a study of the post office may be followed by a study of other places in the neighborhood that provide services for families.

Long-range planning facilitates arrangements for field trips and special events. In takes into account factors such as what time of year is best for neighborhood walks or bus trips or for buying certain fruits and vegetables needed for cooking projects. Community calendars can help you find out about events and places that would be appropriate for your children.

Long-range planning is essential for budgetary reasons: the cost of field trips needs to be factored in, the purchase of special materials accounted for, and the direct and indirect costs of special events allocated. Although long-range planning provides a helpful organizational framework, teachers also need to be flexible in their plans. Current events in the community or within a child's family often suggest changes.

Trip Planning

It is always a good idea to visit a site before you take children on a trip. This enables you to determine its appropriateness for the children, the best route, what will be most interesting to children, where lunch can be eaten, and the locations of bathrooms. You may need to make arrangements for transportation and parent consent forms. It is also helpful to send a letter to parents explaining the purpose of the trip and any other pertinent information about transportation, money, lunch, and the trip schedule.

Before taking a trip, it's a good idea to have several discussions with the class. You may want to show a map, some pictures, or a book. Inviting children to talk about what they think they may see helps them anticipate the experience and often sparks their curiosity. "What do you think we will see when we visit the pet store? Let's make a list of all your ideas." Give clear instructions on what behavior is expected.

Neighborhood walks and trips are a convenient and usually free resource that can enhance children's learning. Here are some suggestions:

- *Trips to local stores*
  bakery
  hairdresser/barber
  fish store
  supermarket
  pet store
  florist
  shoe store

- *Trips to work sites*

  fire station
  police station
  public library
  post office
  construction site
  doctor or dentist office

- *Trips in the neighborhood*

  the school or center
  immediate block around the school
  children's homes
  woods
  gardens
  parks
  backyards

Not all trips require advance planning and arrangements. Spontaneous trips and walks can be taken in the immediate neighborhood of your program. Suggestions for taking "Let's Look For" walks can be found in the Outdoors module.

Weekly Planning

In an environmentally based curriculum, the focus for weekly planning is on setting the stage for what will happen during group activities and in each interest area. Weekly planning enables you to collect and prepare the materials needed for a particular activity or theme. For example, knowing that a visit to a shoe store is planned for the end of the week, a gradual introduction to this theme each day might include playing a circle-time game where children take off and sort their shoes on Monday, reading a story about buying new shoes on Tuesday, and putting a foot measurer and a collection of shoes in the house corner on Wednesday.

Observation is the basis for planning. By observing children, you can find out if the materials you provided have the desired outcomes. For example, what happens when road signs are added to the block corner? Did the props stimulate a new or different type of dramatic play? What types of props might be added next to extend a new theme? Does the theme continue to hold children's interest, or is it time to add something new or change the theme entirely? Answers to these questions enable you to make adjustments if needed.

We recommend that the classroom teaching team discuss the weekly plan daily to ensure that everyone is prepared and in agreement. Each member of the team may have different observations of children to share and may have important suggestions for making adjustments to the plan.

The *Creative Curriculum* Planning Form

The planning form developed for use in the *Creative Curriculum* is designed to focus the planning process on creating a rich environment. There are several sections to complete, as described below.

Skills/Concepts to Emphasize. The theme being studied, as well as your observations of individual children, will help you identify what concepts and skills you want to focus on in planning activities and changes to the environment.

Group Times. When the children gather as a whole group for circle time, it may be for a story, a group discussion, a celebration, a movement and music experience, or the sharing of play and work projects. Group times provide opportunities for children to listen and talk with one another—an important way children learn. Small group activities allow children to practice taking turns, to exchange ideas, to share materials, and to interact with adults. Children benefit from daily opportunities to participate in small and whole group experiences.

Special Activities. Special activities may involve the whole group or a small group of children. Activities such as a walk to the post office, a child's birthday, or making applesauce will require some planning. For example, knowing a parent is coming on Thursday with cupcakes to celebrate a child's birthday, you'll need to change the regular schedule. Preparing children ahead of time helps them anticipate and feel comfortable with changes in their routines.

Changes to the Environment. The *Creative Curriculum* is organized around interest areas; therefore, the materials you select for each area are very important. As you observe children's use of the materials you set out, you will decide if they are appropriate and if the children are using them as you intend. To maintain children's interest and involvement, you will want to make changes to many of the interest areas on a weekly basis.

The *Creative Curriculum* Weekly Planning Form that follows this page can be modified to suit individual programs. To illustrate how it can be used, we have included a sample completed form during a week in which a study of the post office is in progress. Note that although the post office theme is central to the planning of classroom activities, not all activities and materials planned for the week are related to the theme.

CREATIVE CURRICULUM WEEKLY PLANNING FORM

Week of: _____   Theme: _____

Skills/concepts to emphasize: _____

	MONDAY	TUESDAY	WEDNESDAY	THURSDAY	FRIDAY
Group time (songs, stories, games)					
Special activities					
Outdoor activities					

Changes to the environ-ment	House Corner	Art	Sand and Water
	Blocks	Table Toys	Library
	Cooking	Music/Movement	Computers

CREATIVE CURRICULUM WEEKLY PLANNING FORM (Sample)

Week of: _____ *March 15-19* _____ Theme: _____ *Post Office* _____

Skills/concepts to emphasize: _____ *Patterning, writing and mailing letters, how things change, sink and float* _____

	MONDAY	TUESDAY	WEDNESDAY	THURSDAY	FRIDAY
Group time (songs, stories, games)	*Finger Plays Eensy Weensy Spider Wheels on the Bus* *Story: "Mr. Grigg's World" by Cynthia Rylar*	*Story: "A Letter to Amy" by Ezra Jack Keat* *Write group letter to ourselves*	*Story: Selections from "Cat Poems" by M.C. Livingstone* *Variation of Duck Duck Goose—Cat Cat Mouse*	*Story: "Peter's Chair" by Ezra J. Keats* *Music game Fly Through My Window*	*Story: "Post Office Book: Mail and How it Moves" by Gail Gibbon*
Special activities	*Make peanut butter Use grinder Discuss change Introduce patterns with stringing beads*	*Cut up cucumber and carrots for snack*	*1/2 class walk 1/2 class introduce kazoos Introduce wrapping packages in post office*	*Read "Birthday Candles Burning Bright" by Sarah John Preston* *Ron's 4th Birthday Mom-Cupcakes*	*Walk to post office; bring Polaroid* *Make book about trip*
Outdoor activities	*Colored chalk*	*Take a walk to mailbox to mail group letter*	*Bubbles*	*Colored Chalk Big Balls*	*Pebble collecting Feed birds*

House Corner		Art		Sand and Water
Add new post office props: boxes, tape, string Laundry bag in garbage can for packages		*Eraser stamps and paint on trays for printing New collage materials*		*Sink and float toys to water table*

Changes to the environment	Blocks		Table Toys		Library
	Add block people-community helpers Hang picture of UPS truck		*Add different size stringing beads Change sorting collections to keys and pebbles*		*Books about sink and float Add envelopes to writing center Books about post office Stuffed animals/cat and mice*

	Cooking		Music/Movement		Computers
	Introduce grinder		*Make and introduce kazoos*		*Software about patterns (Patterns-MECC) Patterns and Squares (Harley Courseware)*

VII. The Parent's Role in the *Creative Curriculum*

Parents are the most important people in their child's world; they are also their child's first and primary teachers. Research confirms that the most effective early childhood programs are those which involve parents in meaningful ways. In the *Creative Curriculum*, supporting children's learning is viewed as a joint effort between teachers and parents.

Setting the Stage for a Partnership

Although a teacher's primary job is to work with young children, the needs of the child will best be met if the parents are also involved. Teachers who accept this premise are able to create the climate for a working partnership that will benefit all involved, especially the children. This partnership helps ensure that the program will address the needs of each child and that learning and growth will be supported at home.

An effective partnership begins with mutual respect and trust. Each party brings something important to the relationship. You bring a knowledge of child development and early childhood education. You observe how each child interacts with peers, adults, and the environment and are able to assess a child's development in relation to other children at the same stage. As an early childhood professional, you have values and beliefs that underlie the program you plan and implement. This information can be shared with parents.

In turn, parents bring specialized knowledge and experiences to the partnership. They have a wealth of information about their child. They have dreams and expectations that must be considered and respected. As early childhood educators, we have an obligation to respond to parents' expectations and to help them understand and appreciate how a developmentally appropriate curriculum will offer the best opportunity for their children's success now and in the future.

Here are some suggestions for setting a positive tone for a partnership with parents:

- *Hold an Open House for new parents.* Conduct a tour of the classroom. Explain the program's philosophy and goals, and invite questions.

- *Solicit parents' expectations and concerns.* Find out how they feel about having their child enter the program. Listen to what parents have to say, and respond to their ideas.

- *Get to know all the parents.* Learn their last names (sometimes different from each other's or the child's). Find out something about their interests, other family members, and their work. This information enables you to relate to parents more personally.

- *Convey the importance of parent involvement.* Let parents know that there are many ways in which they can be involved in their children's learning.

- *Solicit and try out suggestions parents offer.* When parents feel that their ideas are taken seriously, they are more likely to increase their involvement.

- *Promote a sense of pride in their child.* Noting something a child has done well and conveying this to the parent goes a long way in building a positive partnership.

- *Always maintain confidentiality.* What parents say about their child or their family is best used to help teachers work with that child and not discussed with others.

Setting the stage for a partnership is the first step in ensuring meaningful parent involvement in the program. To nurture this partnership, ongoing communication is essential.

Ongoing Communication with Parents

When young children observe positive and genuine communication between their parents and teachers, they feel that their two worlds are connected. Both formal and informal communication have a place in an early childhood program.

Formal Communication

Formal communication is needed when everyone must receive the same information and when accuracy is required. For example, if policies change, a special event is planned, or a contagious disease has been diagnosed in one of the children or teachers in the class, you'll need to send written notices to all parents.

Suggestions for formal communication include the following:

- *Set up a parent's bulletin board* at the entrance to the classroom. Highlighting important notices will catch parents' attention. Articles of interest can be posted, as well as a calendar of events, reminders of upcoming meetings, the week's menus, and so on.

- *Send weekly messages home.* A consistent format for weekly messages makes it easy for parents to locate important information.

- *Establish a message center.* Provide each family with a box or message pocket. This can be used for general announcements as well as information pertaining to each child.

- *Use journals.* Provide each family with a journal that travels between home and school. Parents and teachers can share information about the child, and flyers or notices can be tucked inside.

- *Develop a parent handbook.* The handbook should be kept up-to-date and might include an explanation of the program's philosophy, goals, and approach as well as policies and procedures.

Informal Communication

Informal communication with parents is an everyday activity. It can occur naturally when children are brought to the program and/or picked up. Although most of these exchanges are casual, some planning will enable you to make the most of these times. Noting something a child has done during the day and jotting it down so that it can be shared with parents at the end of the day is one way to make these brief encounters more meaningful.

Some suggestions for ongoing informal communication follow:

- *Greet parents by name.* Have something specific to say to each one. Make parents feel as welcome as their children. "Good morning, Mrs. Lewis. I hear that your family is going on a trip."

- *Share an event* or something the child has done recently. "I wish you could have seen the building Marie made with blocks yesterday!"

- *Solicit parents' advice* about their child. "We haven't been very successful at getting Onya to paint. Do you have any suggestions?"

- *Give support to parents* when needed. "It's hard for Michael to say goodbye to you today. Perhaps he needs some extra reassurance from you. I know he'll be fine once he gets busy and we have lots planned for today."

- *Be a good listener.* Using active listening skills conveys to parents that their concerns and ideas are being taken seriously. "I can understand how upset you were when Andrea told you about the biting incident. I can assure you that we are dealing with the situation."

- *Check out communication.* If there is any uncertainty about a statement made by a parent, clarify your understanding. "Let me see if I understood correctly. What I heard you say is...."

- *Use "I messages"* to communicate clearly without judging or putting parents on the defensive. "Carrie likes to play with clay, but she worries about her clothes getting dirty. I want to be sure she really enjoys herself here. I thought maybe if she wore clothes that were more easily washable, neither one of us would worry, and Carrie would have more fun."

Taking time to communicate regularly with parents greatly enhances the possibilities for active parent involvement in the program. However, if opportunities for this type of interaction do not exist because, for example, children are bussed to the program, you can converse with parents by telephone, invite them to participate in classroom activities, and schedule periodic conferences.

Involving Parents in the Daily Program

One of the best ways for parents to understand, extend, and enrich the curriculum is for them to participate in the daily program as a volunteer or special guest. By participating, parents can see for themselves how teachers interact with children to promote learning and growth. They can gain first-hand knowledge of the curriculum and how it is being implemented.

When parents participate in the program, children benefit in many ways. An extra adult in the room means more individual attention for children. In addition, parents who bring a special interest or skill enrich the curriculum. Finally, children who see their parents playing a new role find this exciting and a source of pride.

Not all parents can or want to be involved in the daily program. Individual preferences as well as schedules need to be respected. Look for other ways to involve those parents who do not opt to participate in the daily program. Some parents may be able to get away for an occasional meal with their child. Others may volunteer to help with a project on a weekend or evening. Parents can also assist at home by typing up a story, sewing doll clothes, or collecting "beautiful junk." There are

many ways in which parents can be involved in the *Creative Curriculum*. You will find specific suggestions for involving parents in each of the interest-area modules.

Parent Conferences

While much valuable information can be shared in daily, informal communication, parent conferences provide time for a more in-depth exchange of ideas and for problem solving when needed. Conferences are an excellent time for teachers to ask parents to share information that will help them meet individual needs. Conferences also provide a good opportunity to help parents better understand the program's goals and objectives and how their child is progressing in the program.

Preparing for a Conference

When scheduling a parent conference, give parents an idea of what to expect. A brief explanation of the purpose of the conference, its anticipated length, and what will be discussed helps parents prepare themselves. Parental input can also be sought, as parents frequently have specific questions and concerns they want to discuss.

If possible, offer parents several options for scheduling a conference. Some parents may be available only at lunch or in the evening. Additionally, when parents are separated or have joint custody, teachers need to be sensitive about whether one conference or two will be needed.

In preparing for the conference, take time to review the child's file and be sure it is up to date. This will allow you to address questions regarding the child's progress. Anecdotal records and samples of the child's work are especially useful in giving parents a clear picture of how their child relates to the environment, the materials, and other children.

Conducting the Conference

Almost all parents have difficulty being objective about their children. Knowing this can help you think through how best to approach the conference. Listed below are some strategies for promoting a comfortable atmosphere:

- *Establish a relaxed tone.* At the beginning of the conference, take a few minutes for informal social conversation.

- *Set clear expectations.* Explain how the conference will proceed and exactly what time is available. Clear expectations are important to a successful parent conference.

- *Solicit parent's perceptions.* Before you present your point of view, invite parents to share their perceptions. "What does Kelly say about the program? Have you seen any changes in her?"

- *Be descriptive.* Avoid labeling or judging a child's behavior. Rather than saying, "Stephan is shy. He's very dependent on the teacher." Describe what Stephen does: "Stephan tends to watch the other children a lot. He often needs our help to enter a group. But once he does, he is able to play quite well."

- *Focus on the positive.* Talk about the child's strengths and how you use them to promote development and growth. "Tonya is very good at completing difficult puzzles and pegboards. We plan a lot of activities in which she can build on her excellent eye-hand coordination skills."

- *Organize your comments.* Decide what topics you want to discuss with parents. The following are offered as suggestions:

  interest areas that their child plays in most;
  how their child reacts to group activities (stories, music, circle time);
  routines and self-help skills;
  special interests and friends; and
  development in all areas—socio-emotional, cognitive, and physical.

- *Share the curriculum with parents.* Use the questions and concerns that parents raise to help them learn more about the curriculum. Clarify the parents' questions or concerns first. "When you say you want Leroy to learn his alphabet here, am I right in assuming you mean you want us to do everything we can to be sure he is successful here and later on?" "Our most important goal is to help children develop and grow in ways that will ensure success now and when they go to school. Let me tell you how we do this and why we believe this approach is best."

When parents sense that teachers respect their concerns and want to do everything possible to ensure their child's success, they are more open to sharing their viewpoints and supporting common goals. A positive relationship with parents is also a constructive foundation for dealing with problems when they arise.

Problem-Solving Conferences

Conferences may be scheduled to discuss a specific problem that you and/or the parents have identified. Regardless of who requests the conference, it is important to prepare ahead of time by gathering as much information as possible and thinking through possible strategies for dealing with the problem. The following sequence may be helpful in conducting a problem-solving session with parents.

- *Agree on the problem.* Make sure there is agreement on what the problem is by being as descriptive as possible. "Elias kicks and hits other children, sometimes several times a day."

- *Describe the behavior.* Bring observations of the child that will help identify when the behavior occurs, what seems to provoke it, and what the child does afterward. "Elias hit Kwasi when he wanted to play with the red truck and Kwasi had it. Elias had been watching Evan and Kwasi building in the block corner. He sat down next to them, and when Kwasi said, 'We're busy, watch out,' Elias kicked him."

- *Ask parents for their observations and ideas.* "Does Elias ever kick or hit at home? When does it occur?"

- *Identify possible causes.* Discuss what might be causing the problem behavior. "It looks as if Elias wants to communicate with other children but doesn't know how—so he kicks or hits them."

- *Agree on goals for the child.* These might include the following:

  to stop hitting and kicking others,
  to learn to use words to say what he wants,
  to feel better about himself, and
  to play with one or two other children successfully.

- *Discuss strategies for achieving goals.* Explain what you are doing, and ask parents for their suggestions. "This is what we can do here to help Elias relate more successfully to other children. What have you tried at home?"

- *Agree on a strategy and plan to stay in touch.* Clarify your understanding of how you and the parents will proceed and agree to keep in touch periodically.

Problem-solving sessions are not always easy to manage. They are, however, more likely to succeed when teachers are prepared, ready to listen, and able to maintain a nonjudgmental attitude.

Sharing the *Creative Curriculum* with Parents

This chapter has examined ways in which a partnership can be established between parents and teachers. A sense of partnership is an essential first step in helping parents to understand your approach to curriculum. When parents trust the judgment and expertise of their child's teachers, they are more open to accepting the teacher's selection of a curriculum.

All parents want their children to succeed. For many parents, though, success is measured by how quickly the child learns and how early the child accomplishes specific tasks or content that parents judge as important. For example, learning the alphabet, knowing how to count, and being able to read are concrete accomplishments that many parents readily understand. Early childhood educators have an obligation to listen to parents' wishes and to help them see how a developmentally appropriate curriculum such as the *Creative Curriculum* will best serve the child now and in the future.

Each of the modules in the *Creative Curriculum* contains a section on sharing that interest area with parents. Included are suggestions for conducting workshops for parents on how children learn in each interest area, and ways to involve parents in classroom activities. At the end of the module, there is a letter to parents that describes what you do at school and what parents can do at home to extend learning.

Other strategies for helping parents understand the importance of a developmentally appropriate curriculum include the following:

- Share the National Association for the Education of Young Children's publication entitled *Developmentally Appropriate Practice in Programs Serving Children Birth Through Age 8*. Pamphlets summarizing appropriate and inappropriate practices for each age group are available from NAEYC.

- Invite experts to speak at a parent meeting or workshop.

- Show parents the videotape, *The Creative Curriculum*, which illustrates the curriculum in action.

- Develop a brochure on the program that briefly explains the philosophy, goals, and objectives of the program.

- Provide each parent with a copy of the booklet, *A Parent's Guide to Early Childhood Education*, written specifically for programs using the *Creative Curriculum*.

Part II of the *Creative Curriculum* focuses on each of the interest areas that might be included in an early childhood classroom. The original *Creative Curriculum* interest areas—Blocks, House Corner, Art, Table Toys, Sand and Water, Library, and Outdoors—have been supplemented with three new areas: Music and Movement, Cooking, and Computers. Activities in music and movement and cooking can take place without designating a specific area and we have included suggestions either way. Computers are an option for programs serving older preschoolers and kindergarten children. Each module addresses what and how children learn, how the environment is arranged, the role of the teacher, and how to involve parents. A letter to parents concludes each module and explains how children learn in that interest area and what parents can do at home. Appendix B lists resources for those who wish to read further on any of the topics covered in the *Creative Curriculum*.

Part II
INTEREST AREAS

BLOCKS

I. Why Blocks Are Important

Blocks are standard equipment for early childhood classrooms and they are essential to implementing the *Creative Curriculum*. Hollow blocks are ideal for children who wish to set the stage for dramatic play. In a short time these large blocks become a puppet stage, a house, a bus, or fire engine. Unit blocks provide a wealth of learning activities that allow children to acquire important concepts in math, science, geometry, social studies, and more.

Wooden blocks are naturally appealing to young children because they are smooth, hard, and symmetrical. Children like to explore their physical characteristics by touching them, stroking them, and banging them together to find out how they sound. Wooden blocks are open-ended play materials that allow children to create whatever they desire. There is no right or wrong way to build with blocks—children can create whatever they want. Sometimes children start with an idea of what they want to make; at other times the three-dimensional designs grow as children place blocks together randomly or in patterns. Like other art, the creations children produce with blocks are often reminiscent of things they have seen, and so they will begin to name what they build: house, road, or rocket ship.

Block building is important to cognitive development. As children experience the world around them, they form pictures in their minds of what they see. Playing with blocks gives them an opportunity to recreate these pictures in concrete form. The ability to create these representations of their experiences is an important skill necessary for abstract thinking. Moreover, because blocks are designed in mathematical units, children playing with them acquire a concrete understanding of concepts essential to logical thinking. They learn about sizes, shapes, numbers, order, area, length, and weight as they select, build, and clean up blocks.

Blocks are valuable play materials for physical development. Children use their large muscles to carry blocks from place to place. As they carefully place blocks together to form a bridge or an intricate design, they are refining the small muscles in their hands, which is important for writing tasks.

Like the house corner, the block corner is a place for children to play together and share experiences. One child's idea of how to build a zoo may differ from another's, but children learn to respect different viewpoints and they learn from one another. As children build together, they solve problems and learn the benefits of cooperation.

Objectives for Children's Learning

Children can realize many of the benefits of block play when their teachers set objectives that are realistic and appropriate for their stage of development. Listed below are sample objectives that you can address as children work with blocks.

Objectives for Socio-Emotional Development

- Work independently and in a group (deciding when, how, and with whom to play).

- Express needs, concerns, and fears in socially acceptable ways (creating a hospital or cave with monsters and playing make-believe).

- Share and cooperate with others (trading materials and props and planning joint building projects).

- Demonstrate pride in accomplishments and a positive self-concept (sharing their buildings by talking about what they have created).

Objectives for Cognitive Development

- Develop an understanding of concepts of length, height, weight, and area (carrying blocks and using them in constructions).

- Classify and sort objects by size, shape, and function (placing blocks of the same size together).

- Make use of physical principles (weight, stability, equilibrium, balance, and leverage).

- Predict cause-and-effect relationships (seeing how high they can build before the blocks fall).

- Solve problems related to construction (bridging a bridge or making steps to a house).

- Organize in a sequence (laying out blocks from short to tall and counting in correct order).

- Use addition, subtraction, and fractions (judging how many blocks are needed to fill a space).

- Utilize emergent reading and writing skills (making signs for buildings).

Objectives for Physical Development

- Use large and small muscle skills (grasping, lifting, placing, and balancing blocks).

- Develop eye-hand coordination (placing blocks in desired patterns).

- Control the placement of objects (under, over, above, below, on top of, and next to when constructing with blocks).

These objectives are offered as examples of many learning opportunities available to children when they have access to a rich assortment of blocks. You can add to and adapt these objectives to meet the needs of the children in your classroom.

II. Arranging the Environment

The organization of the classroom and the types of materials available to children have a substantial influence on how children behave and what they learn. The space you set aside for block building, the type and amount of blocks, and how you arrange them all send messages to children about the importance and value of blocks.

Creating Space

The size and location of the block corner are important factors in its success as an interest area. No matter how full a selection of blocks is available to children, they will be frustrated if the space allocated for block building is insufficient or plagued with problems. To maximize the potential of blocks as effective learning materials, children need have sufficient room to build, a clearly defined space for block play, and appropriate flooring.

Block building requires a large play area. If the block corner is too small, children will have to build very close to each other. This not only leads to squabbles over "turf" but also inhibits children who like to create large or long structures. An area that is too small sends a message to children that block play is not very important in this classroom.

Some children like to have a defined space in the block corner where they can build on their own. One way to do this is to use cardboard sheets. Thick cardboard makes a good, flat surface on which

to build, which is especially helpful if you have an uneven floor or shag carpeting. Alternatively, tape can be used to define individual areas. Tape is also useful in defining a "no building zone" near the shelf. This prevents children from building too close to the shelf and having their buildings knocked over by builders who are taking or returning blocks to the shelf.

Define the block area on three sides. A well-defined block corner protects children's block structures and gives them a feeling of security. When the area is protected from traffic, there are fewer accidents and less chance that constructions will be knocked over. Defined areas are especially important for children who find it difficult to stay with a task or are easily distracted by what is happening in the rest of the classroom.

Locating the block area in a corner of the room offers the advantage of having two walls as dividers. Furniture or shelving can be used to create additional boundaries. Children are less likely to take blocks into other interest areas when they have a clearly defined space for block play.

Locate the block corner near other noisy activities. In designating a place for block play, try to locate an area that is adjacent to another active, noisy area so that children engaged in quiet activities will not be disturbed. Situating the block corner next to the house corner, for example, is ideal because both areas engage children in active play. The dramatic play in one area can easily overlap into the adjacent area.

Floor covering is important. Effective floor covering for block building serves several functions: it cuts down on the noise level, it makes block play more comfortable for children and adults, and it reduces toppling accidents. Indoor-outdoor carpeting is ideal because it is comfortable to sit on and blocks can stand up steadily on it. Thick-pile or shag rugs should be avoided because they increase the likelihood of toppling accidents. Linoleum is not recommended because sitting on it can be uncomfortable.

Plan creatively for hollow blocks. Large, hollow blocks require a large building area that may not be available in your classroom. If space is limited and there isn't enough room to have a hollow block area in the classroom, consider the following options:

- Take over another area for a week or so, remembering that hollow block play will be a noisy activity. However, because of their size, hollow block structures do not need as much protection as unit blocks do.

- Large hallways can be used for hollow block building.

- Use hollow blocks to help transform the house corner into a new setting.

- Use hollow blocks outdoors. Store them in a shed or take them indoors when they are not in use.

Selecting Blocks and Props

A good supply of blocks and accessories to enhance children's buildings will make the block corner a valuable component of the curriculum. The two types of blocks recommended for use in implementing the *Creative Curriculum* are unit blocks and hollow blocks.

Unit Blocks

Hardwood unit blocks are durable, have no rough edges, and are easy for children to manipulate. Unit blocks come in proportional sizes that allow children to learn math concepts as they build. There are 25 different sizes and shapes of unit blocks. The basic unit block is 5-1/2" x 2-3/4"x 3/8". All blocks in the set are proportional in length or width to this basic unit; for example, the double-unit block is 11" long and the half-unit is 2-3/4" long. The two half-triangles equal one unit, and the four quarter-circles equal one circle.

A set of 390 unit blocks for a classroom of 10 to 15 children is highly recommended. This total should include as wide a range of sizes and shapes as possible, including ramps, curves, and cylinders. The more types of blocks children have access to, the more their creativity will be inspired.

For young children or inexperienced block builders, it is preferable to introduce just a few basic shapes and sizes at the start of the school year, such as the unit, half-unit, and double-unit blocks. As soon as children become comfortable and adept at building and putting blocks away, you can add additional block shapes until the full set is out.

UNIT BLOCKS

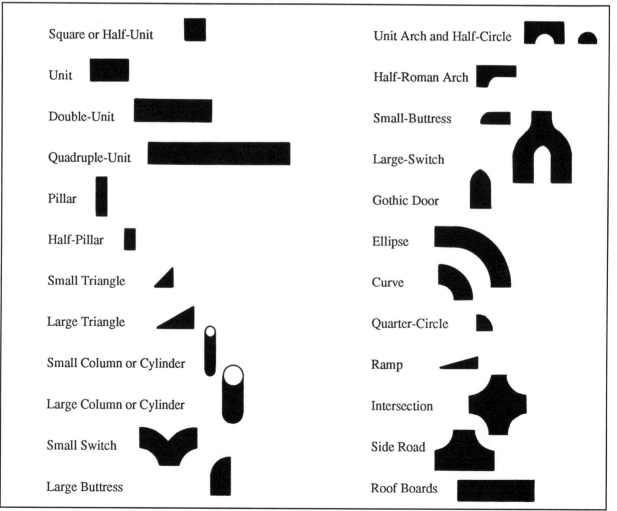

Square or Half-Unit

Unit

Double-Unit

Quadruple-Unit

Pillar

Half-Pillar

Small Triangle

Large Triangle

Small Column or Cylinder

Large Column or Cylinder

Small Switch

Large Buttress

Unit Arch and Half-Circle

Half-Roman Arch

Small-Buttress

Large-Switch

Gothic Door

Ellipse

Curve

Quarter-Circle

Ramp

Intersection

Side Road

Roof Boards

Hollow Blocks

Hollow blocks are made of wood and are much larger in size than unit blocks. The basic square is 5-1/2" x 11" x 11". There are five other pieces in a set: a half-square, a double square, two lengths of flat board, and a ramp. Hollow blocks are open on the sides so that they can be carried more easily. Because children typically enjoy carrying hollow blocks around the block area, these blocks are excellent for children's large muscle development. Young children also enjoy the sense of power they gain by moving something large.

With hollow blocks, children can construct large structures—a boat, an airplane, a rocket—and then climb inside and pretend to be the captain, pilot, or astronaut.

Props and Accessories

Including props and accessories in the block corner is one effective way to encourage children to extend their block play into dramatic play. Here are some traditional props that encourage children to build representations of their world and often lead to dramatic play:

- *People:* family sets, community workers, and others representing various ethnic groups and showing men and women in a variety of roles.

- **Animals:** farm and/or zoo animals.

- **Transportation:** vehicles that include large and small cars, trucks, dump trucks, airplanes, helicopters, spaceships, trains, boats, fire engines, buses, and other vehicles.

Displaying Blocks and Props

How materials are displayed in the block corner influences children's use of blocks as well as what they learn. A well-organized arrangement of blocks and props makes it easier for children to find what they want. Attractive displays invite children to select blocks and props and to use them purposefully. When everything has a place, clean-up is a much easier task.

Arrangement of Blocks

Blocks should be stored on shelves at the children's eye level and grouped by size and shape. The following blocks in the illustration are neatly arranged on the shelf, giving children a clear message that blocks are important. When children can see the different shapes that are available, they can more easily select the ones they need.

Labeling of Block Shelves

To further enhance the display and care of blocks, the shelf should have labels showing where each block shape and size belongs. Labeling conveys a sense of order and reinforces the importance of block play.

Labels can be made by tracing the outlines of the blocks onto solid-colored contact paper. (Blue or red are recommended colors because they show up well on a shelf.) The outlined shapes are then cut out and placed on the shelves. Contact paper labels can easily be removed and replaced if the blocks are rearranged.

Labels for unit blocks should be placed on the shelf lengthwise so that children can see which block is which. (If placed endwise, the unit and double-unit blocks look the same.) Placing the label in the left-hand corner of the shelf reinforces left-to-right directionality, an important reading skill. For blocks that stand up, the label goes behind the blocks on the back of the shelf, as shown in the next illustration.

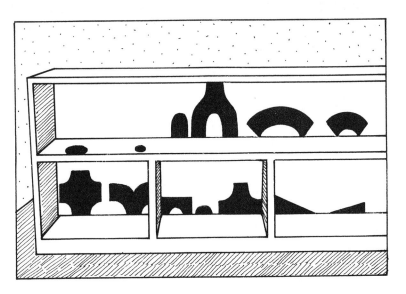

Teachers who use labeling also find that clean-up becomes a much easier task—and one rich in learning as children practice their matching and sorting skills.

Display of Props and Accessories

Props and accessories are more likely to be well-used and cared for if they are displayed in a way that invites children to use them and replace them on shelves when finished. When props are arranged haphazardly, children are less likely to use them or put them away. When props are grouped together, however, children gain a sense of organization.

Labeling Props and Accessories

There are several ways to make labels for props and accessories. An outline of the prop can be drawn on a piece of posterboard or cardboard, cut out, and covered with clear contact paper. In some cases an outline of the object can be traced directly onto colored contact paper.

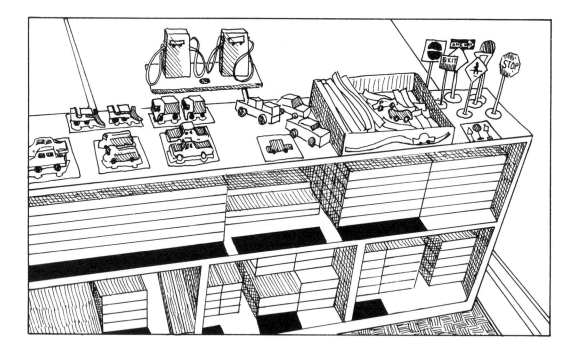

A photo of the object, covered with clear contact paper, can also serve as a label. Make sure that the picture is large enough for children to recognize the object's details.

Many props, such as the traffic signs or transportation toys shown earlier, can be placed directly on the shelf. If there isn't enough shelf space to store each prop on the shelf, plastic basins or sturdy cardboard boxes can be used as supplemental storage space. As shown in the following illustration, each basin is labeled so that children sort the objects as they replace the props.

Caring for Blocks

By thoughtfully laying out the block corner, you can maximize the probability that blocks will be well cared for. Adequate space, storage, and labeling ensure that blocks are well-housed and not thrown against each other during the clean-up process. Wooden blocks, however, are an investment and require some care if they are to last for many years. Sandpaper should be used periodically to eliminate rough or splintered edges. Commercial wood polish or linseed oil can then be applied to provide a protective coating.

Dirty blocks can be washed with oil soap and then scrubbed with a stiff brush and soap and water. They should be dried thoroughly and polished as described above.

Assessing the Effectiveness of the Area

Assessing the effectiveness of the block corner is something you will do daily as you interact with children. These observations are informal, but they form the basis for decisions when you do your weekly planning. Based on your daily observations, you may decide that some props are hardly ever used and should be put away for a while or that you have put out too many block shapes and the children are overwhelmed. Daily observations enable you to plan what changes need to be made to the environment and what activities (such as field trips) you want to schedule to enhance this interest area.

Here are some questions to consider when you observe children's use of the block corner:

- How often is the block corner used?
- Have I made the area appealing and inviting?
- Which children tend to use the block area regularly?
- Which children never or rarely select blocks?
- Which blocks are not being used and why?
- Are children able to put away the blocks and props independently?
- Which props do children select and how do they use them?
- What different stages are evident in children's constructions?
- Are girls and boys using the block corner equally?
- Do children work cooperatively in block building?

These questions are offered as examples of the types of information that you may find helpful in assessing the effectiveness of your block corner. You will have other questions and issues to consider based on what you know about the children, your community, and your resources. This information will help you determine how to intervene and promote every child's use of blocks.

III. Observing and Promoting Children's Learning

Once the block corner is set up, how do teachers stimulate play and creativity? How can teachers be responsive to children and enrich their play experiences? How can children's safety be ensured? And what about cleaning up all those blocks?

The answers to these questions lie in discovering how and when to intervene without interfering in children's play. You can achieve this balance by taking time to observe what children are doing in the block corner and planning your intervention on the basis of what you observe. A good place to start is to become familiar with how children use blocks.

How Children Use Blocks

As with all areas of development, children go through stages using blocks and they progress through these stages at different rates. Understanding the stages helps you gain realistic expectations of what children should be accomplishing as they play. For example, it is appropriate for a child first using blocks to carry the blocks around, and it is appropriate for an experienced five-year-old block builder to construct an intricate tower. Each child is exhibiting behaviors appropriate to his or her current stage of development.

There are four stages in block use, each of which is briefly summarized below.

Stage I: Carrying Blocks (Functional Play)

Young children who haven't played with blocks before will carry them around or pile them in a truck and transport them. At this point, children are interested in learning about blocks—how heavy they are, what they feel like, and how many can be carried at once. By experimenting with blocks, children begin to learn their properties and gain an understanding of what they can and cannot do with blocks.

Stage II: Piling Blocks and Laying Blocks on the Floor

Piling blocks or organizing them on the floor is another stage of exploration. Children in Stage II continue to learn about the characteristics of blocks. They discover how to make a tower by piling blocks on top of each other and what different arrangements look like as they lie on the floor.

At this stage children also begin to apply imagination and critical thinking skills. To young builders, flat rows of blocks on the floor typically suggest a road. Props such as cars and trucks are frequently put to use if they are available to the block builders.

Stage III: Connecting Blocks to Create Structures (Constructive Play)

The use of roads during Stage II marks the transition from piling blocks to making actual constructions. Children who have become comfortable with road building find that they can use roads to link towers. This discovery leads to an active stage of experimentation as children apply their problem-solving skills.

Typically, children in Stage III (three- and four-year-olds) have had some experience with blocks. Their experience enables them to approach blocks in new, creative ways. Typical among the construction techniques developed by children in Stage III are the following:

Making enclosures. Children put blocks together to enclose a space. At first, simply making the enclosure is a satisfying experience. Later, the enclosure may be used for dramatic play with zoo or farm animals. Enclosures help children think about mathematical concepts, particularly area and geometry.

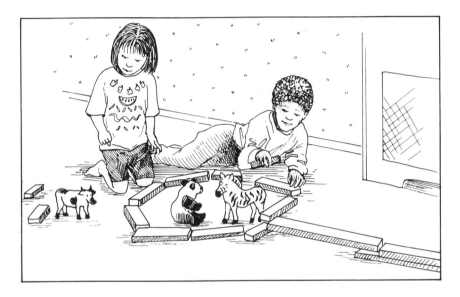

Bridging. To make a bridge, children set up two blocks, leave a space between them, and connect the two blocks with another block. As with enclosures, children use bridges first as a construction technique and later as a part of dramatic play. Bridging also teaches children balance and improves eye-hand coordination.

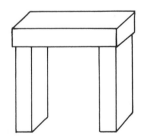

Designs. Children are fascinated with symmetry, balance, and patterns and begin to use blocks to form decorative patterns and symmetrical layouts. Once they have combined a few blocks in a certain way, they may continue the same pattern until their supply of blocks runs out. As they express themselves aesthetically, they notice likenesses and differences and develop motor skills.

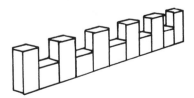

Stage IV: Making Elaborate Constructions (Dramatic Play)

Experienced builders (four- to six-year-olds) are able to put blocks together with dexterity and skill. Children learn to adapt to changes in their building area by curving structures and by building them above, around, or over obstacles. Children in Stage IV are adept in creating structures of remarkable complexity and ingenuity.

During this stage of development, children need a variety of block sizes and shapes so they can make their constructions more elaborate. Another hallmark of Stage IV is that children are able to label their constructions, which are often used as the setting for dramatic play.

Keep these stages in mind when you observe the children in your classroom. You will probably see evidence of all four stages.

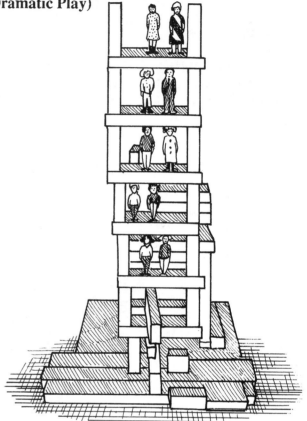

Observing Individual Children

When you have set the stage for children to use the block corner productively, you will have more time to step back and observe how children use blocks and props. Observations enable you to assess where each child is developmentally so that you can plan appropriately to enhance that child's growth and development.

In observing children's individual growth, the stages just demonstrated provide a framework for assessing where each child is developmentally. The objectives for each area of development described in section I provide another set of criteria for observing each child.

Some questions you might ask yourself while observing a child include the following:

- What stages of block building has the child achieved?

- Does the child need more time to practice a particular stage, or should I help the child move to the next stage?

- Does the child build alone or with others? Should I encourage the child to play with others?

- Is the child aware of different shapes and sizes and able to return blocks to their proper place? If not, how can I encourage this awareness?

- Does the child talk about structures and respond to questions? Should I spend more time working with this child?

- Is the child able to solve problems independently? How can I encourage problem solving?

Your answers to questions such as these will help you plan ways of working with each child. You may find, for example, that a child needs more encouragement to use blocks or simply more of your time and attention.

Encouraging All Children to Play in the Block Corner

As with many other activities, block play does not hold the same interest for all children. Some children head straight for the block corner while others never choose to build with blocks. It may be that those who avoid blocks do so because they are:

- afraid to try new activities,
- unsure of what to do,
- afraid of doing it incorrectly,
- uncomfortable with the noise that often accompanies block building,
- too busy doing other activities, or
- girls who view blocks as an activity only for boys.

One way of easing a reticent child into the block area is to invite that child to join you in playing with blocks. If a child is overwhelmed by the noise or the number of children, it is best to choose a time when only a few children are in the block corner. You might say to the child, "I'm going into the block corner, would you like to come?" Or you might simply go into the area, sit down, begin to build, and ask the child to help find a particular block or prop.

Overcoming gender inhibitions about blocks being "boy's play" may take a concerted effort. In some classrooms the boys establish the block corner as "boys only" territory. They tell the girls in words and actions that they aren't welcome. Moreover, girls often get the message in the outside world that construction work is for men. This may be another reason why girls sometimes feel that they don't belong in the block corner. As a result, they may be at an earlier developmental stage of block building than boys of the same age.

It is important, from the very beginning of the school year, to reinforce the idea that the block corner is for everyone. If a boy or group of boys tells a girl that she can't come into the block corner, you might say, "In our class, everyone can build with blocks." Or if a boy says "she doesn't know how to build" one response might be: "In our class everyone makes his or her own buildings. Each one is different and that's what makes them all special."

In addition to verbal messages reaffirming that girls belong in the block corner, subtle messages can be conveyed to help girls feel more secure with blocks. You might display pictures of female construction workers or read a book at storytime about female builders. (Try *Mother Can Do Anything* by Joe Lasker or *Joshua's Day* by Sandra Lucas Surowiecki and Patricia Riley Lenthall.)

Interacting with Children

One of the most effective ways to reinforce children's block play is to talk to them about their structures. Many teachers find this task difficult, especially when the children involved are young and their constructions minimal. For example, talking to a child about the construction shown below might prove challenging for some teachers.

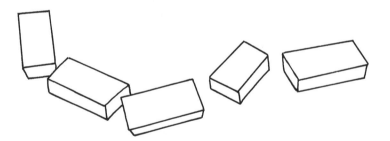

The easiest response to this builder would be to say, "That's a nice building" or "You did a good job." But such judgmental statements say nothing at all about what the child did, nor do they give the child a chance to tell you something about the arrangement of the blocks.

The key to talking to children about their block play is to use statements that describe what a child has done, or to ask open-ended questions that encourage children to talk about their work. This technique is also helpful for children who have difficulty expressing themselves and may be unable, at least in the beginning, to describe what they have built. You can talk about the following:

- *Choice of blocks:* "You found out that two of these blocks make one long block."
- *The arrangement:* "You used four blocks to make a big square."
- *The number used:* "You used more than ten blocks to make the road."

- *The similarity:* "All the blocks in your road are exactly the same size."
- *Noteworthy designs:* "Your building is as tall as the shelf." "Those long blocks are holding up the short ones. It took careful work to be sure the blocks wouldn't fall."

Descriptions such as these enhance children's vocabularies, validate the importance of their work, and enable you to observe how each child is doing developmentally.

It's not always easy for teachers to think of descriptive comments to make about a child's work, especially if the block structures are very simple. Below are two sample buildings and some possible comments a teacher might make to reinforce the child's work.

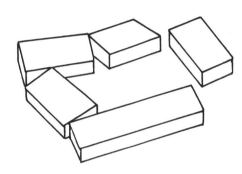

- "I see you used one block that is longer than the others."
- "Look, your blocks make a space in the middle."
- "All of your blocks except one are touching."
- "You used five blocks. You made the whole building with just five blocks."
- "All your blocks are rectangles, but they're not all the same size."

Similarly, for the block structure pictured to the right, a teacher might make the following comments:

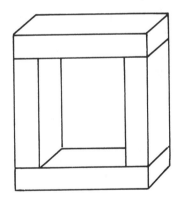

- "You made the top block balance. I bet that wasn't easy."
- "Some of your blocks lie down and some stand up."
- "If I get down on my knees, I can look through it."
- "You had to be very careful when you made this building."

Comments such as these serve several purposes. First, they demonstrate that the teacher values what the child has done. This encourages the child to experiment with new ideas and materials and to learn from mistakes. In addition, the teacher has introduced certain words to describe what the child did. By repeatedly hearing about such concepts as under, on top of, beneath, through, less than, and more than, children learn what the words mean and enlarge their vocabularies. Most importantly, the process—what the child has done with blocks—rather than the final product is emphasized.

Cleaning Up the Block Corner

Clean-up in the block corner can be a real chore that everyone tries to avoid. Children become so involved in what they are making, it is sometimes hard for them to stop. Clean-up often means asking children to undo something they have spent time diligently constructing. With art or table toys, children can usually finish something. In the house corner, they have to stop, but they can pick up in the same place the next day. In the block corner, however, structures eventually have to be dismantled. This may be particularly difficult for older children who have planned constructions and want to continue playing with them.

Another common reason for problems with clean-up is that children become overwhelmed by the task. When the block corner has been well-used, all or most of the blocks and props are on the floor.

There are several strategies you can use to make clean-up easier and more satisfying for children. The key is to offer just enough help so that children begin the task. Eventually, they should be able to start and complete clean-up by themselves. Here are some suggestions:

- *Allow extra time for clean-up* so that children don't feel quite as rushed. If teachers assist, the task usually becomes more manageable.

- *Give children a five-minute warning* that clean-up time is coming. If necessary, tell each child individually how much time is left: "You have enough time to finish the road."

- *Be flexible*. If a child is truly engrossed in block play, allow the child to continue past the work period, if possible. Children appreciate having their work respected in this way and will learn that everyone gets the privilege when it is needed.

- *Help the children get started.* Remind them that the shapes on the shelves tell them where the blocks go. Assign each child a shape or prop to put away. After doing this for several days, the children should be able to organize the task on their own.

- *Make clean-up time into a game.* This is especially helpful at the start of the year. Some examples:

    Give each child a "ticket" with a block shape on it. Children put away all blocks that match the shape on their ticket.

    Say to each child, "Bring me all the blocks that look like this one." As children bring all blocks of one shape, show them where on the shelf the shape belongs by having them compare the shape to the labels until they find the right one.

    Declare a number for the day: "Today we'll clean up the blocks by threes." Each child then collects three blocks at a time and puts them away.

- *Allow block structures to remain standing,* whenever possible, until the next day so that the children can continue their play. This makes it easier to say: "I know you want to keep working on your apartment house, but it's time to clean up. Just put away the blocks you haven't used and we can leave the building up. Then you can work on it again tomorrow (or this afternoon)."

Helping children through the task of clean-up and conveying your respect for their work are effective ways of ensuring that children will use the block corner and benefit from their play.

IV. Extending and Integrating Children's Learning

Children sometimes need a teacher's help to move on to the next stage of building and to expand their ideas. However, it's not always easy to determine when to intervene. You may wonder what to do, for instance, if a child simply piles up blocks day after day. Should such a child be encouraged to move to the next developmental stage?

Keep in mind that piling up blocks isn't just busywork. It's an important and natural stage in block building. Children gain understanding and mastery by repeated interactions with materials. They gain self-confidence when they have time to practice their new skills.

Most children will move on to the next stage when they are ready, often by observing how other children build with blocks. However, if a child truly seems to need help or encouragement to move on, you can try the following suggestions.

- *Get down on the floor* with a child who is frustrated over a problem and offer support in solving the problem. "Let's see if we can find another way to make those blocks stand up."

- *Help the child solve a problem*. For example, ask a leading question: "Do you think another block shape might work there?"

- *Offer pictures of constructions to inspire* a child who has built the same construction every day for a week.

- *Add new accessories and props* to expand construction ideas.

- *Ask questions* about the type of structure and what might belong with it. For instance, you might ask: "Who could live in that building?" or "How will people get to that building?"

Sometimes just a word of encouragement or a small suggestion can inspire a child.

Special Activities

Adding new dimensions to child's work sparks creativity and new uses for blocks. If children see the same props and old materials every day, they sometimes run out of ideas for block building or may avoid the area altogether. You can plan special activities such as trips in the neighborhood, signs for their constructions, or ways to preserve children's buildings to convey the importance of their work.

Neighborhood Walks

When children begin making constructions that represent what they have seen in their immediate environment, you can help them expand their ideas by taking trips. For example, if a child is building a gas station, you might talk about what gas stations look like and suggest a walk if one is near the school. Bring a camera, and have the children take a picture of the gas station and other buildings that can then be posted in the block corner for inspiration.

A construction site offers many insights into how buildings are made. If one is within walking distance, you can visit it periodically. In this way the children can note the stages of building and recreate them in the block corner.

Adding New Props

The addition of new props and materials to the block corner often inspires children to create constructions they hadn't thought of before. Here are some suggestions:

a dollhouse with furniture and dolls	small containers
traffic signs	telephone wire
gas pumps	paper towel rolls
paper, crayons, and scissors	popsicle sticks
hats (construction hardhats, police)	tiles, linoleum squares, rugs
trees (e.g., from a Lego set)	pulleys and string
toy carpentry tools	magazine pictures of buildings, roads, bridges
castle blocks	shells and pebbles
play money	thin pieces of rubber tubing

Sign Writing

Using signs to label children's structures is a good way to support and enhance block play. Sometimes a child will come to you and request a sign. You can say, "Do you want to make the sign yourself, or do you want to tell me what it should say?" If the child wants you to write the words, record exactly what the child says and read it back. The child may want to illustrate the sign.

Keeping markers, paper, and tape near the blocks encourages children to label their buildings, which is beginning writing and reading.

Preserving Buildings

Sometimes when children have made a building that is very special to them, it's difficult for them to dismantle it during clean-up. When there is enough room in the block corner, it is ideal to leave buildings up overnight or even for a week. Doing so allows children to work on a construction over time, which leads to more elaborate building and often to dramatic play. A block construction is more likely to be used as a setting for socio-dramatic play if the children have been allowed to spend an extended period of time creating it.

Unfortunately, in many rooms the block corner has to be used for other group activities such as meetings or story time, or to accommodate cots for naptime. Even in a classroom with a separate block corner, all buildings must eventually come down. However, one way to preserve a block construction before it is dismantled is to take a picture of it. Instant cameras are particularly good to use because children can see the photos right away. Photographs serve the following purposes:

- An important message is communicated to the child: the teacher values the building even though it has to come down.

- Pictures are special. Many teachers have found that when they begin to take pictures, the block corner becomes more popular. Children want to build and have a picture taken of their construction.

- When photos of constructions are displayed in the block corner, they often encourage the builder and other children.

- By taking pictures of a child's work over a period of time, you have a visual record of the child's progress in the block area to include in the portfolio.

Alternatively, block structures can be preserved in a sketch or drawing that can be displayed in the block corner. This also gives children the message that their block building is valued. Older children might be encouraged to draw pictures of the structures they especially like or to help record a structure built by a younger child.

Integrating Blocks with Other Curriculum Areas

Children develop and enhance a range of skills as they build with blocks and return them to the shelves. Blocks can also be integrated into other interest area activities.

Problem-Solving Skills

The construction process is a natural way for children to learn how to solve problems. As soon as children start building with blocks, they are confronted with problems. A road builder may foresee the need for an exit ramp; a house builder may be stymied by the problem of how to build a window. Solving such problems can be a major challenge. Self-motivated children meet the challenge with determination as they search for answers.

Although discovery on one's own is, of course, the preferred problem-solving approach, it does not work for all children in all circumstances. Many teachers ask: "When is it appropriate for an adult to help a child who is working on a block problem?" The best answer is to use good judgment and to intervene only if the problem becomes frustrating for the child. If intervention seems to be the appropriate action to take, the following strategies are suggested:

- *Offer help with the first step* in the solution and then encourage the child to think through the rest: "If I were to hold this block up, how could you make the others reach?"

- *Ask questions that encourage* the child to use information: "It looks like we're all out of the long blocks. What else could you use to fill up the same space?"

- *Plan a walk* in the neighborhood to look at buildings and roads. Help the child relate these real-life constructions to the construction problem experienced in the block corner.

Coming up with a solution demands that the child experiment with ideas through trial and error. With critical thinking, concentration, and persistence, children eventually experience the thrill of discovering an approach that will work.

Acquiring Math Concepts Through Block Play

Unit blocks are ideally suited to teaching many concepts in mathematics. Because the blocks are proportional and can be combined and used in many ways, they are excellent for illustrating abstract ideas in concrete terms. Using blocks regularly, children experience first hand such concepts as these:

- More and less: "I have more blocks than you do!"
- Taller and shorter: "My building is the tallest."
- Twice as big: "I need two of those blocks to match this long one."
- Names of shapes: square, rectangle, triangle, cylinder.
- Numbers: three squares, four cylinders.

When playing with blocks, children also acquire many logical thinking skills, including the ability to make use of classification, seriation, and equivalence. Each of these concepts is illustrated below.

- *Classification:* Putting blocks that are alike together in a group (for example, piling up squares or lining up cylinders). At a more advanced level, children can name the different shapes: "I put the squares here and the cylinders there."

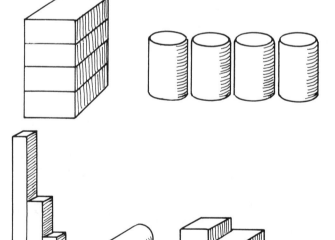

- *Seriation:* Putting items in order (for example, by height from shortest to tallest).

- *Equivalence:* Noticing relations among blocks of differing sizes and shapes (for example, four squares fill the same space as two units, which fill the same space as one double unit).

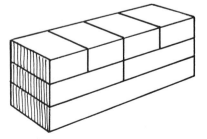

Social Studies

Blocks are used by children to recreate the world around them. For example, children apply their creative abilities to make a zoo, a farm, an airport, a highway, a parking garage, a fire station, a police station, or a shoe store.

How can you encourage and support this important type of play with blocks? By asking questions and making suggestions, you extend children's ideas. Here are two examples that demonstrate how children can recreate their experiences with the teacher's support.

The Apartment House. A three-year-old began by building a tall structure with several cars parked beside it. The teacher entered the area and the following dialogue took place:

Teacher: I see there are a lot of cars parked next to this building.

Builder: It's a parking lot.

Teacher: Where are all the people who own the cars?

Builder: Inside.

Teacher: Is that where they work?

Builder: No.

Teacher: Is that where they live?

Builder: Yes. It's a compartment house.

Teacher: Oh, all these people live in an apartment building. Is there a playground for the children?

Builder: Now there is. (The builder took out the smaller blocks to improvise a playground.)

It is important to note that because the child replied with one word answers, this teacher had to ask several questions to initiate and extend the conversation.

The Zoo. A four-year-old began by getting the basket of zoo animals and some unit and double-unit blocks. She built simple enclosures and put the animals inside.

At this point, the teacher entered, and the following dialogue took place:

Teacher: Tell me about these animals.

Builder: They're at the zoo.

Teacher: Have you been to the zoo?

Builder: Yes.

Teacher: What do you see at the zoo? What kinds of buildings do they have?

Builder: Cages for the animals—where they can go inside and outside.

Teacher: It looks like you've made an outside yard for the giraffe and the elephant. Do they have an inside house, too?

Builder: Yes. (She started to make one.)

When the teacher returned five minutes later, the builder had constructed a round house with a roof and an outdoor enclosure that in fact resembled the elephant/giraffe house at the local zoo.

The child in this example was able to remember what the cages looked like because she had been to the zoo. If she hadn't had any ideas from her own experience, the teacher could have offered a book to look through. In this example, the builder had also used one of the wooden community workers (the street sweeper) to be the "zookeeper." The teacher commented on this and then made more suggestions.

Teacher: I see one of the workers at the zoo. Who else comes to the zoo?

Builder: People, families, children. (She went to the block accessories and took four wooden block figures, which she lined up in front of the building.)

Teacher: How will people know what this building is?

Builder: It would say "elephant house."

Teacher: I have some paper and crayons here. Would you like a sign?

Builder: Yes. It should say "elephant house."

Teacher: Do you want to make the sign?

Builder:	No, you write "elephant house." (The teacher makes the sign and the child taped it on the building.)
Teacher:	How do people get to the zoo from their homes?
Builder:	They drive in cars.
Teacher:	And where do they park their cars while they walk around to see the animals?
Builder:	There's a parking lot and it costs a dollar to park there.
Teacher:	Maybe you could make a parking lot for your visitors.

The teacher left the builder for a short while. When she returned, the builder had added walkways around the building and a parking area with cars.

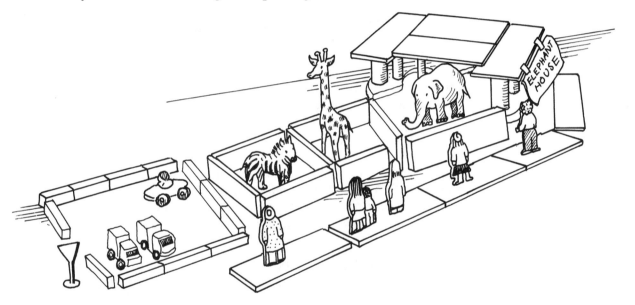

By conversing with the child about visitors and by naming the buildings, the teacher encouraged the child to think about the zoo from several perspectives—who comes to visit the zoo, how they come, where they walk, and where else they go. This example shows how the teacher supported and extended a child's block play in the following ways:

- observing what the child did,
- asking questions to help the child recall experiences,
- listening to what the child said,
- making suggestions based on the child's experiences, and
- helping the child by supplying props and making signs.

By actively participating with children in the block corner, teachers can effectively promote the use of blocks and props as valuable learning materials.

V. Sharing Blocks with Parents

As with all aspects of the *Creative Curriculum,* block play as a tool for learning achieves its fullest potential when parents value its importance. Even parents who have watched children in the block corner may not fully appreciate all the learning that is taking place. You can help parents understand the value of blocks and the role they can play in supporting their child's learning by planning workshops on blocks, welcoming parents into the classroom, and sharing resources such as the letter to parents (at the end of this section).

Conducting Workshops on Blocks

One of the most effective ways to introduce parents to the value of blocks is to have a block workshop. Two types of workshops are suggested: one to explain the value of blocks as part of an early childhood curriculum, and one in which parents can make blocks to take home.

Helping Parents Appreciate the Value of Blocks

Here are some suggestions for involving parents in a workshop where they can experience first hand the value of blocks as learning materials that challenge children's skills and imagination.

- Hold the workshop in the classroom so that parents can use the blocks and props just as their children do.

- Divide the group into two teams. Invite the first team to select any blocks and props they wish and start building. Provide the second team with cards specifying tasks they have to complete. You can select tasks that you have seen children work on, such as building a bridge, making a house with windows and a roof, building steps, or making a zoo.

- While participants are building, talk to them about what they are doing. Ask open-ended questions about their constructions as you would with the children. Allow ten to twenty minutes, depending on how involved the group becomes.

- When the time is up, reconvene the group, allowing the buildings to stand, and lead a discussion of the experience. You might:

    provide a handout of the stages of block building and ask parents which stages they can see in the buildings they created,

    ask each team to share how it felt about the experience, and

    talk about what children learn using blocks and the role you play.

- As a conclusion to the workshop, show the section on blocks from the videotape, *The Creative Curriculum.* Have parents focus on problems that children solve using blocks and the role that teachers play in promoting children's learning in the block corner.

Making Milk Carton Blocks

The second type of workshop is one that parents will enjoy because they can make something to use at home. Milk carton blocks are practically cost-free and have some of the advantages of unit blocks.

Because milk cartons come in proportional sizes—half-pints, pints, quarts, half-gallons, and gallons—they offer another concrete way for children to develop an understanding of math concepts.

To plan a workshop on homemade blocks, you will need to involve parents in collecting the following items:

- cardboard milk cartons (two for each block),
- newspaper,
- rubber bands, and
- contact paper to cover (optional).

Prepare a handout or chart illustrating the steps described below. Make a few blocks yourself first, to be sure you know how to do it. This will enable you to identify and resolve any difficulties prior to the workshop.

You might start the workshop by demonstrating each of the steps and completing one block. Here are the directions for milk carton blocks:

1. Cut out newspaper squares the size of the bottom of the carton you plan to fill. You will need a tall stack of newspaper squares to give the block some weight. (A paper cutter makes this task easier.)

2. Cut the tops off the cartons so they have a square opening.

3. Slit one of the two cartons down each corner. Then hold the sides together with three rubber bands.

4. Pack the slit carton with newspaper squares stacked flat and pressed down. This fills the carton and allows it to stand up.

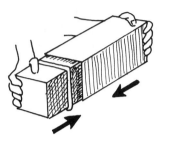

5. When the first carton is filled, put the second carton over the first upside down. The rubber bands can be removed, as the second carton encloses the first. Finish the block by covering it with clear contact paper.

Involving Parents in the Classroom

When parents visit the classroom, you can help them appreciate the value of blocks by inviting them to observe or participate in the block corner. To use this time most effectively, provide parents with specific suggestions of what to look for in the children's buildings. Here are some ideas:

- Refer parents to the stages of children's block building and point out what stages are evident in the block structures being built that day.

- Display the objectives for children's learning in the block corner and explain to parents how block play addresses these objectives.

- Discuss how the blocks and props are arranged and displayed. Talk about how the arrangement helps children use blocks more effectively and how it contributes to their growth and development.

- After intervening to handle a problem or extend a child's learning, explain what you did and why.

- Invite parents to join children in the block corner and build with them if they wish. Not all parents will feel comfortable doing this. It may help if you offer a specific suggestion, such as helping a child who is working on a problem or assisting in clean-up.

Sharing blocks with parents takes time and some planning. The results, however, will be worth the effort, as parents who understand the value of these materials can be more supportive of their children's work at school. You can use or adapt the letter to parents that follows to further enhance parents' understanding of the role of blocks in your curriculum.

A Letter to Parents on Blocks

What We Do and Why

Blocks, the hard wood units that come in proportional sizes and shapes, are one of the most valuable learning materials in our classroom. When they build with blocks, children learn about sizes and shapes, spatial relationships, math concepts, and problem solving. When children lift, shove, stack, and move blocks, they learn about weight and size. Each time they use blocks, they are making decisions about how to build a structure or solve a construction problem.

When children build with blocks in the classroom, we encourage them to talk about what they are doing. For example, we might say:

- "Tell me about your building."
- "How did you decide to put those blocks together?"

We also ask questions that help children extend their thinking about their block play. For example, we might say:

- "You built a tall apartment house. How do the people get to their floor?"
- "How many blocks do you think it will take to fill up that space?"
- "Where do people park their cars when they come to visit the shopping center?"

These questions and comments are designed to help the children become aware of what they are doing and think of ways to extend their work.

What You Can Do at Home

Hardwood unit blocks are expensive, but there are several other types of blocks you might want to have at home to support your child's learning. For example, you might wish to purchase table blocks, colored wooden cube blocks, or cardboard brick blocks.

Small blocks can be stored in shoe boxes or plastic tubs and containers. You can put a picture label on the container so your child knows where these materials belong. Identify a place where your child can build and play with the blocks, either on the floor or a table. As your child builds with the blocks, you can talk about the structure and ask questions. Props such as clothespins, small plastic animals, and cars and trucks will extend your child's play and inspire new ideas. Playing with large or small blocks, your child can learn to:

- judge distance, space, and size,
- create scenes for dramatic play,
- stack blocks carefully (using eye-hand coordination and small muscle control),
- compare and sort by size and shape, and
- use words to describe a construction.

Perhaps the most important contribution you can make to your child's learning through blocks is to take an interest in what your child does, both at home and at school. We welcome you to visit the classroom at any time so you can see for yourself how much your child is learning.

HOUSE CORNER

I. Why the House Corner Is Important

The house corner is the area of the classroom dedicated to "playing house." The work children do in the house corner is called dramatic play, pretend play, or make-believe; it involves taking on a role and engaging in imitative behavior. Socio-dramatic play, a higher level of play, incorporates verbal interactions with at least one other person in the play episode. This will be discussed in more detail in section III.

Children use the house corner to take on roles extending far beyond familiar family scenes and to create environments as strange and exciting as a space station or as typical as a shoe store. Although the familiar home environment is a common theme for dramatic play, children also act out roles of real and imaginary characters. Dinosaurs and goblins can be found in the house corner just as easily as mommies, daddies, doctors, and storekeepers.

Children love playing "make-believe." We have all seen a child's delight in acting like a parent, performing super deeds like a TV hero, or being a demanding baby. In fact, children seem to crave this type of activity. In one research study on this topic, experimenters removed the house corner of a preschool classroom and observed how children reacted. Within three days, children had formed their own area for dramatic play using hollow blocks, tables, and other classroom objects to create a setting for pretend play. Children so missed the house corner that they took it upon themselves to recreate one.

Why is dramatic play so important to young children? As children act out roles in the house corner, they develop many new skills. They learn about themselves, their families, and society around them. Engaging in dramatic play, they collect and draw upon their previous experiences. They learn to judge and select relevant information in order to enact play episodes. This is an essential skill for intellectual development. Children also learn from one another as they interact in socio-dramatic play. They learn to ask and answer questions and to work together to solve problems. They develop the ability to concentrate as they remain in the same play themes for increasing periods of time.

The house corner provides many opportunities for socio-emotional development. Dramatic play offers children a forum in which to act out fears safely and relive life experiences. Through dramatic play, children can take on roles they fear and learn to control their anxieties. For example, a child who is worried about going to the hospital for an operation can pretend to be the doctor. By assuming the role of the doctor, he can feel "in charge" and act out his impressions of being a doctor. In this way the child gains some control over real fears.

Children also learn to be flexible and cooperate with others by negotiating roles and playing together. Knowing how to pretend helps children become better planners. It allows them to anticipate how they will feel and act in certain real-life situations.

Finally, playing in the house corner provides practice in using small motor skills as children put on and take off dress-up clothes. In a well-labeled house corner, children use hand-eye coordination skills and visual discrimination skills as they put away props and materials.

Objectives for Children's Learning

Children benefit from their play in the house corner when teachers set realistic expectations for them based on their stage of development. As teachers participate in children's role playing, make-believe play, and socio-dramatic play, they can facilitate children's growth and development.

Below are some objectives for children's learning in the house corner. You will think of many more based on the ages and abilities of the children you teach.

Objectives for Socio-Emotional Development

- Interact with others (taking on roles and play acting).

- Express individuality and creativity (developing play themes based on individual preferences and experiences).

- Play cooperatively with others (taking turns and sharing materials).

- Demonstrate an understanding of the social expectations and attitudes of others (role playing and reenacting life experiences).

- Anticipate how to act in new situations (developing the ability to imagine).

- Address fears and worries (trying out roles and re-playing difficult and scary experiences).

- Demonstrate empathy for others (developing more complex roles and showing concern for others while in those roles).

Objectives for Cognitive Development

- Use symbols to represent real objects and situations (using a block to represent a telephone or a string for a firehose).

- Identify and plan play episodes with others. ("Let's play store. You be the storekeeper. I'll come shopping.")

- Draw on past information and experience to solve problems. ("Doctors don't give shots in the hand. My doctor gives shots in my arm.")

- Identify solutions to problems that arise during play. ("What are we going to feed this baby? There's no cereal in the house! We'll need to go to the store.")

- Classify props according to common characteristics. ("You put away the cooking utensils and I'll put away the things for eating.")

- Arrange objects according to size (cleaning up props and returning them to labeled places).

- Persevere at a task (remaining involved in a play episode for increasing periods of time).

Objectives for Physical Development

- Improve small muscle control (putting on dress-up clothes and snapping, buckling, zipping, and buttoning).

- Use eye-hand coordination (dressing dolls and matching pots and pans with outlines on the shelves where they are stored).

- Use visual discrimination skills (matching and grouping like objects such as dishes or utensils).

These objectives are offered as examples of the skills and understanding children can develop playing in the house corner.

II. Arranging the Environment

The location and set-up of the house corner, as well as the selection and display of props and furniture, strongly affect how children use this area and the extent of their learning.

Creating Space

In setting up the house corner, you might consider the following suggestions:

Enclose the house corner on three sides. The house corner should be a clearly defined area and a secluded place for pretend play. Enclosure also helps children keep track of the props and materials that belong in the area and return them to their proper places during clean-up.

By placing the house corner in one corner of the room, the two existing walls serve as dividers. A third wall can be made using shelves or house corner furniture.

Another way to set off the house corner from other classroom areas is to put all or part of it on a platform. To create a platform, put a piece of plywood on cinder blocks and cover it with an old carpet or rug samples.

The house corner is best situated near other noisy interest areas. This avoids disturbing children who are involved in quiet activities such as playing with table toys or looking at books. Many teachers

locate the house corner next to the block corner because both tend to be noisy and engage children in dramatic activities. As children become more skilled at pretending, they may want to borrow props from the block area to assist their dramatic play in the house corner.

Create a homelike setting. The primary activity in this area is playing house. It is natural for young children to play out themes familiar to them, and the most familiar of all themes is, of course, home and family life. You can facilitate this type of play by making the house corner warm and inviting.

The house corner can be subdivided into different "rooms" by using furniture. A bedroom or sitting area and kitchen are typically selected, as they represent living spaces that lend themselves well to dramatic play. Dress-up clothes, a doll bed, and a mirror can be placed in the bedroom area; a stove, table and chairs, and empty food containers can outfit the kitchen.

Hanging a decorative piece of fabric on the wall lends both warmth and beauty to the house corner. Real or plastic flowers and photographs of children and families hung at the children's eye level add to the homelike feeling.

If there isn't a real window in the house corner, one can be created on the wall with tape and curtains. Rug scraps or an inexpensive piece of secondhand carpet also help make the house corner a soft, cozy place to play. Additional furniture can be donated or made (e.g., the back seat of an old car can be used as a couch).

Selecting Materials and Props

While too many props in the house corner can be overwhelming, the guiding principle is that the richer the house corner environment, the more expressive and creative children will be in their dramatic play. In selecting materials and props, it's a good idea to consider the developmental levels of the children.

In the first developmental stage of dramatic play (role playing), children require more concrete and realistic objects to stimulate their play. Therefore, the younger the children, the more important it is to equip the house corner with real materials and realistic-looking props. Older children are better able to rely on their imaginations to create props. Children who are unfamiliar with the house corner or are tentative in their dramatic play can be introduced to a limited number of props at a time. More props can be added as children can handle them.

Furniture and materials for a well-equipped house corner would include the following:

- **Furniture:**

  stove
  refrigerator
  child-sized table and chair
  doll bed
  ironing board/iron

  doll highchair
  doll stroller
  rocking chair
  full-length, nonbreakable mirror

- **Kitchen Equipment:**

  pots and pans in various sizes
  eating utensils
  cooking utensils such as serving
    spoons, ladles, sifters, and
    colanders
  dish towels

  dishes—plates, cups, saucers, and bowls
  tea kettle or coffee pot
  clean-up materials such as broom, mop,
    and sponges

- **Basic props:**

  male and female ethnic dolls
  clock
  telephone
  blankets for dolls
  empty food containers and boxes
  plastic food

- **Dress-up clothes:**

  shoes and boots
  ties and scarves
  costume jewelry
  hats and wigs (unless prohibited by local licensing requirements)
  suitcases, pocketbooks, briefcases, wallets, keys

In equipping the house corner, include props and materials that reflect the cultural and ethnic backgrounds of the children in the group. Look for items that best convey the message to children from all backgrounds that "this is my home." Select props that are characteristic of both sexes and nonsexist.

Although young children rarely tire of "playing house," with a little encouragement from the teacher, their play can include themes such as going to the doctor, shopping for food, and going to work. The addition of props (and prop boxes) is one of the best ways to stimulate new themes. The house corner can be converted into many different types of settings. Periodically, you can try converting all or part of the house corner into a different type of setting, such as a supermarket, a laundromat, or an office. (Prop boxes for different dramatic play settings are described in detail in section IV.)

Displaying and Storing Materials and Props

An attractive and orderly layout in the house corner is inviting to children. Because there are many different kinds of props in the house corner, arranging them in a logical way encourages children's creativity, enables them to work independently, and helps them make choices. An orderly area sends this important message to children: the house corner is a special place, and the items in it are to be valued and taken care of. When children can easily find the props they need, less time is spent searching for materials and more time is devoted to dramatic play.

Be sure that all props in the house corner are clean and intact. Children quickly lose interest in dolls that are falling apart or in dress-up clothes that cannot be tied or snapped into place. As props get broken or torn, repair or replace them.

Here are some suggestions for displaying props and materials:

- Hooks, set on a board tacked to the wall or on a pegboard on the back of a shelf, are ideal for hanging hats, bags, and dress-up clothes.
- A shoe rack or hanging shoe bag is suitable for both shoes and other small items.
- A pegboard with hooks can be used for storing pots, pans, and kitchen utensils.
- A small coatrack can be used for hanging clothes and bags.
- Three-tiered wire baskets that hang from hooks are excellent for storing plastic foods.
- Plastic storage bins are useful for costume jewelry and plastic food.

Labeling Materials and Props

Labeling facilitates storage of materials in the house corner. Labels that are visual representations of the objects' shapes and sizes can be used to designate storage areas. For example, labels for pots and pans can be made by tracing an outline of each item onto solid-colored contact paper. These outlined shapes are then cut out and placed on the appropriate storage shelf.

For props such as ladles or spoons hung on a pegboard, center the label under the hooks. If items are stored in cabinets or bins, put labels of each item on the outside cabinet door or on the side of the storage bin. This helps children know what is inside.

Dress-up clothes can be hung on hooks or coatracks with a label or photo of each item posted above each place.

Hats and other props can go on a shelf with a picture label to show where each item belongs. Well-organized storage and an orderly room arrangement go hand in hand in creating an environment that facilitates children's dramatic play.

Assessing the Effectiveness of the Area

You will want to be aware of the how the children in your classroom use the house corner. Observing the entire group lets you know when to add new props, adapt the setting, or provide new stimulus for children's play in the form of a trip or a planned pretend play activity (described in section IV.) You will probably have additional questions as you observe children in the house corner. Discuss your observations with your co-teacher as you plan the changes you want to make. Answers to many of the questions will be addressed throughout this module.

Here are some questions to consider now:

- How often is the house corner used?
- Which children tend to select the house corner regularly?
- Who rarely or never wants to play in the house corner, and how can I involve them in dramatic play?
- Are both girls and boys using the house corner? If only girls use the area, have I included props for boys?
- Are children imitating TV characters or recreating their own experiences?
- Which props are most frequently used? Never used? Do they need to be changed?
- How are props used?
- Are children able to clean up the house corner independently?

By regularly observing to assess the effectiveness of the house corner, you can make changes that are needed to continually inspire children's dramatic play.

III. Observing and Promoting Children's Learning

Observation helps you assess how individual children progress—what aspects of pretend play they use and what skills they have already mastered. Your observations help you decide how you will intervene to support their learning.

How Children Play Pretend

Like all areas of learning, pretend play is developmental in nature, which means that children move through a progression of stages in their play. Knowledge of these stages enables teachers to set realistic expectations for children.

Stage I: Imitative Role Play

In this initial stage of play, beginning as early as age one, children try to act, talk, and dress like people they know. Children use real objects as props. They depend on an element of reality in their play. For instance, a child may pick up a telephone and pretend to "talk on the phone like Mommy" or hold a doll and "feed the baby."

Stage II: Make-Believe Play

In the second stage, children's play is enriched by their imaginations. Now less dependent on concrete props for role playing, children may use a string as a firefighter's hose, or an envelope may be Mommy's briefcase. The ability to make-believe moves beyond the scope of real props or costumes. Children also learn to use their imaginations to invent actions and situations. Dramatic play is no longer confined to real-life events. At this stage children often use such play to help them understand feelings or deal with fears and worries.

Stage III: Socio-Dramatic Play

Socio-dramatic play emerges at the time children begin seeking the company of others, often at about age three or four. Socio-dramatic play includes elements of imitative play and make-believe play; however, it stands apart from the earlier stages in that it requires verbal interaction between two or more children. Because of its interactive nature, socio-dramatic play necessitates planning. One child chooses to be the teacher and the other the student; one child can be a firefighter and the other a would-be victim. Because of its more complex story lines, socio-dramatic play requires that children spend a significant amount of time in this type of play.

Factors Influencing Developmental Stages

Children progress through these stages at their own pace, which may not correlate with their chronological age. One child may pass through the first two stages quickly, while another child may stay in the first stage for many months. There are two reasons for such different rates of development. First, all children have unique developmental timetables. Second, many factors influence children's play, including life experience, parental involvement and attitudes about play, and exposure to television and movies.

Young children begin pretend play by drawing on their own experiences for ideas. To illustrate, almost every four-year-old child has some notion of what a firefighter does. The extent of the child's experiences with firefighters will be reflected in his or her play. Ideas may come from:

- seeing fire engines racing down the street;
- visiting the fire station;
- knowing a firefighter—a relative, friend, or neighbor;
- seeing or experiencing a real fire;
- hearing stories about fires and firefighters;
- seeing fires, fire engines, and firefighters on television; and
- talking with other people about firefighters.

Young children's dramatic play is also affected by parental attitudes about play and fantasy. Children whose parents encourage pretend play and view fantasy as a positive attribute are likely to enter preschool and kindergarten well-equipped to play in the house corner. In contrast, when children come from families where imaginary playmates or storytelling are frowned upon, they tend to have less developed dramatic play skills.

The media—particularly television—influence children's stages of development. The media bombards children with a steady flow of fantasy creations and imaginary happenings. Depending on the child, this exposure can elicit two different reactions. For some children, viewing fantasy on TV fulfills their need for creative and imaginative expression. These children are content to let TV do their dramatic play for them. Other children watch the fantasy on TV and incorporate many of the characters and situations in their own play. If they only imitate what they see, rather than building on these characters or events, they will remain at a beginning level.

In sum, children come to school with a range of experiences that influence their dramatic play. While all children have a tendency to pretend, they may need your intervention to begin playing at higher levels.

Observing Children's Pretend Play

To assess individual children's growth and development in dramatic play, you can use the stages of development previously described as a framework. Also, the objectives for children in the house corner can be used in conjunction with the Child Development and Learning Checklist in Appendix A as a way for you to evaluate and plan for each child's growth.

The ability to pretend involves six skills. As you observe children, you'll want to find out which of these skills children already have and where you need to intervene in order to help children acquire new skills. Dr. Sara Smilansky, an Israeli psychologist who has conducted extensive research in dramatic play, identifies the following six skill areas:

1. imitative role play,
2. make-believe using props,
3. make-believe in actions and situations,
4. time spent in dramatic play,
5. interactions with other children, and
6. verbal communication.

In imitative role play, the child assumes a make-believe role expressed through imitative behaviors and verbalizations. As you observe each child, ask these questions:

- What role(s) does the child play?
- What type of role is this (family member, animal, TV character, self)?
- Does the child select the same role day after day or experiment with different roles?
- How many different aspects of the role does the child play?

In make-believe with props, children use props in many ways. First they rely on real objects; then they use objects to represent other objects (e.g., a piece of paper for a steering wheel). Children with the highest level of pretend ability can substitute words and actions for real objects (e.g., they use hands in circular motion for a steering wheel). As you observe each child, ask these questions:

- Does the child use props?
- Which props does the child use? Clothes? Hats? Tools? Dolls? Furniture?
- How does the child use the props? Is the child simply interested in playing with the prop, or does the prop serve as a part of make-believe play?
- How many different props does the child use?
- Does the child think of symbolic and inventive uses for props, such as using a string of beads to represent spaghetti and meatballs?
- Can the child perform in the role using movements and/or words instead of real objects?

In make-believe actions and situations, children use words to describe real-life actions or events. They also engage in fantasy—enacting situations that aren't drawn from real-life, such as dragons and witches. As you observe each child, ask these questions:

- Does the child pretend with make-believe actions or situations? (For example, does the child point to the table and say, "I'm the doctor— pretend this is my office." Or, having invented this situation, does the child say, "We just went shopping—let's unpack the food in the bag.")
- Does the child's play include fantasy?
- Are the elements of fantasy used by the child simple or complex in structure?
- Do the child's ideas for make-believe come from stories, TV, or the child's own imagination?

As children become more adept at role playing, they can remain in play episodes for **increasing amounts of time.** Ask these questions as you watch each child:

- How much time does the child spend in a dramatic play episode?
- How much of the child's time is spent in group play?
- Which play themes hold the child's attention longest?
- How persistent is the child in carrying out the role selected?

Socio-dramatic play means that a child is engaged in a play episode that involves **interaction** with at least one other person. As you observe each child, ask these questions:

- Does the child play alone? With one other child? As part of a group?

- Who initiates group play? Is it always the same child who assigns roles and gets things started?

- How does the child let other children know of his or her interest in group play?

- How does the child resolve problems in sharing props, selecting roles, and giving directions?

If **verbal communication** is taking place, children are engaged in socio-dramatic play. As you look at each child, ask these questions:

- What does the child say during play?

- Does the child use language to communicate ideas? Give directions? Explain things? Ask for information? Request props?

- Does the child's voice change when he or she is taking on a role?

Observing these aspects of dramatic play allows you to compile a profile of each child's pretend ability and know when it is appropriate to intervene. The following chart outlines the progression of dramatic play skills.

LEVELS OF ABILITY IN SOCIO-DRAMATIC PLAY

CRITERIA	BEGINNING LEVEL	ADVANCED LEVEL
ROLE PLAY **Role chosen**	Role relates to child's attempts to understand the familiar world (e.g., mommy, daddy, baby, animals)	Role relates to child's attempts to understand the outside world (e.g., firefighter, police officer, doctor)
How child plays role	Child imitates one or two aspects of role (e.g., child announces, "I'm the mommy," rocks the baby, and then leaves the house corner)	Child expands concepts of role (e.g., child announces, "I'm the mommy," feeds the baby, goes to a meeting, prepares dinner, reads the newspaper, goes to work, talks on the phone, etc.)
USE OF PROPS **Type of prop needed**	Child uses real object or replica of object (e.g, real or toy phone)	Child uses any object as prop (e.g., block for phone) or a pretend prop (e.g., holds hands to ears and pretends to dial a telephone)
How child uses prop	Child enjoys physically playing with objects (e.g., banging receiver of phone, dialing)	Prop is used as part of play episode (e.g., child calls a doctor on phone because baby is sick)

HOUSE CORNER

CRITERIA	BEGINNING LEVEL	ADVANCED LEVEL
MAKE-BELIEVE	Child imitates simple actions of adult (e.g., child moves iron back and forth on ironing board, holds phone receiver to ear)	Child's actions are part of a play episode of make-believe (e.g., "I'm ironing this dress now so I can wear it for the party tonight")
TIME	Fleeting involvement (e.g., child enters area, plays with doll, puts on hat, and leaves area)	Child stays in area more than 10 minutes (e.g., child is really involved in play episode and carries through on theme)
INTERACTION	Solitary play (e.g., child acts out role alone with no apparent awareness of others)	Functional cooperation (e.g., child interacts with others at various times when the need arises to share props or have a partner in play) Cooperative effort (e.g., child acts out role cooperatively with others, recognizing the benefits of working together)
VERBAL COMMUNICATION	Verbalization centers around the use of toys (e.g., "Bring me that phone" or "I had the carriage first")	Dialogue about play theme—constant chatter about roles children are playing (e.g, restaurant scene: "What do you want to eat?" "Do you have hamburgers?" "Yup. We have hamburgers, french fries, and cokes")

Interacting with Children

Although children from an early age can play pretend, they usually need support from teachers to develop the many elements of pretend ability that are important for their academic success. Do children need to be introduced to more props? Would it be beneficial to provide encouragement to move to the next developmental stage? Are children getting stuck in their choice of dramatic roles?

Ongoing assessments will help you know when it's appropriate to let children be and when it's appropriate to intervene. In the *Creative Curriculum*, intervention refers to strategies you can use to facilitate learning. Nondirective interventions such as a smile or a reassuring glance can be effective ways to convey approval to a child busily at play in the house corner. Strategies for more direct intervention to facilitate children's pretend ability are discussed below.

The Teacher as a Stimulator of Play

Many teachers do not feel it is appropriate to take an active role in children's dramatic play—yet some children need this type of support and encouragement. One effective strategy is to enter the house corner as an observer and comment or ask questions about what you see happening. This makes children more aware of what they are doing, and it can help redirect negative behaviors, as the following examples illustrate:

A child has placed a doll in the carriage and is pushing it around. The teacher says, "I see you are taking your baby for a walk. Where are you going?" The child doesn't respond, so the teacher says, "Are you taking your baby to the park or to the store?" The child says, "To the store," and the teacher makes a suggestion: "Don't forget your pocketbook because you'll need some money."

A child is putting a doll in the bed and says, "Now, baby, you go to bed and shut up." The teacher says, "Do you know a song the baby might like to hear? Sometimes a lullaby helps babies go to sleep."

Offering suggestions at the right moment enables you to help children use props effectively:

Two children are making a cake in the house corner. One is using the rolling pin, and the second child says, "I need the rolling pin." The teacher says, "Have you sifted your flour yet? Here's a sifter you can use first."

A child is playing shoe salesperson. She measures another child's foot and says, "Here are your new shoes." The teacher asks, "Do you have a shoebox for those shoes or a bag to carry them in?"

When children are using the house corner but not engaging in any interactions with one another, you can encourage interaction by making suggestions relevant to what they are doing:

A child is standing by the stove, and the teacher says, "You've been very busy cooking. What are you making?" or "Mmm, it sure smells good! I'd love to have some lunch." Then, to the other children, the teacher says, "Is anyone else here hungry for some lunch?"

One child is holding a doll. The other is by the stove. The teacher says, "How is your baby today? Is she hungry? Maybe Robbie can make some food so you can feed your baby."

In these examples, teachers facilitated children's play but remain outside the actual play episode.

The Teacher as a Participant in Play

You may find that there are times when it's necessary to take a more active role in children's play. This is usually the case when children are at a very beginning level of dramatic play.

To be an active participant in children's play, the teacher takes on a role and demonstrates a particular skill such as how to make-believe with objects and situations. Consider these examples:

One child takes out the dishes and starts to set the table. The teacher says, "I would love to have a cup of coffee. Do you have any?" The child responds, "Sure do." The teacher invites another child into the play episode by saying, "Do you have enough for a friend?"

To a child playing with the cash register, a teacher says, "I'm planning a party and I need some food. Can you help me, Mr. Storekeeper? Do you have any eggs? How much are they?"

For children who seem to be running out of ideas for a play episode, a teacher might help the group extend the role-playing situation, make the theme more complex, or include more actions for the role being played. Here are two examples:

Three children are playing restaurant. Two are sitting at the table eating, and one is serving the food. The teacher sees that the episode is ending because the children have run out of ideas. He says, "Does anyone besides me want to order dessert? Waiter, what kind of desserts do you have?"

Two children have been playing doctor and the "doctor" has examined the "baby" but doesn't seem to know what else to do. The teacher suggests some ideas: "What's wrong with the baby, doctor? She won't stop crying? Do you think she needs some medicine? Can you write down the prescription for the mommy so she can have it filled? Let's call the drugstore and see if anyone is there."

The house corner is first and foremost a place for children to play and interact. As you participate in children's dramatic play, avoid dominating the conversation and/or "running the show."

Responding to Pretend Play That Makes Adults Uncomfortable

Many teachers feel uncomfortable when they observe some of the things children incorporate into their pretend play. Knowing how to react in these situations requires careful thinking as well as sensitivity to children's personal lives. Keep in mind that dramatic play is an opportunity for children to work out difficult feelings and experiences and to begin to understand the adult world. Instead of stopping children's behavior, you can respond in a pretend role. In this way you allow the play episode to continue as you redirect children's actions and help them find alternative behaviors.

Children sometimes exhibit anger and aggression by hitting, cursing, or using weapons in their dramatic play. Anger is a very real emotion. Guns are often a way in which children express their desire for power. You can show the child that you understand these feelings while also demonstrating appropriate ways to express them, as illustrated in these examples:

> A child is running around the house corner pointing his finger, as if a gun, at another child. The teacher might say to the child with the gun, "Excuse me, sir, are you a policeman? I need your help. Someone has stolen my purse." In this play episode the gun is helping the child feel powerful. By redirecting his actions in the role of policeman, the teacher demonstrates a more appropriate way to assume a powerful role.

> Three children are playing house and eating dinner. The "baby" is whining and the "mother" hits the child and says, "Shut up, baby. No more food for you, go to bed!" Rather than criticizing the "mother" for this behavior, you could ask, "Is there another way we could get this baby to stop whining? My baby stops crying when I hold her on my lap."

Children may incorporate embarrassing and inappropriate behavior in their play, such as sex acts or the use of drugs and alcohol. Children's dramatic play most often reflects real-life feelings and events. For many children violence, sex, and drugs are part of their everyday experience—if not at home, then in the media. Again, within the context of a pretend role, you can prescribe rules or redirect behaviors, as the following examples illustrate:

> Two children are sitting on the couch and pretending to use drugs. The teacher comes into the room and says, "I'm the father. In my house you can't use drugs because I don't like them. They aren't good for you."

> The teacher notices that two children are lying on each other as if they are having sex. Realizing that they are re-playing roles they can't really understand, she redirects this play by saying, "I just got home from work. Is dinner ready? What should we have?"

By intervening in the ways illustrated above, teachers avoid making judgments about the events portrayed. It is best to discuss rules about behavior outside of dramatic play episodes, during a private conversation with a child, or at circle time with the class.

Sometimes children's play simply imitates themes seen on TV. Re-enacting the characters and actions of super-heroes from movies and TV is the same as playing a game with rules. It isn't socio-dramatic play. Teachers often find that discouraging children from this kind of play is ineffective. Rather, provide children with special times for pretending to be superheroes (particularly outdoor times). This allows them opportunities to play these games and also to try out other roles in the house corner.

Only by observing children's dramatic play regularly can you determine the individual abilities, concerns, and interests of the children in your group and make appropriate decisions about when and how to intervene.

IV. Extending and Integrating Children's Learning

Teachers extend learning in the house corner as they participate in children's spontaneous play, stimulate new ideas within existing play episodes, and introduce new themes into the house corner. Group experiences focusing on pretend skills can also help children extend the repertoire of their imaginations.

Introducing New Themes

An effective house corner will offer children an array of dramatic experiences that go beyond "playing house." When is it best to introduce new themes? One obvious choice is when children seem bored or tired of playing house and have trouble continuing their play. Even if the children don't seem stuck, introducing new themes can spark their imagination and facilitate learning. You may want to introduce a new theme for a day or two in response to a special event. Or you may decide to turn the house corner into a new setting in response to a theme you are developing in your classroom.

Special events or situations constantly arise in the early childhood classroom. For example, a trip to the fire station or post office provides an ideal stimulus for children to reenact the experience through dramatic play. If someone in the class is moving away, children might wish to take on the roles of movers and actually play out the move to a new town.

Some teachers may prefer to implement a planned sequence of themes in the house corner. For instance, a teacher may wish to begin the year with family play and gradually move on to dramatic play related to places in the community, such as the supermarket, gas station, or library. Thus, the planned sequence of dramatic activities would reflect actual places in the community that children have visited.

Using Prop Boxes

As their name suggests, prop boxes are filled with materials relevant to a particular theme. A "hospital" prop box, for example, might include bandages, stethoscopes, white "lab" jackets, black bags, pill bottles, hot water bottles, white sheets, and other medical-related paraphernalia. The prop box is thus a way of instantly converting the house corner into a hospital or another setting for dramatic play.

If you are using prop boxes to introduce themes, you may wonder how best to do this. Is it preferable to expose children to all the props at once or only a few props at a time? Here are several suggested ways to introduce a new prop box.

- *Select one item* from the box most likely to stimulate the theme, such as a firefighter's hat, a stethoscope, or a cash register. Put the item in the house corner before the children arrive and see what the children do with the new prop. Add more props if the children demonstrate an interest in the new theme.

- *Place the entire prop box in the house corner* before the children arrive. Leave it open. Without talking to the group about the box, watch what the children say and do and how they use the materials. Add new materials as the children request them or need them.

- *Include only two or three items* in a prop box. This can stimulate a play theme but still enable you to help children develop the skill of making believe with props. After an item is in use, you can demonstrate for children how to have a stethoscope using a string or simply their hands.

No matter how themes and props are introduced, keep in mind that the goal is to extend children's dramatic play. By doing so, you help children gain a better understanding of the world around them.

Ideas for Themes and Prop Boxes

- *Supermarket.* Children often accompany their parents to buy food. Hence, the supermarket theme evolves quite naturally in the house corner. To set up a supermarket, the following props and materials can be used:

table or crates to create sections of the supermarket	empty containers of food
shopping baskets made from cartons with a string for pulling or a dowel for pushing	cash registers made from cardboard boxes
signs for different sections—meat, dairy	paper or plastic money
plastic fruits and vegetables	paper bags for groceries

- *Laundromat.* Clothes in the house corner get "dirty," and children will note the need to wash, dry, and iron the clothing. A laundromat can be a natural extension of house play if you include props such as the following:

large cardboard carton made into a washing machine with a door cut out in front for loading clothes	chairs for patrons to sit on
	clothes to wash
dryer made from a carton	laundry baskets
table for folding clothes (can be borrowed from another area)	empty detergent bottles
ironing board and iron	clothesline and clothespins

- *Shoe store.* The shoe store is another popular theme for dramatic play. Props for a shoe store can be quite simple:

chairs to sit in	a shoe-shine kit with clear polish and rags
assorted old shoes	
shoeboxes	a box with a shoe-shaped wedge cut out of wood
a cash register	a ruler to measure feet or a real foot measurer from a shoe store

- *Barbershop/hairdresser.* Not all children have had their hair cut by a barber or hairdresser. However, a well-equipped setting will encourage them to try out this experience. It might be equipped with the following items:

combs and brushes	hat-style hair dryer (minus electric cord)
empty shampoo bottles with labels	hand-held dryer without electric cord
curlers and pins	shaving cream and empty razors
sheets cut into smocks	magazines for the waiting room
hand and table mirrors	basins
towels	

- *Garage/repair shop.* Young children are often fascinated by the workings of machinery. Cars in particular hold a great deal of interest for both boys and girls. A garage setting provides children with an opportunity for dramatic play while at the same time allowing them to work on motor skills development. Some elements for a garage can include:

  cars made from cardboard or wooden crates (complete with a real license plate and steering wheel)

  gas pump (can be created from a box with a hose attached)

  jack

  old credit cards to buy gas

  traffic signs made from cardboard and wooden dowels

- *Office.* An office workplace is another natural extension of house play, particularly for children with family members who work in an office. To create an office area, you might include the following props:

pads of paper	adding machine or calculator
stapler	telephone
paper clips	pencils, pens, markers
typewriter and/or computer	stamp pad and stampers
briefcases	

- *Camping.* Some children have been on camping trips with their families. Camping props can inspire some very creative dramatic play. Props to consider might include the following:

pup tent	compass
canteens	boxes of food
cooking utensils	knapsacks

We encourage you to supplement this list with your own ideas as well as those suggested by children's play.

Planned Activities

Teachers using the *Creative Curriculum* understand the importance of pretend play and know that very often children need help learning how to pretend. Sometimes these pretend skills can be demonstrated in the house corner within the context of a play episode, as in the examples given in the previous section. Teachers can also undertake a more systematic approach to teaching dramatic play skills.[1]

Circle-Time Activities

At certain points you may want to use circle time to teach children new pretend skills. In this setting you can demonstrate to children the importance of dramatic play and stimulate their curiosity and interest in the house corner. The following examples illustrate ways in which teachers can use circle time to enhance dramatic play skills:

> With the goal of helping children learn how to make-believe with objects, a teacher brings a toy steering wheel, a paper plate, and a scrap of paper to circle time. She asks the children, "Who would like to pretend to be a truck driver?" Taneka comes to the center of the circle, and, using the toy steering wheel, drives around the circle. The teacher asks again, "Who else wants to drive a truck?" Travis comes to the center and waits for Taneka's toy. "You can use this plate," the teacher explains, showing him how to drive with the plate. The circle time continues, and other children have chances to drive a truck using a variety of pretend objects.

> Based on her observations, a teacher wants to support children's learning about how to develop many aspects of a role. She brings a doll to circle time and rocks the "baby" in her arms. "I'm the mommy," she says. "My baby is sleeping now that I'm rocking her in my arms. Who would like to be the mommy or daddy and show us some other ways to care for the baby?" As each child comes up to take the baby, the teacher asks the other children if they can figure out what the mommy or daddy is doing for the baby.

> After a trip to the post office, a teacher gathers her children in the circle and says, "Who were some people we saw at the post office?" The children share ideas such as mail carrier, person buying stamps, mail clerk, mail truck driver. After the children talk, the teacher announces, "Let's pretend we're at the post office." Then she pretends she is carrying a heavy box. She says to the children, "I'm a lady coming into the post office. What am I doing?" The children respond enthusiastically. She adds, "Who would like to come up and show us something you saw at the post office?" As each child comes up and acts out a role, she asks the children to guess the role being played.

These examples are just some ideas of how circle time can be used to facilitate children's pretend ability. If you try these ideas, you will probably find that the children bring their new skills to their play in the house corner.

---

[1] We wish to acknowledge the work of Dr. Sara Smilansky (1990), which has greatly influenced our thinking about teaching children dramatic play skills.

Playing Pretend with Small Groups of Children

Another way to inspire children to use the house corner and to ensure that children are developing pretend skills is to plan group activities. You may decide to have part of your class remain in the room with you while the rest of the children go outdoors to play, supervised by your co-teacher. With a smaller group of children, you can extend the house corner to include the block area and use the entire space for dramatic play. The following is an example of how one teacher used such a situation with a group of eight children:

> The teacher said, "Today we are going to play pretend all together. You may use all the space in the house corner and block area. I have added the doctor prop box and the firefighter prop box if you would like to use these props. Let's begin our play." Some children immediately went to choose a prop and began various play episodes. Others, more tentative, simply watched to see how the play evolved. The teacher moved over to one hesitant child and said, "I need to see a doctor for this rash I have on my arm. Would you like to be my doctor?" After a while everyone was involved in play, some in groups of two and others in three and four. The play period lasted for a half-hour.

Experiences like this help children feel more relaxed with dramatic play. Because children can engage in their play without distractions, they learn to stay involved in play episodes for longer periods of time. Teachers also find that settings such as the one described above offer excellent opportunities to observe children for extended periods of time.

Integrating Pretend Play with Other Curriculum Areas

Because so much of young children's learning is expressed through dramatic play, the house corner is often a place where we see children trying out new skills and concepts. The previous section discussed means of adapting the house corner to reflect themes being developed in your classroom. This is an important way in which the house corner serves an integrator of the curriculum.

The section on arranging the environment described the value of placing the house corner next to the block corner. This arrangement will usually invite children to find connections between these two interest areas. As children build with table toys, they often engage in dramatic play. For example, as a child uses construction toys to create a plane, he may begin to fly it overhead and to provide sound effects. Questions such as "are you the pilot?" or "will your plane be landing in the airport?" let the child know that you value his or her dramatic play.

Emergent Literacy

Props such as signs, menus, receipts, and notepads in the house corner stimulate children's thinking about the uses of print as a means of communication. As you participate in children's play, you might say, "I am the waiter. May I take your order?" Using a pad and pencil or pretending to write something on your hand (a make-believe pad), you jot down an order. In this way you model a role, use a pretend object, and demonstrate a functional use of print. Or you might say to a child holding a doll, "Would you like to read your baby a story?" Placing a magazine rack with a few magazines in the "living room" can add to a homelike feeling and generate ideas for imitative role-play.

If your house corner is set up as a supermarket, you can encourage children to make signs for it. In so doing, you help them think about the kinds of print they've seen at different stores. You might take some children on a walk to a grocery store to refresh their memories or spark new ideas.

Certain types of dramatic play settings lend themselves to reading and writing experiences. An office, a library, and a post office will stimulate children's involvement in literacy activities. Adding a typewriter or a computer to an office setting enables children to play the roles of people who use print in their work.

Emergent Mathematical Thinking

Introducing props such as cash registers, scales, and play money into the house corner provides children with opportunities to think about how math is used in everyday life. It isn't necessary for children to use these props "correctly"—it is the experience which is most important.

When a child counts out money as he buys some groceries at the store, he may say, "One, four, three, eight, one hundred dollars." He is using information he has learned about number names in his role as shopper. This is an important part of his emerging knowledge of how money is used in everyday life.

Following a trip to the shoe store, children may begin measuring their feet for shoe sizes because a shoe measurer has been added to the house corner. In this way they can see the important and practical uses of measurement.

In a carefully labeled house corner, children use math skills such as seriation, one-to-one correspondence, and matching as they choose materials and clean up at the end of their play. The house corner thus provides diverse, rich learning opportunities for children and enables them to develop skills that they will use throughout their lives.

V. Sharing the House Corner with Parents

A guiding principle of the *Creative Curriculum* is that children benefit most when teachers and parents work together to support children's growth and development. Play is the child's work. Conveying to parents the important role of dramatic play in a child's development and academic success is key to helping them understand the *Creative Curriculum*.

Conducting Workshops on Pretend Play

A parent workshop is particularly effective because it enables parents to see first hand the uses of dramatic play and imagination in learning. Here are some suggestions for planning such a workshop:

- Encourage parents to visit the classroom during the week prior to the workshop to observe children at play in the house corner.

- Give parents a copy of the chart on stages of dramatic play while they are observing the children's dramatic play.

- At the workshop, present the videotape, *The Creative Curriculum,* which shows children engaged in dramatic play and illustrates the role of the teacher as a participant.

- Share with parents the types of themes children enact in the house corner and how you enrich and extend their play.

- Show parents the prop boxes that are available and describe their purpose.

Some teachers also find it helpful to have an outside expert attend the parent workshop to talk with parents about the importance of play. The selected person may be the director of another early childhood program, someone from a local community college or university, or a parent in the education field. By adding "expert" opinion to the discussion, some teachers find that parents accept the information presented more readily.

Involving Parents in the Classroom

Teachers using the *Creative Curriculum* encourage parents to visit or volunteer in the classroom as often as their schedules permit. Seeing children busy at play in the house corner is an effective way to help parents understand the importance of this interest area for children's learning.

Some parents feel at home in the house corner and will readily take on a role themselves. By providing them with a few simple suggestions, they can be valuable helpers.

Parents are also a wonderful resource for equipping your house corner. Ask them for suggestions on props and decorations that reflect their culture. Parents might also be willing to help you equip a prop box for a particular theme.

The letter to parents that follows is another strategy for helping parents understand and support their children's dramatic play in the house corner.

A Letter to Parents on the House Corner

What We Do and Why

The house corner is a very important part of our classroom. The work children do in the house corner is called dramatic play or pretend play. In the house corner children take on a role and recreate real-life experiences. They use props and make-believe about a wide variety of topics.

The ability to pretend is very important to children's later academic success in school. When children pretend, they have to recall experiences they've had and re-create them. To do this, they have to be able to picture their experiences in their minds. For example, to play the role of a doctor, children have to remember what tools a doctor uses, how a doctor examines a patient, and what a doctor says. In playing the role of a doctor, children have to be able to cooperate with other children and defend their own ideas.

When children are engaged in dramatic play in the classroom, we encourage them to talk about what they are doing. For example, we might say:

- "What do mothers do when children are sick?"
- "What kind of cake are you going to make: chocolate or vanilla?"
- "Why does your baby cry so much?"

We ask questions that help children extend their thinking and their play.

What You Can Do At Home

You can encourage the same kind of pretend play at home by having a box of dress-up clothes available or by putting a sheet over a card table and making a hideout for your child. Such activities are particularly good for a rainy day.

One way to extend your child's dramatic play is to collect different kinds of dress-up clothes and put them in boxes with picture labels showing the contents. For instance, one box might contain an apron, bibs, cups, plates, spoons, small cooking utensils, a whisk broom, and other objects for use in the kitchen. Another box might include hats with visors or recognizable insignia denoting an occupation, shoes, neckties, shirts, vests, coats, or trousers. A hospital prop box could hold nurses' hats, white coats, toy thermometers, stethoscopes, empty pill bottles, a small pillow, an eye patch, and a watch.

When the time is appropriate, you can give your child one of the boxes and encourage play by asking questions such as these: "What can we do about this sick baby?" or "Will you make grandmother a birthday cake?"

When you play pretend with your child, you are teaching important learning skills and spending valuable time together.

TABLE TOYS

I. Why Table Toys Are Important

Table toys are games, manipulatives, puzzles, and collectibles that children can play with at a table or on the floor. They offer children a quiet activity that they can do alone, with a friend, or with a teacher.

Table toys are of great value in an early childhood classroom. Children enjoy their variety and versatility. Rich in texture, color, and shape, table toys offer children challenging opportunities to learn new skills. When teachers work with children individually or in small groups, table toys can also serve as excellent teaching tools.

Children grow in all areas of their development as they play with table toys. Self-esteem can be developed as children experience the satisfaction of completing a task successfully, using puzzles and other self-correcting toys. Children learn to cooperate with one another by sharing and taking turns as they play a game or build an intricate design.

Table toys offer many opportunities for children to experiment with construction and invention. As they build with table blocks or make designs with pattern blocks and parquetry blocks, children use creative problem-solving skills. Table toys offer extensive opportunities for children to work on emerging math skills such as seriation, matching, and classification.

Physical development is enhanced as children practice eye-hand coordination while completing puzzles or placing pegs in a pegboard. As children string beads or construct with interlocking cubes, they refine small muscle skills.

The table toy area thus provides a setting in which learning is both satisfying and ongoing.

Objectives for Children's Learning

Specific objectives for children in the table toy area need to reflect the backgrounds, interests, and capabilities of the children in your program. For instance, you might set objectives related to learning about patterns for a child who consistently makes repetitive designs with pegs or pattern blocks. Or you might focus on objectives related to self-confidence if certain children seem tentative in their approach to using materials. The following objectives are suggested as a starting point.

Objectives for Socio-Emotional Development

- Work cooperatively in small groups (playing lotto, dominoes, and memory and matching games).

- Develop self-control (sharing toys and waiting for a turn with a desired toy).

- Demonstrate perseverance and self-discipline (working with a puzzle until it has been completed).

- Experience pride in accomplishments (seeing a task through from start to finish).

Objectives for Cognitive Development

- Demonstrate creative abilities (experimenting with open-ended toys).

- Sort and match objects by attributes such as color, size, texture, and shape (using collections such as buttons, shells, or bottle caps).

- Demonstrate an understanding of number concepts related to sequencing, seriation, and classification (using table blocks, parquetry, and attribute blocks).

- Develop emergent reading skills such as directionality, figure-ground discrimination, matching like objects (using such table toys such as pegboards, puzzles, dominoes, and collectibles).

Objectives for Physical Development

- Develop fine motor control (placing pegs in holes, stringing beads, piecing together puzzles, and manipulating buttons, marbles, or shells).

- Develop eye-hand coordination (sewing with yarn, sorting buttons, and returning puzzle pieces to their frames).

- Demonstrate visual discrimination skills (sorting objects according to attributes of size, color, and shape).

- Refine sense of touch (learning to distinguish toys made of different materials).

This sample list of objectives can serve as guidance for the many learning possibilities in the table toy area of your classroom.

II. Arranging the Environment

Children can most easily enjoy using table toys and learning objectives can best be met when the area is arranged to facilitate learning. Both the location of the table toy area and how toys are displayed have an effect on how children use, learn from, and take care of these materials.

Creating Space

In setting up a classroom area for table toys, it is important to create an environment where children can concentrate on the toys with as few outside distractions as possible. The picture below illustrates an arrangement in which the table toy area is enclosed on three sides by using an L-shaped shelf to create boundaries.

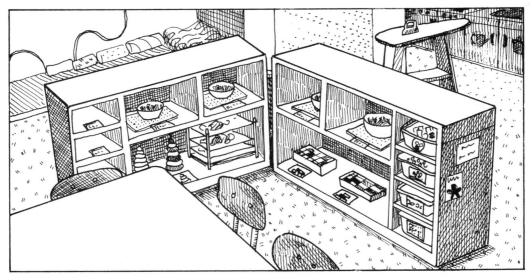

In this illustration the toys are stored on shelves near the tables. Materials are accessible to the children and clean-up is made easier.

Another design feature shown in the illustration above is ample, unobstructed floor space for children to use the toys on the floor, which some children prefer doing.

If space or furniture is limited, teachers can use rug scraps or tape to define individual floor spaces where children can play with the toys. To help children concentrate, the table toy area should be placed next to other quiet areas such as the library or art area.

Selecting Materials

Table toys can be grouped into four categories: self-correcting, structured toys; open-ended toys; collectibles; and cooperative games.

Self-correcting, structured toys are those which fit together in a specific way—for example, a puzzle. A child using this type of toy can readily determine if the toy has been put together correctly. Self-correcting toys include the following:

- puzzles: wooden, rubber inset, and durable cardboard;
- wooden cylinders;
- self-help skill frames (buttoning, zipping, tying);
- geometric shape sorters;
- graded circles that fit on a cylinder; and
- nesting boxes.

Open-ended toys have no right or wrong solution. These toys can be put together in a variety of ways, depending entirely on the child's creativity and level of development. Many are excellent for developing motor skills and eye-hand coordination. Open-ended toys include the following:

- sewing cards with yarn
- felt boards
- Legos
- colored cubes
- beads and yarn for stringing
- pegs and pegboards
- Cuisenaire Rods

- Unifix Cubes
- attribute blocks (three-dimensional blocks)
- manipulatives: any put-together toy (e.g., JiGan-Tiks, snap blocks, Tower-ifics, Ring-a-Majigs)
- equipment for weighing and measuring
- multi-links

Collectibles, like open-ended toys, can be put together in a variety of unspecified ways. They differ from open-ended toys in that they are composed of sets of like objects. Attractive collections encourage children to sort, match, and compare in many inventive ways. Examples of collectibles include:

- plastic bottle caps,
- buttons,
- keys,
- seashells,

- seeds,
- different colored plastic coffee scoops,
- rocks,
- plastic fasteners (from bread or other grocery items), and
- baby-food jar tops.

Cooperative games encourage children to work together in matching pictures, numbers, symbols, and objects. The emphasis is not on winning or losing. Cooperative games provide children with the opportunity to improve visual discrimination skills as well as social skills. Games in this category include:

- lotto,
- dominoes,
- concentration,
- matching games, and
- card games.

Some table toys can be used in different ways, thus falling into more than one category. To illustrate, parquetry blocks could be considered a structured toy when used in conjunction with pattern cards, when the child chooses to replicate the design on the card. However, their function is open-ended when children create their own patterns.

As you plan for the selection and purchase of materials to include in the table toy area, here are some considerations that may be helpful:

- *Safety.* All toys should be safe to use and in accordance with standards outlined by the Consumer Product Safety Commission, a Federal agency that sets safety standards. There should be no sharp points or edges, no pieces small enough to be swallowed, and no pieces that can be used as projectiles.

- *Durability.* Because of their constant use, materials in a program for young children need to be more durable than those purchased for home use. For example, puzzles made of wood or rubber are more long-lasting than cardboard puzzles.

- *Construction.* Make sure toys are made well and work as intended. Nothing is more frustrating to a child than a toy that doesn't do what it is supposed to. This means that all pieces of a puzzle or interlocking toy actually fit together and all the pieces of a lotto game or domino set are intact.

- *Flexibility.* Interlocking and manipulative table toys can be used in many ways by children. The more flexible a toy, the more ways it can be used and the longer it will hold children's attention. Children quickly tire of gimmicky toys that have a single purpose and don't require any thinking or creativity.

- *Price.* The cost of a table toy should be balanced against its flexibility. Some expensive toys may be good investments because they can be used in many ways and will last a long time. Before purchasing, consider these questions: How many different ways can the toy be used? Can children use it in more complex ways as their skills develop? Can it be used in different ways by children of different ages?

Displaying and Storing Table Toys

Because of the large number of toys in this interest area, the display and storage of table toys is of great importance. Children will be drawn to the table toy area only if it is attractive and uncluttered. Random piles of toys are likely to go unused if children cannot independently select what they want.

Here are some guidelines for displaying table toys.

- *Place toys at children's eye level* so they can easily see what materials are available.

- *Group toys by type:* puzzles in one area, pegboard and pegs in another area, and so on.

- *Remove any broken toys* or ones with missing pieces.

- *Store extra toys* (for replenishing the area) outside the table toy area (in a teacher cabinet or on high shelves).

- *Use bins or plastic tubs* to maximize storage space for collectibles, table blocks, and other toys with multiple pieces.

Labeling Table Toys

Careful labeling makes it possible for children to find what they need and return it to the right place when they are finished with it. Labels can be made in several ways. Teachers may, for instance, wish to take a photograph of each individual toy or draw a small picture of the toy on heavy cardboard or posterboard. These pictures can then be covered with clear contact paper and attached with masking tape to the shelf areas where the toys are to be stored. If several toys are housed in a storage bin, pictures of all the items can be displayed on the label. Placing labels on the shelves as well as on the

storage bins helps children know where to return items during clean-up. Shelf labels can be placed directly under the place where the storage bin will be or above the height of the bin on the back of the shelf.

For young children, picture labels are best. Four- and five-year-olds often enjoy having the name of the toy or game written below the picture.

Caring for Table Toys

Because of their many pieces and the extent of their use, table toys undergo inevitable wear and tear. Cardboard games such as lotto eventually wear out. However, purchased games can be preserved in much the same way as homemade items. Two procedures are recommended for increasing the shelf life of cardboard toys:

- dry-mounting and lamination with a dry-mount machine that can be used at many frame or art supplies stores, and

- covering with transparent adhesive-backed paper (e.g., clear contact paper), purchased at most houseware or hardware stores.

Missing puzzle pieces can be replaced by laying a piece of plastic over the empty space and filling it with Plaster of Paris or wood putty. When the piece dries, it can be painted. Alternatively, if you write to the company that made the puzzle and enclose an outline of the missing piece, they will sometimes replace it.

Most manipulatives can be washed with soap and water and sterilized by adding a little bleach to the solution. An occasional routine cleaning of all the table toys will increase their attractiveness and in some cases help them last longer.

Assessing the Effectiveness of the Area

Observing the effectiveness of the table toy area is something you can do informally each day as you interact with children. Your observations can help you with your weekly planning as you make decisions about what materials to put away for a while, what toys to add, or what you may want to put out on a table to inspire children's play. For instance, observation may reveal that a particular table toy is not being used, perhaps because it's too simple or too complex for the group. Or perhaps the toy has been out too long and the children have lost interest in it. In either event, the toy can be put away for a while. If observation shows that children are continually fighting over building toys, a larger supply is probably necessary.

Here are some questions to consider:

- How often is the table toy area used?

- Is it interesting and appealing to all the children, or are the same children using it each day?

- Are all the materials being used? Which ones should be put away or put on a table to stimulate interest?

- Are toys varied enough to maintain the children's interest?

- Are the available materials flexible? Are children using toys in a variety of ways?

- Are the toys providing opportunities for children to play both individually and cooperatively?

Through careful and regular observations, you can gather important information on how well the table toy area is working as an activity area. By rotating toys and regularly introducing new and more challenging materials, you can ensure that this area is an effective setting for learning.

III. Observing and Promoting Children's Learning

Once the table toy area is arranged, the teacher's role is to provide encouragement, help children get involved with toys, introduce new skills, and talk to children about their efforts and accomplishments. You can do this in the table toy area first by observing and then by responding to and reinforcing what children are doing. To do this most effectively, it is helpful to understand the developmental stages of play with table toys.

How Children Use Table Toys

As we have seen in earlier modules, children approach materials in fairly predictable stages. Depending on the children's previous experiences with table toys and their physical skills, they will move from tentative, simple types of play to more complex, integrated modes of play.

Exploration

Children approach a new object by first exploring and getting to know its characteristics. Their exploration helps them answer questions such as the following:

- How does it look?
- How does it feel? What kind of texture does it have?
- How big or small is it? How heavy or light?
- What shape is it?
- What color is it?

The goal at this stage is for children to investigate the physical properties of the toy. The explorations children do at this stage help them acquire emerging science and math concepts.

Experimentation

The experimentation stage involves using the object. During this stage, children test the toy to see how it works, experimenting with both function and cause and effect. If the toy is structured, they may attempt to put it together as intended. If the toy is unstructured, their efforts typically incorporate creative problem-solving strategies. Children in this stage work at answering the following questions:

- How does it work?
- What can be done with it?
- Can it be put together?
- Can it be used to build?
- Do pieces match?

As children experiment with table toys, they invent more and more ways to use materials, gaining new skills as they play. A child's development through these stages is enhanced when teachers make good decisions about when and how to introduce new and increasingly complex materials.

Observing Individual Children

Careful observation lets you know which toys and materials the children are selecting and how they use the materials they select. Based on what you see, you can plan ways to enhance each child's development through table toys.

As you observe individual children, the stages of development described above will help you determine where children are in their use of table toys. The Checklist in Appendix A can also be used to document a child's progress.

Here are some questions to consider as you observe individual children:

- Is the child exploring the table toys or creatively experimenting with them?
- Does the child need more time practicing at this stage? Should I intervene?
- Does the child choose the table toy area only when a teacher is present?
- Does the child play alone or with other children?
- What logic and reasoning skills is the child using in playing with table toys?
- Is the child able to solve problems independently? How can I promote more independent use of table toys?
- Does the child look either overwhelmed or bored with a particular toy?

Such information can give you an understanding of what each child is doing in the table toy area so that you can respond appropriately.

Interacting with Children

A child reluctant to use table toys may be willing to go to the area if a teacher is sitting there. The promise of personal attention for a few minutes can be a powerful incentive.

At times you may need to teach specific skills necessary to work with certain table toys. For example, a child who has had little experience with puzzles may need to be shown, step by step, that to complete a puzzle one has to:

- spill out the pieces;

- turn them all over so that the painted side is in view;

- start putting them back along the edge matching the outline;

- put each piece in next to one that is there until the whole picture is made; and

- either do the puzzle a second time or return it to the designated place on the shelf.

Knowing how to break down a task into steps is an important skill for children to acquire. The table toy area is a good place to work on this skill. The steps used unconsciously by the experienced child present a challenge for the beginner. And all children are beginners with materials they haven't seen or used before.

By talking with children about their play in the table toy area, you can foster their self-esteem and learning in the following ways:

- Introduce new vocabulary and encourage conversation.

- Help children become more aware of what they are doing, what they are discovering, and what they are thinking and feeling.

- Give children the message that you care about them and recognize their increasing skills and competence.

- Help them identify concepts and label them: "These are the smaller blocks" or "You have the red pegs."

When talking with children about their play, first ask them to describe what they are doing. For children who have difficulty expressing themselves, you can take the lead in conversation by providing nonjudgmental observations of their work:

- "Tell me about the puzzle you put together."

- "I see you are using all the red pegs and some of the purple pegs."

- "You matched the two elephants. Here's a picture of a giraffe. Can you find the other giraffe?"

- "I see you've put all the circles in one pile and all the squares in another pile."

- "You used the parquetry blocks to make your own design."

With experience, even reluctant children can begin to express themselves and describe their efforts. By focusing on the process—what they are doing and how they are doing it—children develop thinking, planning, and organizing skills.

IV. Extending and Integrating Children's Learning

You can enhance children's play with table toys by making new materials and introducing special activities. Play with table toys becomes richer and more meaningful for children when it is integrated with other curriculum areas.

Making Materials for the Table Toy Area

Most teachers want to have a wide variety of table toys available to children at all times, yet few program budgets permit this. Cost is usually a prime consideration as you select materials for the table toy area. But, you can enhance the area with many wonderful homemade toys and games, which save money and can be designed to reinforce specific concepts or topics. A matching game, for example, can be used to illustrate objects seen on a trip. To assist you in constructing your own table toys, some sample designs are illustrated below.

Flip Books

Matching games can easily be made using inexpensive ring binders. A 7" x 4" binder with six rings is suggested.

Cut cardboard or posterboard into cards that will fit into the binders as shown in the illustration below. Make two copies of each card. Paste an identical picture on each pair of cards and then laminate or cover with clear adhesive-backed paper. Punch holes in both sets of cards so that they fit into the binder.

To play a matching game, a child chooses a picture to be matched from one set of cards and then flips through the other set of pictures until the matching picture appears. Four pictures in each set is a good number to begin with for very young children. A book for older children can have more choices. When all the pictures relate to a theme (such as birds, transportation, numbers, houses, letters, people, or flowers), the activity is a more meaningful learning experience for children.

Here are some examples:

- Birds (a simple game)   Binder open to matching cards

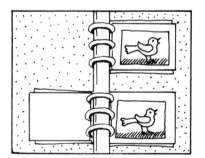

- Patterns (a more difficult game)

This example uses one set of large cards (four holes) and one set of smaller cards (two holes). Each large card is covered with a different pattern. Each small card shows just a part of the corresponding large card pattern. This "part-to-whole" matching is an advanced perception game.

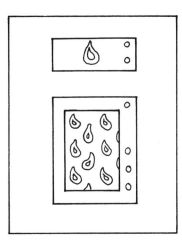

Puzzles

Puzzles can be constructed using either photographs or pictures. Family photos provide a personalized, always popular choice of subjects. Magazine pictures that illustrate classroom themes are another favorite choice.

Mount the selected photo or picture on cardboard and then cut it into sections. The pieces are then dry-mounted and laminated or covered with clear adhesive-backed paper for protection. Matching puzzles can be made using two copies of the same photograph or picture. One copy is mounted intact and the other picture cut into pieces as described above.

Spool Boards

Several interesting matching toys can be made from scrap wood, empty thread spools, and wooden dowels. Often parents, tailors, or lumber yards will donate these materials. If none are available, they can be purchased inexpensively.

To make a spool board, start with a thick block of wood, a selected number of spools, and dowels of varying length that are a little thinner than the spool holes. Drill holes the width of the dowels into the wooden block at points where the dowels are to go. Glue the dowels to the board and place the spools on the dowels.

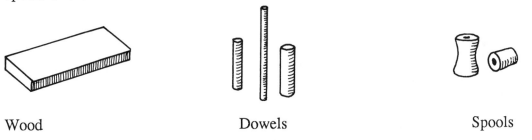

Wood   Dowels   Spools

Shoebox Sorting Game

Use a shoebox to make a toy for sorting and classifying. Make multiple compartments by gluing in cardboard inserts. Slots leading to each compartment can be cut out of the shoe box lid. The sizes of the slots need to be large enough to allow either bought or homemade picture cards to pass through them into the box. Slots can be labeled using symbols or clothespin "flags" to identify which cards go into each slot.

To make the game illustrated below, you need 25 cards. Make five cards each of five different pictures. Put one to five items on each card.

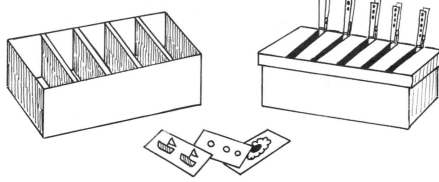

Grouping Games

Grouping games are constructed from cardboard or posterboard that is lined horizontally and vertically into a grid. At the top of each column, place a picture or label identifying a category. Cards can then be placed in the squares according to their identifying attribute. In the following illustration, gummed stamps (stickers) are mounted on cardboard and covered with clear adhesive-backed paper. To make the game last longer, laminate or cover the pieces with clear adhesive-backed paper.

Self-Help Boards

Boards that give children practice in lacing, snapping, buttoning, and zipping can be made by nailing or stapling material to a wooden frame. Cut the material in the center and add a zipper, button hole, snaps, and so on.

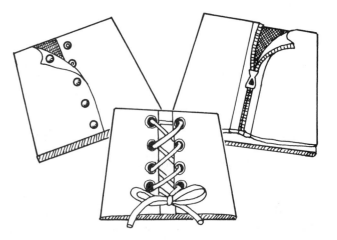

Special Activities

You can extend and enrich children's play with table toys by helping them discover new ways to use familiar materials. The examples below illustrate how you can introduce new vocabulary and concepts, foster the development of thinking and planning skills, and enhance socio-emotional development as children play with table toys.

- "I see you've picked out blocks that are all the same. How are they the same?"

- "You've stacked five Ring-a-Majigs. What would happen if you added two more?"

- "You've built a whole city with the Lego blocks. Does anyone live in your city'?"

- "I see you figured out a way to make all the pattern blocks fit together. What other patterns could you make with the same blocks?"

- "You put all the cylinders in the holes. How did you know which cylinder fit in which hole?"

- "Look at the pattern I made on the matrix board. One peg is missing. Can you put the missing peg in the box?"

Play can also be extended by having children follow simple directions:

- "Can you make a tower with two blue cubes and two purple ones?"

- "Can you line up these bottle tops so the tallest pieces are on the side of this table and the smallest caps are on the other side?"

Making Up New Games Using Familiar Objects

In addition to giving verbal suggestions and initiating spontaneous games, teachers can set the stage for further play by creating new games and activities for children. The following six examples all use common table toys and objects.

Feeling Shapes. This is a matching game that uses the sense of touch and teaches the concept of "same." An adult plays this game with one child or a small group.

- Take a small cloth bag or any other type of bag that the child can reach into but cannot see through.

- Put a selection of beads, parquetry blocks, or attribute blocks in the bag (start with two; add more as children get used to the game).

- Give each child a bead or block to hold and feel, and ask the child to find (by feeling, not looking) a bead or block of the same shape inside the bag.

- The child brings out the bead or block to show and compare. Are they the same shape?

- Talk about the name of the shape and how it feels.

- Try again with a different shape.

Once the child knows the name of each shape, the game can be made more complicated.

- Use only beads or parquetry or attribute blocks that have a clearly recognizable shape such as round, square, or oval.

- Put a selection in the bag.

- Ask the child to find the shape you name (by feeling, not looking).

More and Less. This is a counting game that helps children develop visual skills and reinforces the concepts of "more" and "less." It can be played by two people. An adult's assistance may be necessary if children are unsure of the meaning of more and less.

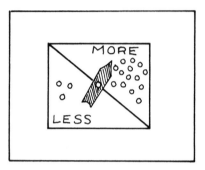

Make a spinner by drawing a diagonal line between the corners of a square piece of cardboard. This divides the square in half. Label one half "MORE" and the other half "LESS." Cover with clear adhesive-backed paper for durability. (For a sturdy spinner, mount the cardboard on a square board of scrap wood.) Make a wide cardboard arrow and cover it with clear adhesive-backed paper. Punch a hole in the arrow and attach the arrow to the cardboard (and its mounting board, if one is used) with a nail at the center.

- Each player chooses a color and gets 20 objects (pegs, beads, or cubes).

- At each turn, both players put out any amount of objects from none to five.

- Adult asks "who put out more?" and "who put out less?"

- One player spins (children can take turns spinning).

- If the arrow stops on LESS, the child with less out takes all the objects that are out. If the arrow stops on MORE, the child with more takes all that are out.

- The game continues as long as the children want to play.

- The objects are divided again and the game starts over.

Following Instructions. This game enhances language development, spatial relationships, and visual discrimination. It can be played in pairs by older four- and five-year-olds.

- Give each child the same set of materials (cubes or pegs of different colors, a string and some beads, or a set of attribute blocks).

- Have each child put up a "screen" (a box top works well) so no one can see what anyone else is doing.

- Make a pattern piece by piece, telling the children what you are doing with each piece. Have them do exactly what you are doing.

- Take down the screens and see if everyone's pattern came out the same. If they are different, talk about why differences might have occurred.

- Let the children take turns giving the instructions.

Sequence or Patterning Activities. Using stringing beads, pegs, cubes, or parquetry blocks, lead the child from random designs to complex patterns. This activity helps develop reading readiness skills. It may require some preparation by the teacher, but the children can work on it alone.

- Give the children a chance to explore the objects. Let them make several "necklaces" or designs over a period of time.

- After several days, say to a child, "I like your design. I'm going to try to make one just like it." Then do so, describing the process. The child will get the idea that a pattern can be copied and is usually quite pleased that the teacher is interested in copying his or her design.

- Make a pattern in beads on a string or in cubes on the table and suggest that the child make a similar one. This is an exercise in copying a three-dimensional pattern.

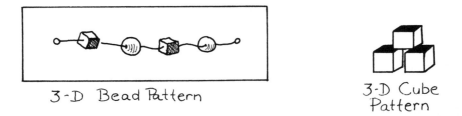

3-D Bead Pattern   3-D Cube Pattern

- Cut out paper forms that match the color and shape of the beads, cubes, or blocks. Cut strips (3" x 12" is a convenient size) from white cardboard. Store them in a box. When the child has made an interesting pattern, invite the child to make a reproduction of it, finding the right colors and shapes in the box and pasting them onto a strip.

Beginning Math Games. Use pegs and pegboard to introduce addition and the concept of "sets," a basic math principle. This activity requires an adult.

- Ask a child to put one peg in the first row and two in the second, adding one more for each row. Have the child count pegs in each row. Encourage the child to observe patterns, particularly the step design made by pegs.

- Give the child addition problems such as this: "Put one red peg and two blue pegs in the first row. Fill the second row with yellow pegs until it is just as long as the first. How many yellow pegs did you use?"

Duplicating Patterns. Use parquetry or pattern blocks. This activity can enhance visual discrimination and fine muscle development.

- Make a series of pattern cards for children to duplicate. The cards can be made increasingly complex.

    Very simple—one block, two in a row

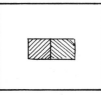

Simple figures with each block drawn in color and shape

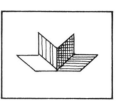

Figures with shapes outlined but not colored

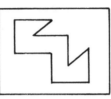

Outline of figure only

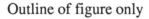

- Copy an original design made by a child and have the child match blocks to the design.

- For a complex picture like this one, have the children sort out the necessary pieces and put them in a plastic cup or can; have them available with the picture.

Integrating Table Toys with Other Curriculum Areas

Table toys can provide opportunities to develop children's emerging math, science, and literacy skills as well as to develop their problem-solving skills and creativity. For very young children, this happens simply as they handle materials again and again. As children get older, they can begin to make patterns, sort and classify, or work with computers on mirroring activities.

Problem-Solving Skills

When young children play with table toys, they construct, design, and assemble materials. As they put together puzzles, make designs with parquetry and pattern blocks, sort and classify a collection of buttons, or construct a building with Legos, children pose and solve problems by themselves, with a friend, or with the help of a teacher.

An essential part of the problem-solving process is planning and experimentation. When children feel comfortable with the process of trial and error, they are more able to approach math and science problems later on in their schooling. Learning how to develop problem-solving strategies in nonthreatening situations helps children become intellectual risk-takers and critical thinkers.

Emergent Math

Table toys offer an unlimited number of ways to help children with their emerging mathematics learning. The games described earlier suggest ideas for teaching and reinforcing concepts such as more and less, addition, and sets. Patterning, matching, seriation, sorting, and classifying can all be learned by children as they play with table toys.

As children work on patterns using table toys, you can encourage them to observe how patterns appear in everyday life. Helping children notice patterns in the block area, patterns on clothes, or patterns in their artwork are ways to reinforce this important math concept for children. You can take children on a walk in the neighborhood to observe patterns in nature and the environment (on sidewalks, on leaves, or on the fence).

Emergent Literacy

Talking with children about their play with table toys provides a rich opportunity to develop language skills. Visual discrimination and sequencing, important pre-reading skills, can be learned and reinforced as children use stringing beads or parquetry blocks to make patterns or as they handle and play with attribute blocks. Children can be encouraged to draw and write (using scribbles or invented spelling) about the designs and constructions they make in the table toy area. Hanging children's drawings of their constructions at eye level in the table toy area is one way to inspire their work.

Computers

There is a natural connection between the work children do with table toys and the computer area. The module on computers describes the process of mirroring. This means that after a child has made a construction, design, or pattern using certain materials in the table toy area, the same experience can be replicated using the appropriate software on the computer.

We have described only a few of the ways that table toys can be integrated in the classroom. You will be able to think of many more ideas as you observe and interact with children in the table toy area.

V. Sharing Table Toys with Parents

An underlying principle of the *Creative Curriculum* is that children learn best when the program is supported by the child's parents. Of all the materials in a preschool and kindergarten classroom, table toys are the ones most commonly found in the home. You can help parents understand the importance of table toys as rich learning tools by planning workshops on table toys, welcoming parents into the classroom, and sharing resources such as the letter to parents that follows this section.

Conducting Workshops on Table Toys

Most parents at one time or another purchase a variety of table toys for their children. Parents know that their children enjoy playing with these toys, which is usually the motivation for such purchases. However, helping parents recognize that table toys enhance learning opportunities will extend the usefulness of materials parents typically have at home. An especially effective technique is to plan a workshop on the subject of table toys in which parents have an opportunity to see and use toys. The following guidelines may be helpful in planning such a workshop.

- Hold the workshop in the classroom and set up a display of different types of toys.

- Explain the four categories of toys—self-correcting, open-ended, collectibles, and cooperative games. Have the participants divide into four groups, and assign each group one category. Ask them to gather all the toys in their category.

- Give parents time to experiment with the toys they have selected. While the groups are working, talk to them about what they are doing. Pose open-ended questions as you would with the children.

- After the play period is over, have each group describe their experience in exploring the toys and what they think children could learn with each type of toy.

- As a conclusion to the workshop, show the section on table toys from the videotape, *The Creative Curriculum*. Have parents focus on problems that children solve and the role of the teachers in promoting children's learning.

As part of the workshop, talk with parents about the types of table toys they generally purchase for their children. Many teachers find that parents welcome suggestions on toys and materials that would be most appropriate for their child's age and abilities. Parents are also interested in knowing which table toys their children use in school and which are their favorites. Parents may appreciate a written summary of the value and importance of table toys, based on the information found in sections I and II of this module.

Another workshop might be scheduled in which parents can make table toys either for use in the classroom or to take home. The suggestions on making toys in this module may be useful in planning this type of workshop.

Involving Parents in the Classroom

When parents volunteer or visit in the classroom, you can help them appreciate the importance of table toys by encouraging them to observe and participate in the table toy area. Here are some suggestions you can offer them about what to look for:

- Refer them to the section on stages of table toy play in the *Creative Curriculum* and point out examples of each.

- Talk with them about how the area is set up and how materials are displayed. Let them know how this arrangement helps children use the materials more effectively and how it affects their learning.

- After you have intervened in a child's play, explain what you did and why.

- Display the objectives for children's learning in the table toy area and explain how table toys address these objectives.

- Encourage parents to work with children in the table toy area. Remember, not all parents will feel comfortable doing this. When you offer a specific suggestion, such as "would you like to see if Tracey wants some help stringing her beads?" or "can you assist children in their clean-up?" parents may feel more comfotable about joining children in their play.

Sharing table toys with parents takes time and planning, but the results are well worth the effort. The following letter to parents about table toys can be used or adapted to further enhance parents' understanding of the role of table toys in the curriculum.

A Letter to Parents on Table Toys

What We Do and Why

Table toys include puzzles, various table blocks, and other small construction materials such as Legos, Ring-a-Majigs, and collections of objects (including shells, bottle caps, and buttons). When children use table toys, they learn many new skills and concepts, including:

- sorting and classifying things according to their own categories;
- judging distance, direction, right and left, up and down; and
- describing what they are thinking and doing.

When children use table toys in the classroom, we encourage them to talk about what they are doing. For example, we might say:

- "Tell me about those blocks you are using."
- "How did you get those rings to fit together?"

We also ask questions that help children extend their thinking as they play with table toys. For example:

- "You grouped all the bottle tops by color. Can you put them together any other way?"

- "You've picked out all the pegs that are the same. Can you tell me how they are the same?"

These questions and comments are designed to help the children become aware of what they doing and develop their thinking skills.

What You Can Do at Home

Small colored cubes, those about one inch square, offer many opportunities for your child to build patterns and designs. These cubes can be made into a tower, a corral, or other formations, depending on the child's interest. Colored cubes such as beads can be used to make patterns of colors and sizes: red, blue, yellow, and then repeat; large, small, medium, and then repeat.

You might collect various small objects such as buttons, seashells, rocks, and plastic bottle tops. You can give your child a tray to use on the floor if the surface isn't level, or let your child sit at a table to play. Make suggestions such as sorting all the buttons that are the same color or all the beads that are the same size. Encourage your child to tell you about the design he or she is making or why things belong together.

Playing with table toys at home promotes a child's development in many important ways. However, the most important contribution you can make to your child's learning with table toys is to take an interest in what your child does, both at home and in school. We welcome you to the classroom at any time. In this way you can see for yourself how much your child is learning.

ART

I. Why Art Is Important

Most young children naturally delight in art. They love the process of applying paint to paper, gluing things together, and pounding a lump of clay. Working with art materials offers children opportunities to experiment with color, shape, design, and texture. As they engage in art activities, children develop an awareness and appreciation of pleasant sensory experiences—which is the beginning of aesthetic development.

Using art materials such as paint, clay, markers, crayons, cornstarch, and collage materials, children express their individual ideas and feelings. As they view their own creations and those of other children, they learn to value and appreciate differences. For young children, the process of creating is what's most important, not what they actually create.

Artwork benefits all aspects of children's development. As children draw, paint, and make collages, they experiment with color, line, shape, and size. They use paints, fabrics, and chalk to make choices, try out ideas, plan, and experiment. They learn about cause and effect when they mix colors. Through trial and error, they learn how to balance a mobile and weave yarn.

Through their art, children express how they feel, think, and view the world. Art is an outlet that lets children convey what they may not be able to say with words. Involvement with a rich variety of art materials instills confidence and pride.

Art also offers opportunities for physical development. As children tear paper for a collage or use scissors to cut, they refine small muscle movements. Making lines and shapes with markers and crayons helps children develop the fine motor control they will need for writing.

Art is enjoyable and satisfying for young children. It enables them to learn many skills, express themselves, appreciate beauty, and have fun—all at the same time.

What Art Isn't

Many teachers wonder if coloring books, patterns, and pre-cut models are appropriate methods for enhancing children's art play. The *Creative Curriculum* takes the position that these materials have no proper place in the preschool or kindergarten classroom. These materials leave little room for imagination, experimentation, individuality, or discovery. They not only inhibit creativity but can have a negative effect on a child's self-esteem if the child is unable to follow the model.

Many of these materials are frustrating to three-, four-, and five-year-olds who don't have the manual dexterity or eye-hand coordination to stay within the lines, to cut along the lines, or to reproduce a model made by an adult. Beyond this, when children are given coloring books rather than pieces of paper on which to draw, they receive a subtle but powerful message: "We don't think you can draw things of your own design."

Some teachers defend using coloring books or cutting out pre-drawn patterns on the grounds that such activities are good for developing fine motor skills. However, there are many other more developmentally appropriate ways for children to develop these skills in art—for instance, by cutting out their own designs or learning to use glue, tape, a stapler, or a hole punch. Instead of coloring books and dittos, the *Creative Curriculum* recommends that teachers rely on activities that allow children to be creative and individualistic in their art play.

Objectives for Children's Learning

Teachers can select many important objectives for children to work on as they explore and use art materials. Although the actual choice of objectives should reflect the ages and interests of the children, you might want to consider the objectives below:

Objectives for Socio-Emotional Development

- Express feelings (selecting bright colors for a painting to match a playful mood).
- Learn to channel frustration and anger in a socially acceptable way (punching and pounding clay).
- Assert individuality (drawing a pumpkin that differs in color and design from the traditional).
- Experience pride (making a mobile that is hung in the classroom).
- Share and cooperate with others (working together on making a group mural).

Objectives for Cognitive Development

- Enhance creativity (combining materials and textures for a collage in a unique way).
- Develop an understanding of cause and effect (observing what happens when blue paint is added to yellow).
- Label shapes and objects (painting a yellow circle and calling it a "sun").
- Solving problems (figuring out how to get a mobile to balance).
- Develop planning skills (determining which color finger paints to assemble before starting work).

Objectives for Physical Development

- Develop small muscle skills (coloring with markers).
- Refine eye-hand coordination (pouring tempera into an easel paint can).
- Learn directionality (painting a circle with one continuous brush stroke).

Taken together, these learning objectives can help teachers plan appropriate art experiences. By targeting specific objectives, you can more easily select the art media and activities that will help children expand and increase their skills.

II. Arranging the Environment

There is a direct relationship between how the art area is set up and how effective this interest area will be in facilitating children's learning. If the area is inviting, children will want to become involved with art materials. But if the art area looks messy, overwhelming, or barren, it is not at all likely that children will want to be here. Children's creativity flourishes in an environment that is both appealing and well-organized.

Creating Space

When selecting an area of the classroom for art, you may want to consider several physical factors that have a strong influence on the environment's effectiveness.

There needs to be enough space for children to work comfortably. If possible, children should have the option of working at easels, at a table, and sometimes on the floor.

A water source should be nearby. Because painting and many other art activities need water both for use and clean-up, it is helpful to locate the art area close to a water supply. If this is not possible, buckets of water can be brought to the art area and used to wash brushes as well as hands.

Traffic flow should bypass the area. Such an arrangement promotes independent work and also reduces the chances that a child will trip over an easel or be accidentally painted.

Selecting Materials

Art materials can be as diverse as creativity and funds allow. Before gathering exotic or highly challenging materials, however, teachers should first ensure that the art area is stocked with the basics—that is, something to:

- paint on (e.g., an easel with paper),
- paint with (e.g., brushes, tempera, finger paint),
- draw on (e.g., a variety of paper, chalkboard),
- draw with (e.g., crayons, markers, pencils, chalk),
- put things together with (e.g., paste or glue),
- cut with (e.g., scissors),
- mold (e.g., clay, playdough), and
- clean up with (e.g., mops, sponges, brooms, towels).

Basic art supplies fall into three categories: painting materials, drawing and pasting materials, and sculpting and molding materials.

Painting Materials

An important part of every preschool and kindergarten classroom, painting entails the use of easels and different kinds of brushes, paints, and paper. It also requires protective clothing for children—that is, smocks. If possible, easels should be set up and available to children every day. Brushes, paint, paper, and smocks can all be stored near the art table. When everything they need for painting is nearby, children can paint and clean up independently with little help from their teachers. Although painting is essentially an individual activity, children sometimes enjoy talking to each other while painting, and they like to see what other children are doing. Therefore, consider including at least two easels in the art area to promote socialization and reduce the amount of time children have to wait for a turn.

Easels

There are two types of easels to choose from; either is appropriate in the classroom. **Free-standing easels** have two sides so that two children can paint at the same time. They should be sturdy, in good repair, and adjustable in height. These easels can be bought or made by a teacher or parent who is good at carpentry.

When space is a problem, **wall easels** are an alternative. Commercially made wall easels can be attached permanently to the wall. Or, you can cover the wall with a large piece of plastic or a dropcloth and tack easel paper at an appropriate height for the children.

Brushes

The best brushes for use in the painting area are those with metal bands and no seams. This construction secures the bristles so that they don't slide. Brushes come in either flat or round shapes. Flat 1" bristle brushes are suggested for younger preschoolers; older preschoolers and kindergarten children can use round brushes for variety. Both types of brushes are most easily handled by children when they have handles 5" to 6" in length. Older preschoolers and kindergarten children might also enjoy using pastry brushes and wall-painting brushes.

Paints

Several different kinds of paints are available, each offering a different kind of art experience:

- liquid tempera (already mixed),
- powdered tempera,
- water-based paint, and
- finger paint.

Liquid tempera lasts long and produces vibrant colors; however, it is costly. Powdered tempera is less expensive, but it must be mixed to the right consistency. If you choose to use powdered tempera, try adding a few drops of alcohol or oil of wintergreen to keep the mixture from going sour. Ivory Snow ™ also improves the consistency of tempera and makes it easier to remove from clothes.

Water-based paints, which include poster paint and water colors, are good to use at a table. With both these paints, smaller brushes are better.

Finger paints can be purchased or made. Some popular recipes for homemade finger paint are these:

Recipe 1: Easy finger paint

3 cups Vano™ starch
1 tablespoon powdered tempera (color of choice)

Mix all the ingredients together.

Recipe 2: Brilliant finger paint

1 cup Vano™ starch
1 cup cold water
3 cups boiling water
1 cup Ivory Flakes™
1 tablespoon powdered tempera (color of choice)

Mix starch and cold water until smooth.
Add boiling water and simmer, stirring constantly until thick and glossy.
Add soap flakes and tempera and beat with a wire whisk until smooth.

Another variation for finger painting that children enjoy is shaving cream. You can use it as is or with food coloring.

Paper

For finger painting, glossy paper is preferable but can be expensive. An alternative is to let children finger paint on a table top. This gives children more room to move and emphasizes the importance of experimenting with paint rather than making a picture. Alternatively, you can use cafeteria trays or a large piece of heavy-duty plastic (such as a shower curtain) stretched over a table and taped in place. If children want to have a copy of their finger paintings, any type of paper can be placed on top of their picture and pressed down to create a reverse imprint.

For painting with tempera or water-based paints, you can offer several different types of paper:

- manila paper
- newsprint
- construction paper
- butcher paper

- sandpaper
- wrapping paper
- wallpaper samples
- styrofoam packing pieces (for table painting)

Manila paper is of high quality but quite expensive. Most teachers prefer to use less expensive newsprint. Younger preschoolers painting at an easel should be given paper that is 24" x 36" in size. Older preschoolers and kindergarten children do better with 18" x 24" paper. Wallpaper and other painting papers can be cut into different shapes and sizes to vary the painting experience.

Smocks

Smocks can be purchased, but you may find it more economical to use old adult-size shirts. Trim the sleeves of long-sleeved shirts and have the children put them on backwards for maximum protection. Alternatively, an old sheet can be made into a smock by cutting a hole in the center of the sheet that is large enough for a child's head.

Drawing and Pasting Materials

For drawing and pasting, children need materials they can use independently. In preparing the art area, you might consider using the following:

- *Markers* that are water-based for easier cleaning. A variety of colors, including the vibrant "neon" shades, should be available.

- *Crayons* that color evenly and steadily. Jumbo crayons that are easy to grasp are recommended for younger children. Older children can do well with smaller ones.

- *Chalk* in both white and colors. Younger children should be given jumbo chalk; older children can use both jumbo and narrow varieties.

- *Chalkboards* in black, white, or green. Younger children will enjoy wall-mounted boards or easel-like chalkboards. Older children can use lap-top chalkboards.

- *Scissors* for both left- and right-handed children. For preschoolers who are just beginning to learn how to cut, safety scissors should be provided.

- *Paper* in a variety of colors, sizes, and textures. Most teachers prefer using newsprint. Computer paper (18" x 11"), which can frequently be found through donated sources, can also be used for drawing. Matboard (also often obtainable free from a local frame shop) has a high-quality drawing surface. It's a good idea to collect as many types of paper as possible and to use program funds to purchase paper that can't be collected (such as construction and butcher paper).

- *White glue* that is water-based and *school paste*. Epoxy, instant glues, and solvent-bond glue are toxic and don't belong in a preschool or kindergarten classroom.

Sculpting and Molding Materials

Children will benefit from having access to both clay and playdough. Each offers a different type of art experience, and each can be made in the classroom

Playdough

Although playdough can be readily purchased, most teachers prefer to make their own with the children. Doing so not only saves money but allows the children to vary the texture and color. By adding different amounts and colors to the mixture, teachers can create flesh-colored dough to simulate a variety of skin colors.

There are many recipes for playdough. Here are three that are recommended.

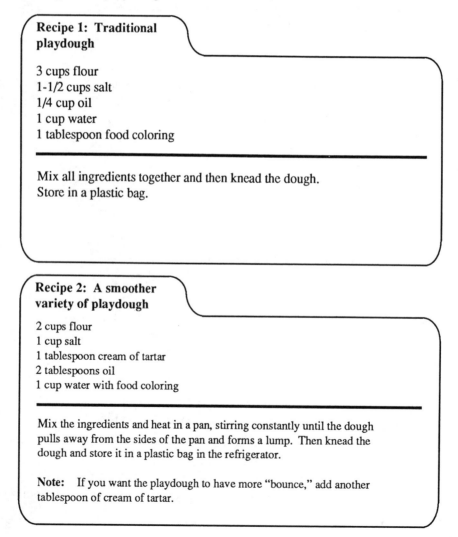

Recipe 1: Traditional playdough

3 cups flour
1-1/2 cups salt
1/4 cup oil
1 cup water
1 tablespoon food coloring

Mix all ingredients together and then knead the dough.
Store in a plastic bag.

Recipe 2: A smoother variety of playdough

2 cups flour
1 cup salt
1 tablespoon cream of tartar
2 tablespoons oil
1 cup water with food coloring

Mix the ingredients and heat in a pan, stirring constantly until the dough pulls away from the sides of the pan and forms a lump. Then knead the dough and store it in a plastic bag in the refrigerator.

Note: If you want the playdough to have more "bounce," add another tablespoon of cream of tartar.

Recipe 3: Playdough that hardens and can be painted

2 cups corn starch
1 cup baking soda
1 cup water with food coloring of choice added

Mix all ingredients and cook, stirring constantly until a ball forms.
Knead the dough as it cools (it will have an unusual and appealing texture).
Store it in a plastic bag in the refrigerator.

Clay

Two types of clay are appropriate for young children: **modeling clay** (soft clay) and **baking clay**, which can be baked in a kiln or left to harden on its own. Modeling clay is useful for those times when children want to manipulate the clay and perhaps make balls, snakes, or different shapes. Soft clay is also fun to use with rolling pins, plastic knives, or tongue depressors. Clay that hardens can be painted and the resulting creations saved.

Like playdough, clay can be either purchased or homemade. If you're fortunate, it can even be dug from its natural source—the earth. Homemade clay is recommended over store-bought varieties because unlike some commercial products, it's not harmful if swallowed. Some recipes for homemade clay follow:

Modeling clay

1 cup salt
1-1/2 cups flour
1-1/2 cups warm water
2 tablespoons oil
1 tablespoon food coloring

Mix all ingredients together.
Store it in an air-tight plastic container.

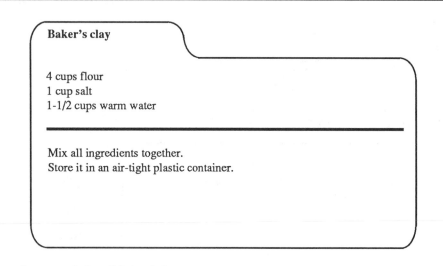

Baker's clay

4 cups flour
1 cup salt
1-1/2 cups warm water

Mix all ingredients together.
Store it in an air-tight plastic container.

Supplemental Art Materials

Once you've equipped your art area with the basic materials for painting, drawing and pasting, sculpting, and molding, you can augment the area with whatever your imagination and budget allow. The listing that follows offers some suggestions.

SUGGESTED SUPPLEMENTAL ART SUPPLIES

Natural Items	Fabrics (any size scraps)	Kitchen/Laundry Items	Miscellaneous
Acorns	Acetate	Aluminum foil	Business cards (old or used)
Dried flowers	Burlap	Bleach bottles	Cardboard tubes
Dried herbs	Canvas	Bottle tops	Clock parts
Driftwood	Corduroy	Candles	Confetti
Feathers	Cotton	Cellophane paper	Containers of any kind (e.g., baby
Pine cones	Denim	Coffee cans	food jars, margarine tubs)
Seeds	Felt	Corks	Glitter
Shells	Fur (fake)	Egg cartons	Hangers
Stones and pebbles	Gloves (old)	Grocery packages	Hole punch
Sewing Items	Hats (old)	Juice cans	Marbles
	Lace	Milk containers	Paint rollers
Beads	Leather	Paper bags	Paper clips
Braid	Oilcloth	Paper cups	Pipe cleaners
Buttons	Socks (old)	Paper doilies	Shoe boxes
Cotton balls	Terry cloth	Paper plates	Stamp pads and stamps
Hooks and eyes	**Building materials**	Paper towels	Stapler and staples
Large plastic needles	**(any size scraps)**	Parchment	Styrofoam or other packing
Macrame twine		Plastic wrap	materials
Ribbon	Linoleum	Popsicle sticks	Tongue depressors
Shoelaces	Masonite	Steel wool pads	Wire
Snaps	Metal pieces	String/rope	Wooden beads
Spools	Nails	Toothpicks	Wooden dowels
Thread	Tiles		
Yarn	Wallboard		
	Wire mesh		
	Wood scraps		

Displaying and Storing Materials

When the shelves in the art area are orderly and inviting, children tend to to use and put away the materials they need. To facilitate both the use of art supplies and the cleaning-up process, items can be stored and displayed together.

To further enhance the display of art materials, the *Creative Curriculum* offers teachers these practical suggestions:

Egg cartons can be used for *scissors* or *pencils*. Tape the carton's edges together so it remains closed when carried.

An empty coffee can makes a good *scissors* holder. Turn the can upside down and use a can punch to make holes for the scissors. Then glue the plastic lid to the open top (now serving as the bottom) so that the edges won't be exposed.

Another *scissors* holder can be made using elastic nailed to a wall or back of a cubby.

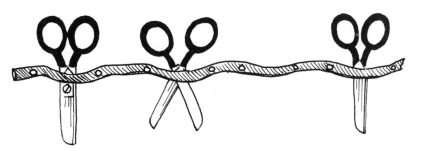

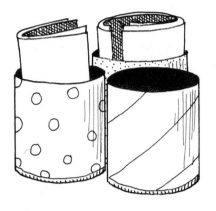

Ice cream containers or newspaper cylinders make good *paper* holders.

Ice cream containers or cylinders can also be used to store *collage materials*. Several containers stapled or bolted together can house a variety of small art items. If the collage materials are very small, cover the bottom half of each open circle with a strip of cardboard so the materials won't fall out.

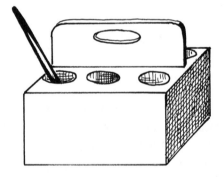

Paint caddies can be made using six-pack cardboard beverage containers. Place clean orange juice cans lined with contact paper in each of the six slots. Fill each container with a different color of paint. Children can pick up the caddy and a brush. This is especially handy when easels don't have a paint drawer attached or when a wall easel is used.

Clay should be kept in airtight containers, either plastic with a tight-fitting lid or metal with a plastic liner. Margarine containers, coffee cans, or gallon mayonnaise or mustard containers all serve this purpose.

Baby-food jars make good *glue* or *paste* containers. It is a good idea to have enough jars on the shelf so each child can have his or her own supply.

Frozen juice cans are excellent *crayon* holders. Colored paper labels tell the children where each color of crayon goes.

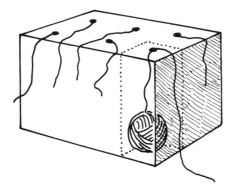

A *yarn* dispenser can be made from a cardboard box with corrugated cardboard dividers. These divided areas make convenient space for individual balls of yarn and prevent tangling. Punch a hole in the top of the box over each space and draw the strands of yarn through.

Supplemental materials can be stored in a closet or on a high bookshelf until needed. A curtain in front of an open cupboard will close it off from the children.

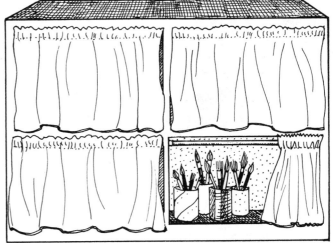

Free storage containers such as empty shoeboxes, fruit baskets, or sturdy cardboard boxes are also useful for storing *supplemental materials*. When storing different types of materials, the set-up illustrated here is effective.

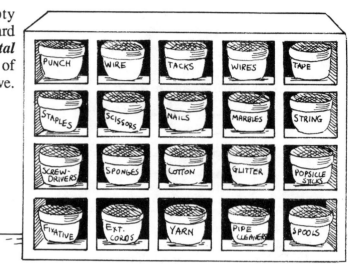

Labeling Materials

Storage and display are always enhanced by the use of labels. Labeled shelves help children know where to find materials and where to put them back.

Picture labels should be displayed directly on the shelf where items are to be stored. Labels for storage containers should be attached on the outside of the containers.

For young preschool children, picture-only labels are recommended. Older preschoolers and kindergarteners might want to see the name of the object written beneath the pictures as a further means of identification.

Drying and Displaying Children's Artwork

Finding enough space for children's artwork to dry can be a challenge. Most classrooms have limited space for hanging paintings or laying down glued collages to dry. It's important to keep in mind that how you handle children's art when it is finished says a lot about how much you value their efforts.

One idea is to hang paintings with clothespins on a line that is high enough so that it doesn't interfere with other play activities, yet low enough so that children can see their creations as they are drying. If the clothesline is tacked to a wall, each child can be assigned a specific spot. For younger children, a photo can mark their places. Older children can also have photos or have their names written on

cardboard labels. Completed artwork can then be attached by clothespins to the line beneath each child's place. This arrangement makes it easy for children to "eye" their artwork during the day and know where to find it when they are going home.

Another idea is to use a clothes-drying rack with space for many paintings. Clothespins can be used to hang paintings or wet collages until they're dry. Children can use a drying rack more independently.

Artwork that cannot be hung such as baked clay that has been painted or styrofoam creations that are wet with glue or paint, also need places to dry. Once all available shelf space has been used, it may be possible to put these items on newspaper on the floor of a hallway or to use the tops of cubbies for additional space.

Selecting Artwork to Be Displayed

Selecting which creative pieces to display is often a challenge. Most teachers want to give all children in the classroom a chance to see their artwork on the walls. Too often, though, teachers assume responsibility for deciding which pictures to feature. A better alternative is to ask the children to make that choice. Giving them the opportunity to decide which pictures they want displayed conveys a sense of respect for their judgment. Moreover, the children's opinions may be quite different from the teacher's.

Assessing the Effectiveness of the Area

Because of the flurry of activity that takes place daily in the art area, it is easy for this area to become disorganized. On an informal daily basis, however, you can observe the area and assess its effectiveness. You'll want to check not only that supplies are neatly organized and accessible but also that there is room for children to paint at easels and work at the art table or on the floor. Based on your observations, you may decide to rearrange the area to give children more room, or you might want to add new collage materials and supplies.

Here are some questions you might want to ask yourself as you observe the area:

- Do children use the art area daily? Are art supplies readily accessible?
- Do both boys and girls join in art activities? What supplies would encourage more play?
- Do children tend to choose the same art materials day after day? Do children need help using other art materials?
- Are children regularly engaged in art activities—drawing, painting, sculpting—on their own? Are the materials overwhelming or too advanced?
- Are spills commonplace? Do children have enough room for play?
- Do children clean up on their own? Are shelves and containers sufficiently labeled so children know where items belong?

By planning and maintaining an art environment in which children can independently paint, make collages, and play with clay and other art materials, you set the stage for creative art experiences.

III. Observing and Promoting Children's Learning

Children's previous experiences with art materials, the attitudes of teachers and parents toward art, and the number of children who can comfortably use the art area at one time all affect children's involvement in art activities. Probably most important, though, is allowing children to use art materials on their own, in their own ways. If a teacher does the artwork for the child, the child gains nothing but an opportunity to watch the teacher at work. At the same time, materials that are too simple do nothing to challenge a child's creativity. Only when materials are developmentally appropriate will meaningful learning take place.

To ensure that art activities are at an appropriate level, it's important to know where children are developmentally. To do this, you need to know how children grow and develop in the area of art.

How Children Use the Art Area

As with all areas of development, children's abilities in using art materials increase in predictable stages. Children move through these stages at their own rates, reflecting their own timetables for development.

Drawing and Painting

In drawing and painting, children go through four specific stages as they learn to hold and manipulate a crayon, pencil, marker, or paintbrush and use it to create something of their own design. The four stages are:

1. disordered scribbling,
2. controlled scribbling,
3. naming a picture that wasn't planned, and
4. representational drawing or painting.

Disordered Scribbles

Infants make their first artistic gestures when they flail their hands and "write in the air." At about a year and a half, they begin to pick up a crayon, pencil, or paintbrush and use it. They go through

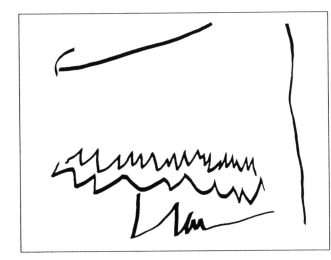

a long period of experimenting and developing muscle control—that is, learning to hold the crayon or paintbrush and make marks on paper. Then, often rather suddenly, they start experimenting with different colors, lines, pressures, and directions. Children's first experimentations make use of large motions and lines of differing lengths.

Controlled Scribblings

Gradually, children begin to gain mastery over their disordered scribblings. Through continued drawings and paintings, they begin to make patterns, to repeat patterns, and to see designs in their scribblings.

Naming an Unplanned Picture

Once children learn to control a crayon or paintbrush, they begin to see reality in their work. They name what they have done: what adults see as scribbles becomes a house or a person to the young preschooler. Children in this stage don't always plan their pictures beforehand. Often they start to draw or paint and what shows up on the paper makes them think of something.

Representational Art

As older preschoolers and kindergarten children gain experience, they gradually begin to plan their drawings and paintings. By about age five, most children are doing representational art, though some children reach this stage earlier than others.

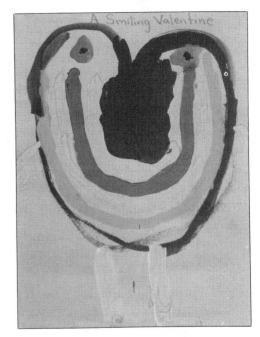

Stages in Using Other Art Materials

Children approach other types of art media and experiences, such as clay, collage, and weaving, in a similar, gradual way. Although the stages children go through in working with other media aren't as clear-cut as the stages in drawing and painting, children's use of these media is nonetheless developmental. Children move from a stage of *exploration* (functional play) to one of *experimentation* (constructive play).

Initially, children familiarize themselves with the medium: What does clay feel like? How is a loom set up? What makes the collage items stick? Children like to use all their senses to learn about a particular medium before they begin to use it purposefully. Gradually, as they become familiar with the new medium, they experiment with it. They roll playdough into worms. They attach potholder loops to prongs in a loom (not necessarily those that will lead to successful weaving, though). They paste pictures on cardboard to see how they look when glued to a surface.

With increased practice and experience, these experimentations become more purposeful and skilled. Eventually, children are able to turn clay into a dinosaur, to weave ribbons on a loom, and to make a collage representing a class trip to the zoo. Their increasing skills enable children to become ever more creative.

Observing Individual Children

Knowing how children develop in their art play gives you a framework for identifying where each child is developmentally. By observing each child, you can design approaches that will help them grow and expand their skills.

As you observe a particular child, think about the objectives you have set for his or her learning. Then, ask yourself questions such as these:

- How does the child hold a crayon or paintbrush? Are the materials too small for the child to grasp easily? Do I need to change the materials or modify them?

- Does the child prefer tearing paper to using scissors? Is the child developmentally ready to use scissors? What activities can I plan to strengthen small muscle skills?

- Are the child's paintings at the same level of sophistication as crayon drawings? Does the child need more time at the easel or more encouragement?

- Does the child explore playdough or try to make creations with it? Is the child still in the beginning stages of play? How can I make playdough more interesting?

- Does the child continue working with one art medium until satisfied with a creation, or does he or she jump from activity to activity? Is the child overstimulated by all the supplies? How can I work to maintain interest?

- Is the child able to talk about artwork? What questions might I ask to encourage reflection?

Interacting with Children

Spending time in the art area talking to children is one of the best ways to show them that you value their work. By talking with children and asking questions, you can use art as a time for vocabulary development (e.g., learning such words as texture, pastel, collage); concept development (e.g., shapes, colors, thick versus thin); and problem solving (e.g., learning about what happens if, what goes first, what do we need)—as well as for aesthetic appreciation and the development of creativity.

Because so much of children's art is experimentation—seeing what mixed colors look like or how water affects clay—your words can help children review and think through what they are doing and discovering.

Reinforcing children's learning takes some skills. When presented with a painting of lines and squiggles, some adults might say, "That's pretty!" or "What is this a picture of?" Children are better served when adults ask such questions as these: "Can you tell me about your picture?" or "What did you enjoy about doing this?" Such questions encourage children to talk about their creations without feeling judged or pressured to describe something specific.

When you comment on or ask children about their work with art materials, you convey the following messages:

- I am aware of what you are doing.
- I am interested in your efforts and therefore in you.

- I will help you look closely at your own work.
- I am aware of your growing confidence.

In summary, when talking with children about their artwork, teachers should **avoid** the following:

- using general words such as "pretty," "great," or "lovely;"
- telling children what you think their work represents; and
- asking children "what is it?"

When you talk to children engaged in art activities, you can do the following to support their efforts:

- *Describe what you see:* "I see you used all the colors on the easel today." "You were very careful about what materials you used in your collage and where you wanted to put them."

- *Talk about children's actions:* "You really are pounding that playdough." "You made some lines going up and down and some going back and forth on the page."

- *Ask children about the process:* "How did you make that new color?" "What part did you enjoy most?" "Did your hand go round and round to make these circles?"

- *Ask open-ended questions* that encourage children to think and respond: "What are some ways you could fill up this paper?" "What would happen if you mixed these two colors together?" "How is this collage different from the first one you made?" "What are some different ways to make these stick together?"

- *Use words to encourage and support* the children's efforts: "You made a lot of paintings today. Which one should we hang up on the wall?" "You spent all morning playing with the clay and thought of so many different ways to use it."

Sometimes children get stuck or seem uninspired in the art area. By observing and analyzing the problem, you can respond appropriately. Here are some ideas for restoring a child's confidence in handling a problem:

When the child...	Try saying...
Needs encouragement	"What do you think you could do with these pieces of felt?"
Is reluctant to join in	"You can put on a smock if you're worried about getting paint on your new shirt."
Ends an activity abruptly	"Is there anything else you would like to add to your collage?"
Is unsure about the next step	"Here is some colored chalk. What do you think will happen if you dip it in the starch?"
Wants you to make a drawing of a cat for him	"Let's see what you have in mind. What's the biggest part of the cat? Can you draw that first?"

In each of these examples, the teacher has tried to restore the child's confidence. These kinds of interactions are very important in helping children develop self-confidence and self-esteem.

IV. Extending and Integrating Children's Learning

Although basic art supplies are always available to children, teachers can add new life to the art area by introducing new approaches and materials. By providing children with enough guidance to enable them to explore on their own, teachers can help children achieve new levels of problem-solving ability and creativity.

Special Activities

There are a number of books you can purchase that offer ideas for art projects. Keep in mind, however, that appropriate art experiences for young children aren't "cute projects" but enjoyable and satisfying adventures in self-expression and exploration. The activities suggested here focus on the art experience itself rather than on producing something to be admired by adults.

Exploring Painting Materials

By combining different types of paints, papers, and tools, teachers can introduce new experiences.

- *Exploring texture.* Provide paper, tempera paint, and brushes. Put out the following in separate containers: sawdust, sand, salt, and powdered tempera. Allow the children to experiment with what these substances do to the paint and paper. They can add a substance to the paint beforehand, sprinkle it on the paper and paint over it, or sprinkle it on afterward. When talking about these experiments, encourage children to talk about "what happened when...."

- *Exploring color.* Provide primary-colored paint (either finger paint or tempera). While the children are painting, add a container of white paint. Observe the children's reactions as they mix white and colored paint to create pastels. Encourage children to try mixing other colors to see what happens.

- *Using different types of tools.* Let children experiment with these painting tools:

rollers	sponges cut into various shapes
whisk brooms	vegetables (e.g., potatoes) cut into shapes to make
straws	stamps
marbles	corks
plastic squeezable	leather thongs
dispenser bottles	string

To use these painting tools, children will need a flat, wide paint container. As an example, an aluminum pie plate can be lined with moistened paper towels and a small amount of paint poured in. The children can then dip the roller, string, thong, or other material into the paint and move it around on the paper. For printing, children can dip a sponge or stamp into the paint and press it on the paper.

For "marble pictures," put a sheet of blank paper inside a shallow open box. The child can then roll the marble in a pie plate of paint, put the marble in the open box, and move the box to make the marble roll. Different colors can be tried on the same piece of paper. These experiences are good for eye-hand coordination and experimentation with line and motion.

Children can also "paint" with a straw by dripping the paint onto the paper with a brush and then blowing it around with a straw to make a pattern. Glossy finger-painting paper is best for this activity.

Printing with Body Parts

To introduce this activity, you might read *The Snowy Day* by Ezra Jack Keats. After reading about making "angels" in the snow, and providing the weather is cooperative, children can try this same activity. Alternatively, if the weather is warm, children can run water over their bare feet and make foot imprints on a sidewalk.

To do handprinting, you will need:

- a washable work surface,
- one, two, or three colors of finger paint,
- a large (about 2' x 3') piece of solid-color paper tacked to the wall, and
- a bucket of warm water nearby for washing hands.

Have the children put a blob of one color on the table or surface. Let them move the paint around. Ask the children how it feels, what it smells like, and so on. Then, invite the children to make a handprint on the paper on the wall.

To extend the experience, you might ask the children to do the following:

- Talk about how everyone cooperated to make the mural.
- Note how each handprint is different. Children like to identify their own prints; teachers can label prints with names or photographs.
- Put their hand over someone else's handprint (to teach concepts of bigger and smaller).
- Point out that some prints go up, down, or to one side or the other (to teach directionality).
- Point their hands in the directions of the different prints (to teach directionality and enhance motor control).
- Note how many hands there are in each color (are there more red hands or more blue hands?).

Making Etchings

Another fun and easy printing activity is to scratch a picture into a printing block and then make a print from it. Materials needed include:

- styrofoam meat trays;
- scratching tools such as a nail, fork, bottle cap, or old ballpoint pen (look for items that are sharp enough to make cuts but not so sharp that children cannot handle them safely);
- paint and a small paint roller; and
- paper at least as large as the styrofoam trays.

Give each child a tray. Let the children cut, scratch, or gouge a design on the outside of the tray. Have the children roll paint over the design as to "ink" it. Lay paper onto the design and then lift it off.

Extending Experiences with Texture

In addition to the everyday texture experiences that children have using clay and playdough, you might consider introducing children to the wonderful sensations of cornstarch mixed with water. These two ingredients mix together in ways that are unexpected and surprising for children. Here are the three steps involved:

1. Give children 3 cups of dry cornstarch to play with. Ask them to describe what they feel.
2. Gradually add 2 cups of warm water. Have children mix in the water, using their hands.
3. Continue to have the children mix the cornstarch and water with their hands. The substance will turn from lumpy to satiny smooth. Ask children to describe what they feel throughout the mixing process.

Most children are intrigued with this activity because the cornstarch and water combine to form an unstable solid. When it is punched, it offers resistance; but if a finger is held lightly on the surface, it will sink into the cornstarch. When left to set on a counter, the substance turns rock hard; cupped in your hand, it will turn to liquid. The contradictions between the way this material looks and the way it feels provide a lesson in science as well as art.

Extending Art with Collages and Assemblages

"Collage" refers to the pasting of all kinds of things onto a flat surface. An "assemblage" is a three-dimensional piece of art made by putting various things together.

Assemblages and collages are wonderful opportunities for creative expression. When children are offered a variety of materials, each child creates something original. New creations can be made by adding materials such as fabric scraps, ribbon, wood scraps, styrofoam, or feathers.

When first introduced to collages and assemblages, children need time to experiment with the materials, explore the different textures, and try out ways of attaching one material to another. Try putting out paper, a random assortment of materials, and something to attach the materials to each other. Both

white paste and glue can be offered; children will quickly discover that paste works when attaching paper to paper, but glue is needed to hold wood scraps together or to attach pieces of felt to cardboard.

Glue can be watered down (half glue/half water) to make a kind of starch. This mixture is good for fabric or yarn collages. Children can put the fabric into the mixture, place it on a cardboard surface, and let it dry in that form.

Collages can be created on a variety of papers, including cardboard, heavy corrugated paper, or construction paper and posterboard. Newsprint isn't recommended because it is too thin. Computer paper can be used as long as the children are just attaching paper scraps.

After the children have had many experiences with this process, they can use scissors to cut pieces of paper or thin materials, such as wallpaper samples or ribbon, to the size and shape they want.

Making Puppets

Puppets are not only fun to create but also very useful for developing body awareness, language concepts, and spatial relationships. Puppets naturally lend themselves to imaginative dramatic play. Even children who don't talk very much will often become verbal when their puppet is talking. There are many ways to make puppets. Three of the more popular types of puppets are sock collage, newspaper, and papier-mache.

As their name implies, *sock collage puppets* are made from socks and a "collage" of assorted fabrics, scissors, and glue. To create the puppets, place the collage materials in one pile and the socks in another. Invite children to pick a sock and then cut and glue on facial features.

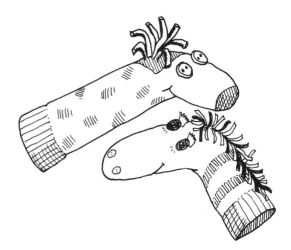

Three- and even four-year-olds probably won't be able to cut shapes that look like eyes or even to get the eyes in the right place. Their puppets

186

will be three-dimensional counterparts of their scribble pictures. Nonetheless, they are sure to enjoy making their puppets "talk." The teacher can use the experience as a chance to ask young children questions such as these: "How many eyes do we have?" and "Where are our eyes?"

Yarn or string can be added to make hair and fabric scraps to make clothes, thus creating a puppet with a body as well as a face. This is a chance to offer different textures—silks, velvets, and different patterns. Buttons can be glued on for some individuality of features. Sock puppets can, of course, be animals as well as people. One favorite is the dragon—the eyes go on top and a tongue goes in front.

Newspaper puppets can be made from newspaper, sturdy rubber bands, crayons, pens, buttons, fabric, and fasteners. Creating these puppets is a four-step process:

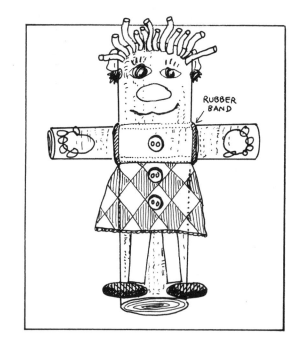

Step 1. Take a section of newspaper and fold it in thirds.

Step 2. Take a sheet of newspaper and roll it up.

Step 3. Put the rolled sheet across the folded section to make "arms." Secure the puppet's arms with a rubber band.

Step 4. Decorate the puppet.

When done, lead a discussion about how different each puppet is: "Let's look at what we made. Just like we are all different, the puppets we made are all different."

Papier-mache puppets can be made by using an inflated balloon or a wad of aluminum foil as the base for the puppet's head. Strips of newspaper are then dipped into wallpaper paste and placed all over the "head" until it is entirely covered with paste-soaked paper. After a day or so, the paper will dry and harden. At this point the papier-mache can be painted to resemble a human or animal head. Clothing can be sewn around the "neck" area to give the puppet a full-body look.

All these puppets lend themselves to play in the house corner and library area as well as the art area.

Weaving Experiences

Weaving is a challenging task and therefore most appropriate for older preschoolers or kindergarten children. Weaving can be introduced through games that help children relate the activity to physical motion:

- *In and out the window.* The children stand in a circle holding hands. One child is chosen to be "it." This child goes around the circle under each pair of arms, alternating going into and out of the circle (three times). Everyone sings: "Go in and out the window (3 times) as we have done before. Now go and pick a partner (3 times) as we have done before."

"It" then chooses someone to be "it" next. The game is repeated until each child has had a chance to go in and out of the circle. You can point out to the children that they have been weaving with their bodies.

- *A line game.* Line six chairs in a row with space in between them. Have everyone join hands and play follow the leader; you can serve as leader. Weave in and out of the chairs. Point out the connection with weaving in the art area by saying, "We are weaving with our bodies! See how we're going in and out?"

To begin weaving activities, children need materials they can manipulate easily. To encourage creativity, consider giving children choices in the materials they select. Children will need something to weave on, such as:

- chicken wire, which comes in two sizes (those of a puzzle board with large holes or small holes),

- weaving mesh, which can be found in a school supply store (mesh vegetable bags are also available in some supermarkets),

- scraps of pegboard,

- plastic berry containers, and

- styrofoam trays punched with holes.

If chicken wire is used, fold the sharp ends down and cover them with duct tape or heavy masking tape. Once made, the wire mats are reusable. The large holes in chicken wire make weaving easier for younger children. It is a good idea to have both large- and small-holed wire available for older, more skilled children.

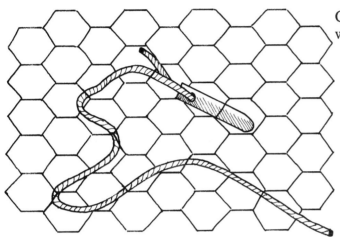

Children will also need something to weave with, such as:

- pipe cleaners,
- straws,
- yarns (rug weight or heavier is best),
- ribbon,
- twine,
- wire with the ends taped (including florist wire), and
- toothpicks.

Finally, children will need tools for weaving. When they first begin to weave, they may not be ready to use a needle. A good alternative is to make yarn into its own needle. Wrap the end of the yarn in tape or dip the end in glue and let it dry; it will harden to the texture of a shoelace tip.

Some other weaving materials, such as wire or pipe cleaners, are stiff enough to use without a needle. For children working on large-holed mesh, a tongue depressor with a hole in it (use a drill to make the hole) makes a needle that is easy to handle. After the children have had experience with taped yarn and tongue depressors and as they start to use smaller-holed materials, they will be ready for needles. Plastic or metal needles with large holes and safety tips are sold in knitting and embroidery stores.

Weaving can be a very satisfying activity. It can also become a long-term project which the children can put away for a while and return to periodically.

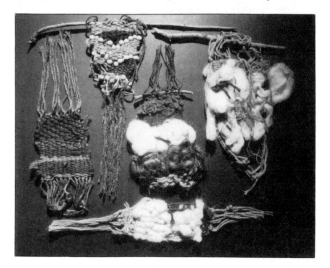

There are also ways to make weaving a group experience for the entire class. A large loom can be created out of wood or Triwall™ (thick cardboard building material). Outdoors, you can string a "loom" between tree branches. Once the loom is made, any child can weave a row with any material (e.g., yarn, ribbon, shoelaces) that will go in and out of the warp strands (the threads that run lengthwise on the loom).

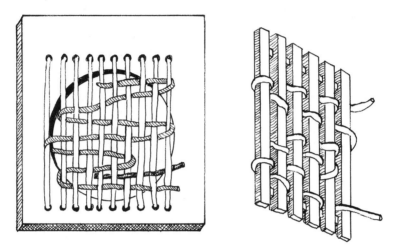

Leave the loom up in the classroom or outdoors and let the children add to it all year long—a ribbon from a birthday present, feathers collected on a walk, straws from a visit to a restaurant; anything that can fit between the strands can be woven in. During the year the loom can be used to start discussions of past experiences: "Remember when Shantay found this velvet ribbon?" or "Remember when Peter's shoelace broke and he wove the broken piece in our loom?" The loom can thus become a living history of your class.

Stitchery Experiences

Stitchery is a process similar to weaving. Children use a needle or yarn made into a needle that goes in and out of material. They can also learn to stitch or sew one material to another. Materials recommended to stitch on include the following:

- tagboard (cut into the size of a puzzle);
- burlap (stapled to a frame made of wood, cardboard, or styrofoam, cut into the size of a puzzle);
- styrofoam trays; and
- felt.

Paper is not recommended for stitchery because it tears easily. Heavy-duty cardboard will work, however, as will buckram.

Children can be introduced to stitchery by being provided with materials to stitch on and with and by being allowed to choose what they like. Over time, a hole punch can be provided so they can create a series of holes to sew

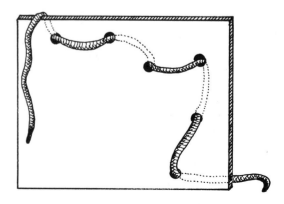

through. Just finding out how to punch holes builds children's understanding of spatial relations and develops eye-hand coordination. Most beginners will punch holes around the edge of the cardboard and stitch overhand or in and out, or a combination of both, as shown in the preceding illustration.

Later on, older children (four- and five-year-olds) may create their own designs.

Creating Holiday-Related Artwork

Holidays present a challenge to early childhood teachers. This is often a time when teachers want to decorate the classroom or have the children make gifts to bring home to family members. There may even be pressure from parents to receive specific objects from the children.

Many people's ideas of holiday art, however, is that everyone should produce an identical picture of a jack-o'-lantern for Halloween or paste up an identical profile of a Thanksgiving turkey. Teachers who are committed to a creative art program in which children use materials in different ways without adult supervision find it difficult to deal with such expectations.

There are many ways to include holiday-related art activities without resorting to dittos, coloring books, or adult-made models. Consider these ideas:

- *Mother's or Father's Day.* Trace the children's bodies on large pieces of butcher paper or brown wrapping paper. Provide crayons or paint and let the children decorate themselves any way they like (some may make faces, others clothes; still others will paint everything one color). On the back, let each child individually dictate a story about the parent. You can say "Tell me about your Mom" or "What do you want to say to your Daddy?" These paper figures make wonderful gifts and meet all the criteria of creative art.

- *Music drawings.* Play music associated with a holiday and have the children draw pictures to the music. These pictures can decorate the classroom and lead to a discussion of what the holiday means to the children.

- *Halloween and Valentine's Day.* Put pieces of orange paper cut like a pumpkin, or red or pink paper cut like a heart, on the easel. The children can then paint anything they want on them.

- *Photos as decoration.* Prepare foods in class that are associated with a holiday. Have a "feast," and ask one of the parents to take pictures. You can then mount the pictures on paper frames that have been cut from drawings made by the children for this purpose. The framed pictures then serve as decorations.

It is also helpful to keep the holidays in perspective and remember what is important to the children. In spring, introducing white paint to create pastels may be far more interesting and important to a group of three-year-olds than drawing pictures of baby chicks. Ask the children for ideas of things to create for the holidays and display in the room. A group mural using seasonal materials is always appropriate—for instance, a fall mural that is a collage of leaves, sticks, and acorns can take the place of an entire bulletin board full of look-alike pilgrims or pumpkins.

Developing an Appreciation of Art

In addition to the many active art activities described above, one special way to extend children's learning is to help them develop what museum educators term "art criticism." Art criticism involves training oneself to enjoy diverse works of art. For young children, this includes their own work as well as museum-quality art.

Art criticism involves using guided discussions to focus children's attention on the process of art and what it means to them as individuals. This may seem like a sophisticated concept, but even young preschoolers can begin to develop an aesthetic sense.

Many ideas for helping children develop a critical eye are based on the work of Edmund Feldman, a researcher in the field of art criticism. Feldman has named four areas that teachers can use as discussion points for guiding children's viewing of art: description, analysis, interpretation, and judgment.[1]

In the **description** phase, teachers focus children's attention on a particular piece of art:

- "Tell me everything you see in this painting."
- "Suppose you were talking to me on the telephone. How would you describe this mobile to me so that I would know just what it looks like without seeing it?"
- "Close your eyes and tell me everything you remember seeing in this picture."

In **analysis,** the teacher encourages children to relate the things they talked about when they were describing the art:

- "Can you find a line in that drawing and follow it with your finger?"
- "Are the colors in this painting friendly?"
- "Does one of the shapes in this sculpture seem stronger than the others?"

The **interpretation** phase helps children identify feelings with what they've noticed thus far:

- "What do you think the artist was thinking about while painting this picture?"
- "Would you like to play with the boy in that drawing?"

---

[1] Edmund Feldman. *Becoming Human Through Art.* (Englewood Cliff, NJ: Prentice Hall, 1970.)

- "How does the finger painting you made make you feel when you look at it now?"

Finally, during the **judgment** stage teachers ask children to make value judgments about their work:

- "Would you like to have this painting hanging in our classroom?"
- "Which of the drawings you made today do you like the best?"
- "Why do you think the artist made this type of sculpture?"

Art criticism is an exciting approach for stimulating children's critical thinking skills at the same time that you help them learn to appreciate their own art and the art of others.

Integrating Art with Other Curriculum Areas

Art lends itself well to many of the activities going on in other areas of the classroom. Music and movement are both arts. An effective music activity tied to visual art involves playing a piece of classical music for children, such as Moussorky's *Pictures at an Exhibition* or Prokofiev's *Peter and the Wolf,* and having children draw or paint the way the music makes them feel. Children doing this activity also develop a sense of the narrative possibilities in all art forms; in this way, they connect art with language and communication.

Cooking, too, has natural links with art. Vegetable dyes made from beets or onion skins make much better (and safer) colors than cold-water or commercial dyes, which usually contain chemical additives. Similarly, potatoes and turnips make easy-to-use, creative printing tools. Art can also be brought into the cooking area in the form of international posters and prints that focus on foods native to foreign countries. For example, Latin American and Caribbean posters that show people carrying bananas or casavas (a food similar to the potato) can be hung in the cooking area next to recipe cards for banana bread or casava soup.

Art is naturally found in sand and water play as children use these materials aesthetically. Bubble-blowing through straws, plastic six-packs, and berry baskets gives children an opportunity to experiment with bubbles of varying shapes and sizes. Sand play also affords children an opportunity to make artistic constructions, castings, and patterned creations in sand.

The outdoors is the artist's natural studio. Moving an indoor activity outdoors for inspiration gives many children added joy; they love to paint a fence with water, draw a mural, or finger paint on an oilcloth spread on the ground. Art experiences sometimes become more expansive and free outdoors.

Finally, it's important to remember that children's art is the best resource for decorating your classroom. By displaying children's artwork prominently, you convey to children that the classroom belongs to them and that their work is important. You also send parents and other visitors the message that yours is a program that treasures children's artistic creations.

V. Sharing Art with Parents

One of the strongest beliefs underlying the *Creative Curriculum* is that the child's experiences at school are enhanced when supported at home. Most parents realize that their children love art, and many give their children crayons and paper for drawing. Yet a great many parents are unaware of the ways in which art experiences promote socio-emotional, cognitive, and physical growth.

Teachers can perform a valuable service by sharing information with parents on the relationship of art play and learning. By helping parents appreciate the stages of growth in children's art and the value of art experiences, parents will be better able to support and value this important area of the curriculum.

Conducting Workshops on Art

One effective way of capturing parental support is through workshops. A good beginning is to plan a workshop on children's art. The following suggestions may be useful in planning such a parent workshop:

- Before the workshop, prepare a one-page written summary for parents describing the value of art, based on information presented in this module.

- Select several different types of art media for the parents to try: for example, a collage, a type of painting, clay or cornstarch and water, and crayons and paper for drawing.

- As the parents come into the workshop, invite them to use the materials and create something to bring home for their child. Interact with them as you do with children, commenting on the process and asking open-ended questions.

- When the parents are finished, use their art as the starting point for a discussion on the value and role of art in an early childhood classroom. Emphasize the importance of the process; ask parents to describe how they felt when they were using the materials.

- Conduct a follow-up discussion on the value of children's art, based on the parents' conclusions.

Some teachers find it helpful to have an outside expert such as an art teacher or art therapist address the parents. By hearing expert opinion, parents can then verify their own discoveries about art.

Involving Parents in the Classroom

Another important way of strengthening the bond between home and school is to encourage parents to volunteer in your classroom art area. Many parents enjoy art experiences and will welcome an opportunity to help. If parents have a particular skill area or talent they would like to share with children, you might focus a special activity around this.

For those parents who are reluctant to be in the art area, you might suggest that they help by collecting supplemental materials. Parents can be encouraged to take their children on walks to gather leaves, pine cones, flowers, feathers, and other natural materials that might be used in art projects.

Similarly, you might ask for the parents' assistance in taking a field trip to an art museum. Before this event, you might also consider holding a workshop on how to ask guiding questions that help children learn about art criticism, as described in the previous section.

By actively soliciting parental support, you send children and parents the message that art is an activity to be valued both at home and school.

A Letter to Parents on Art

What We Do and Why

Art is an important part of our curriculum. Every day, children find a variety of art materials available on our shelves. Drawing, painting, cutting, pasting, and playing with playdough are not only enjoyable but also provide important opportunities for learning. Children express original ideas and feelings, improve their coordination, develop small muscle skills, learn to recognize colors and textures, and develop creativity and pride in their accomplishments by exploring and using art materials.

When children are engaged in art activities, we talk with them about what they are doing and ask questions that encourage them to think about their ideas and express feelings. For example, we might say:

- "I can see you like the new colors we put on the easels today."

- "You made a lot of pictures. Which one do you want to hang up?"

- "You worked a long time with the clay today. What did you like doing best?"

As you can tell, we like to focus on what children are doing—not on what their finished artwork looks like. We say such things as these:

- "Tell me about your picture" instead of "What did you make?"

- "It looks like the playdough is sticking to your fingers. What could we do to make it less sticky?" instead of "You're not having much success with the playdough."

What You Can Do at Home

Art is a very easy way to bring your child's school life into your home. Here are some things you might wish to try:

- Designate a drawer in the kitchen or living room as an art drawer, or use a bookshelf or sturdy cardboard box. In this space include crayons, marking pens, paper, a pair of scissors, and a separate box for collage materials.

- Let your child know where art materials can be used—at the kitchen table, at a small child-sized table, on the kitchen floor, or outside. Some of the most enjoyable art materials are a bit messy and you want to be sure that the space you choose is one that can be cleaned easily.

- Encourage your child to take out the art materials and use them independently at any time.

- Find places to display your child's art—on the refrigerator, on a wall in the child's room, or in a hallway. Displaying children's art lets them know you think it's important and attractive.

Children's natural love for art is something we can support together!

SAND AND WATER

I. Why Sand and Water Are Important

Nearly everyone enjoys the relaxing sensations of walking barefoot on a sandy beach or soaking in a warm tub of water. Children, like adults, are almost instinctively drawn to sand and water. The natural attraction that children have for these materials makes them perfect for the early childhood classroom. Because most children are already familiar with these substances, they enjoy exploring them. The refreshing coolness of water against their skin or the sensation of sifting sand through their fingers is hard to resist.

Children's explorations with sand and water naturally help build various skills. By sifting sand and scooping water, children improve their physical dexterity. By joining others in blowing bubbles or making a sand castle, they develop social skills. At the same time, they enhance their cognitive skills as they explore why certain objects sink in water and others float.

Sand and water play can be two separate activities. Each one on its own provides children with many learning opportunities. As a liquid, water can be splashed, poured, and frozen. As a dry solid, sand can be sifted, raked, and shoveled. Play with each substance separately can be used to foster children's socio-emotional, cognitive, and physical growth.

However, in the *Creative Curriculum* we have combined sand and water play for two reasons. First, sand and water are both natural materials that are pleasurable for children; they encourage similar types of exploration and learning. Second, sand play and water play are enhanced when the two are merged to form a third type of play—wet sand play. You can, of course, use water or sand play as independent activities. However, by housing the two types of play in one area, you can expand the separate benefits of both.

Wet sand play allows children to encounter principles of math and science firsthand. When children mix sand with water, they discover that they have changed the properties of both: the dry sand becomes firm and the water is absorbed. The textures of both materials change, too. Unlike dry sand or liquid water, wet sand can be molded. Individually and together, sand and water play can be used effectively to challenge and soothe children's minds and bodies.

Objectives for Children's Learning

Children benefit the most from sand and water play when teachers guide their interactions. By designating specific learning objectives for children, you can nurture their growth and development. The following list presents some suggested objectives for children's play in this area.

Objectives for Socio-Emotional Development

- Play cooperatively with others (sharing water play props with another child).
- Explore social roles (washing dolls and dishes).
- Develop pride (requesting that a castle made in the sand tub not be knocked down at the end of play).
- See a task through to completion (mixing up and using a bubble solution and then cleaning up).

Objectives for Cognitive Development

- Observe materials to see how they compare and contrast (adding water to dry sand to see how it changes).

- Understand cause-and-effect relationships (predicting what will happen when soap flakes are added to water).

- Observe conservation of volume (pouring sand, water, or wet sand into differently shaped containers and comparing them).

- Develop problem-solving skills (figuring out how to dig a tunnel in wet sand so that it won't collapse).

- Develop creativity (molding wet sand into a variety of shapes).

Objectives for Physical Development

- Strengthen fine motor control (using a tongue depressor to trace figure-eights in the sand).

- Develop eye-hand movements (shaking sand through a sieve).

- Improve coordination skills (filling measuring cups and spoons).

This listing is provided to spark your own thoughts. You can add or change objectives to meet the specific needs of the children in your program. Your choice of objectives will guide you in planning appropriate experiences with sand and water that will promote children's learning.

II. Arranging the Environment

Creating Space

The placement of the sand and water area and how it is laid out have a major effect on the type and extent of learning that occurs through sand and water play.

Many classrooms have an area devoted to sand and water play outdoors, such as a covered sandbox. The module on the outdoor environment presents ideas for setting up a sand and water area outdoors. In this module, however, we are focusing on setting up a distinct sand and water area in the classroom. Including sand and water play as a classroom interest area is recommended even for those programs with outside play areas because it enables you to allow more time for children to use these soothing materials. Also, younger children and/or children who have limited experience with sand and water play may be more comfortable in a controlled indoor environment.

In setting up an area for sand and water play, it's important to create an environment in which children can concentrate on what they are doing with as few distractions as possible. The drawing below illustrates an environment that does this effectively.

As shown, two distinct areas exist—one for sand play and one for water play—yet both activities take place near one another. This arrangement allows children to play with sand and water independently and also to have wet sand play with a minimum of confusion and mess.

A good location for the sand and water area is near the block or house corner. These areas, like the sand and water play area, tend to be noisy. By locating the sand and water area near other active areas, teachers can avoid disturbing children who might be looking at books or concentrating on an art activity.

It is also preferable to have the sand and water area out of the range of main traffic patterns. Because water play often leads to wet floors that can get slippery, the sand and water area should be out of bounds to other children who might come scurrying through, only to slide or fall on a wet floor.

Selecting Materials

Equipment for the sand and water area can be purchased through school supply catalogues or locally. Most sand and water play equipment can be assembled relatively easily and inexpensively. For example, two flat containers such as plastic dishwashing tubs, baby bath tubs, or cement-mixing tubs can be used to hold the sand and water. These tubs can be purchased at department stores, hardware stores, or lumber suppliers.

The size of the tub selected can vary; probably a tub with a capacity of 20 to 25 gallons is the most comfortable size for preschoolers and kindergarten children. In addition, a depth of at least nine inches is recommended so that the tubs can be filled with a sufficient amount of water or sand to engage children in play.

The water tub should be filled daily to a height of about three to four inches. At the end of the day, the tub should be emptied, as water left overnight can grow bacteria. This process is made easier by locating the water play area near the classroom's water source.

Fill the sand tub with dry, finely textured sand. Bags of sterilized play sand can be purchased at lumber or building supply stores. Dirt or coarse-grain sand should not be used, as it will not hold together as well as fine-grain sand and is thus difficult for children to work with. The sand tub should be filled only halfway so that children have room to use props and the sand can dry out overnight.

If sand is not available or if you wish to add variety to sand play, the following materials can be used as substitutes:

- sawdust,
- beans,
- rice,
- large wood shavings, or
- aluminum pie crust beads.

A word of caution when using food as a play material: many parents have strong feelings about wasting food. Therefore, parents' views should be solicited before using beans or rice as a substitute for sand.

Miniature Sand and Water Trays

Another variation is the use of individual miniature sand and water trays. A dishpan makes an ideal miniature sand or water tray. These pans are not intended to be used as a substitute for the larger tub areas but as supplements to the main play activity. They are especially valuable for younger preschool children who are in the beginning stages of sand and water play and may want to explore the properties of sand and water quietly on their own.

The smaller trays also provide an ideal environment for artistic and scientific endeavors that older preschoolers and kindergarten children might enjoy, such as making shell patterns in sand or watching a beetle track across a smooth layer of sand.

You may wish to set up two of these individual trays side by side on a small table and let pairs of children play at the same time. Or, if the floor is well-protected and children are more comfortable doing so, they may wish to use the trays directly on the floor.

Selecting Props

Initially, children will enjoy exploring dry sand and then wet sand with very few toys, tools, or equipment. Children (especially the younger ones) need time to explore sand before they feel free

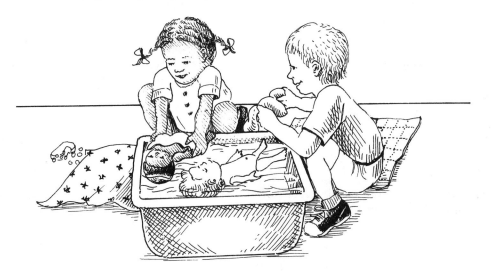

to experiment with it. Similarly, children should be given an opportunity to play in water with only a few simple props, such as plastic bottles or dolls to wash.

Gradually, children's play will expand when props are added. Measuring cups and funnels greatly increase the range of experiences available to children. Floating toys add other possibilities. In the sand area, digging and sifting tools open up new worlds for exploration.

Giving children access to props for sand and water play challenges their minds and their senses and tends to hold their interest. In selecting props, look for ones that are versatile, but don't limit your selection to props that have to be used in both areas. Wooden and metal props (other than aluminum or stainless steel) are not recommended for long-term use, as they tend to crack or rust.

Props for Sand Play (dry or wet)

Bowls
Buckets and shovels
Cookie cutters
Dump trucks
Gelatin molds
Ladles
Magnifying glass
Marbles
Measuring cups
Measuring spoons
Muffin tins
Pebbles and rocks
Plastic doll dishes
Rolling pin
Rubber animals and people
Scales
Scoops
Seeds
Shells
Sticks
Straws
String
Toy cars
Whisk broom

Props for Dry Sand Play

Colander
Funnels
Rake
Sieves
Sifter
Strainer

Props for Water Play

Boats
Bubble-blowing materials (straws, soap flakes, glycerine)
Buckets
Egg beater
Corks
Eye dropper
Food coloring/vegetable dye
Funnels
Ladles
Measuring cups
Measuring spoons
Nonbreakable dishes
Paint brushes
Plastic squeeze bottles
Plastic tubing
Rubber or all-plastic baby dolls (of varying ethnicity and gender)
Scale
Scoops
Siphon
Soap: liquid, solid, flaked
Strainer
Sponges
Troughs
Water wheels
Wire whisks

Many of the items listed here can be used interchangeably with both sand and water. You will probably be able to find other items in your classroom or outdoors that would enhance the sand and water area.

Caring for Materials

Care of this area is simple and straightforward. Yet because the area is prone to messiness, care must be ongoing. Children should wear waterproof aprons, especially for water play. It's advisable to put towels, sheets, newspapers, old shower curtains, or dropcloths to catch falling sand and absorb spilled water.

Equipment and props need to be checked periodically for cracks and rusting. Any worn or rusted materials should be removed and replaced.

Clean-up needs to be supervised daily. Water cannot be allowed to stand in tubs overnight for health reasons. All surfaces, including tables, tubs, and floors, need to be mopped regularly so that no one slides, trips, or falls. If you keep a broom, dust pan, sponges, mop and paper towels on hand, children can help maintain the area.

Children should be taught two basic rules of safety:

- Water stays in the tub—no squirting or splashing.
- Sand cannot be thrown.

Displaying and Storing Materials

Materials should be accessible to children so they can independently select the ones they want. The key to displaying props is to keep the area attractive and uncluttered. Some general ideas for storing props follow:

- Place props at children's eye level so they can readily see what is available and select the ones they want.

- A pegboard with hooks on it can be used to store many of the kitchen-related items used in sand and water play, such as ladles, sieves, and measuring cups.

- Narrow drawers can be used to hold collectible props such as seashells, marbles, or feathers.

- To maximize storage, plastic dishbins can be used to hold props. These are especially recommended for props used in water play, as props may need to be put away while they're still damp. Alternatively, damp props can be hung in nylon or string bags to air dry.

- Props can be grouped in boxes or tubs by function, such as filling, pouring, floating, or measuring. To illustrate, a bubble-blowing box might contain the following:

      bubble solution,
      bubble pipes,
      plastic berry boxes,
      plastic straws,
      plastic rings from a six-pack of soda,
      pipe cleaners, toothpicks, and plasticine clay for homemade bubble frames,
      sponges and styrofoam cups, and
      small containers (plastic/metal) opened at both ends.

Labeling Props

To make the storage and retrieval of materials in the sand and water area easier for children, use labels. By drawing a picture or using a photograph, you can show children where each prop is stored. This approach is especially useful for illustrating those items stored in bins, boxes, or drawers. By looking at the pictures of the props stored in a particular bin, children can readily tell if a prop they want is in that bin without having to wade through its contents. This saves the child frustration and cuts back on mess.

For young children, picture labels at eye level are most appropriate. Older children, however, may like having the written name of the prop posted along with its picture. In either instance, it is suggested that labels be covered with clear contact paper to protect them from water, sand, and dirty fingers.

Assessing the Effectiveness of the Area

By following the simple procedures suggested in this section, most teachers find that the sand and water area operates smoothly. Frequent observations of the area let you know if sand and water play are supporting children's development and learning. Perhaps the placement of the tub is interfering with traffic flow or props are difficult for children to reach. Maybe children are being overstimulated by props or perhaps not enough cleaning supplies are available. Observing children's use of the sand and water area allows you to make changes to the environment when they are needed.

Here are some ideas you might focus on when making your observations:

- How often do children choose to play here?
- Do the same children habitually select this interest area?
- Do boys play here as frequently as girls?
- Do children help themselves to only a few props at a time, or do most of the props stay out during play?
- Do children get into fights over props or over having a turn to play in the area?
- Does the area get very messy during play, or is the mess relatively controlled?
- Do children clean up after themselves?

When the area is arranged effectively, children can focus on their work and benefit from sand and water play.

III. Observing and Promoting Children's Learning

You can facilitate children's learning with sand and water play by observing to see where they are developmentally and then determining how best to ensure their continued development. An understanding of how children's play with sand and water develops will help you with your observations.

How Children Play with Sand and Water

Functional play is the first developmental stage for both sand and water play. Children become familiar with the properties of the materials. What does sand feel like when it is sifted through one's fingers? What does water feel like when it is splashed? What happens to water when soap is added? Do individual grains of sand disappear after being sifted through a strainer? During this stage of development, children use their senses to become comfortable with sand and water. As they sift, pour, poke, splash, and combine these substances, they acquire information about what these materials are like and what can be done with them.

Constructive play follows this exploratory stage. Children apply what they have learned about sand and water. Instead of simply scooping wet sand in and out of pails, they now do this activity as a planned event. In their constructive play, they make an unmolded sand structure into a building that can be named or that becomes part of a bridge support to be built. Activity during this stage is more intentional and part of a series of experiments.

Dramatic play is an extension of the preceding stage. Activity becomes even more finely planned and executed. Children experiment with building intricate moats around castles or channeling tunnels. Water play may involve socio-dramatic elements that rely on children's imaginations. Children's activities during this type of play are largely symbolic of their experiences.

Play activities in this later stage also reveal a higher degree of cooperation. In the beginning stages, children are often content to explore sand and water by themselves. As they begin applying what they know, they like to join in shared projects and their play reflects team efforts to build and experiment.

Observing Individual Children

In making observations, it's useful to begin with the objectives you've set for the children's learning. Then, using your knowledge of how children's play with sand and water develops, carefully observe individual children. The questions that follow are offered as starting points for your observations:

- How often does a particular child choose to play with sand and water? What could I do to encourage a reluctant child to play here?

- Does the child show a preference for sand play over water play or vice versa? Is the preference a result of being more familiar with one type of material?

- Does the child prefer to play with sand and water outdoors?

- Does the child explore props or experiment with them? How can I extend the child's play to the next stage of development?

- Does the child play alone or cooperatively with other children? What group projects could I introduce that would encourage teamwork?

- Does the child stay involved for a sustained period? What open-ended questions could I ask to find out what the child is thinking?

With the information you collect during your observations, you can tell what type of play children are engaged in. Knowing this, you can then interact with them in ways that will help them progress even further.

Interacting with Children

You can build on children's intrinsic interest in sand and water by responding to their play in ways that will encourage them to develop further. One of the simplest but most effective approaches is to talk with children about what they are doing. When you do this, you:

- help children become aware of what they are doing and why, and

- give children the message that their activities are important and valued.

First, ask them to describe what they are doing. For children who are reluctant to express themselves, you can ask questions such as these:

- "How does the water sound when you pour it?"

- "Do your two pitchers of water hold the same?"

- "How does the sand feel?"

- "What did you find out when you used the water wheel?"

Once children have described their actions to you, focus their attention on what they have done. Open-ended questions will encourage them to reflect on their activities.

- "Can you tell me about what you made?"

- "Why do you think the mud pies didn't hold their shape?"

- "You really made that water wheel go fast. What could you do to make it turn slowly?"

- "I see you're trying to pour the sand into that little opening. What could you use to get the sand in the bottle without spilling it?"

- "How could we use these cookie cutters in the sand tub?"

The process of reacting to and reinforcing children's play allows teachers to guide learning while encouraging children to take the lead.

Helping Children Who Are Reluctant to Play

For those children who appear to be stuck at a particular level or who are reluctant to participate in sand and water activities, it is important that teachers know when and how to intervene. Here are some strategies:

- Start with basic props and observe children's play to see when new props can be added (e.g., when children are experimenting with how to fill a bottle, a funnel can be introduced).

- Present materials to children sequentially (e.g., first dry sand and then wet; first clear water and then colored water or soapy water).

- Provide raw materials that children may need for experiments:

    different surfaces they can pour water on, such as waxed paper, a blotter, a sponge, or plastic;

    objects that will sink or float;

    a series of cans with holes punched in them so children can see how long it takes for the different cans to empty; and

    materials that are proportional, such as measuring or nesting cups.

Using strategies such as these, you can create an environment in which children are comfortable experimenting on their own.

IV. Extending and Integrating Children's Learning

By working with children in the sand and water area, teachers can enrich and extend learning. By introducing new props and special activities, you can turn the sand and water area into an exciting setting for learning.

Special Activities

Blowing Bubbles

Children of all ages—as well as most adults—enjoy this activity. Young preschoolers will need assistance from you or older children; older preschoolers and kindergarten children can do much of this activity on their own. Introduce this activity into water play by providing materials for making bubble solution and frames for blowing. A good water-to-soap ratio for bubbles is one cup of dishwashing detergent to one gallon of water. Most teachers prefer to use a high-quality liquid detergent because the bubbling effect is better. To produce longer-lasting bubbles, corn syrup, gelatin crystals, liquid pectin, or glycerine can be added to the bubble solution. One tested recipe suggests that you add about 50 drops of glycerine to the above recipe for bubbles that are truly spectacular to behold.

With your guidance, children can construct or use "as is" a variety of frames for blowing bubbles, such as:

- empty eyeglass frames,
- plastic rings from a six-pack of soda,
- coat hangers or electrical wire fashioned into shapes,
- plastic lids of margarine or coffee containers cut into shapes, or
- plastic berry boxes.

Bubbles are made by dipping frames into the bubble solution and blowing bubbles or by moving the frames swiftly through the air so that the soap film slips through the frame, thus forming a bubble. Children will learn on their own that bubble blowing works best if both the frames and hands are wet; dry surfaces cause bubbles to burst.

One creative variation on this theme can be undertaken outdoors on a day warm enough for children to wear bathing suits. In this activity, children become part of the bubbles themselves. In a wading pool filled with

210

bubble solution, a child stands on a towel. (The towel keeps the child from slipping.) The child then slips a Hula Hoop™ over himself or herself and drops it down so that the hoop becomes submerged in the bubble solution. With your help, the Hula Hoop is raised over the child, enclosing the child in the emerging bubble. This activity is bound to give children a new appreciation for bubbles!

Washing Rocks

Younger preschoolers love to wash things. Begin this activity with a hunt for rocks that need to be washed. Using soft sponges and a bucket of water, children can begin transforming the rocks they find. Encourage children to observe how water changes the color of rocks as they are washed.

Sand Combs

Using posterboard or stiff construction paper, you can help children design and cut out combs that can be used to make patterns in the sand. If children want to preserve their combed designs, plaster of Paris can be used. First, pour the plaster over the combed surface; once the plaster is hard, it can be pulled from the sand. The resulting sculpture will be a reversal of the combed design.

The Sands of Time

Older children can construct a timer similar to that used in many board games by using a can, string, and sand. A small hole is punched into the bottom of the can and three additional holes punched at the top. String can then be threaded through the holes and tied together in the middle so that the can may be suspended and hung. The container is then hung over a bowl and sand poured into it. Using a watch, children keep track of when three minutes (or another time period of their choosing) are up. Any remaining sand is emptied; the sand collected in the bowl now becomes the timing sand. Children can use this timer to keep track of three-minute activities, including taking turns.

Integrating Sand and Water Play with Other Curriculum Areas

Even though sand and water play is relegated to one particular place in the classroom, you can use sand and water to support activities you are working on with children in other interest areas. One of the most natural linkages is with science. Here are some science-related activities you can do with children to extend their learning:

How Water Changes Things

For this experiment, assemble a variety of substances, such as a blotter, salt, jello crystals, paper, sand, a sponge, and so on. Children can then use a medicine dropper to moisten these materials gradually. As these materials become wet, ask questions to encourage children to describe what it is they see and what they think is happening:

- What changed color when you added water to it?
- Did anything change its shape when you added water to it?
- How does the blotter look different when it's wet and then when it's dry?
- What will happen if you add water to a glass of orange juice?

You can follow up this activity with a discussion of what actually takes place when each material is made wet.

Sinking and Floating

For this activity, collect a number of objects that float (e.g., a piece of wood, a plastic bottle with a tight cap, a leaf, an acorn) and a number of objects that don't float (e.g., a paper clip, a nail, clay, washers, a stone). Children of all ages can take turns placing each object in the water and noting whether it floats or sinks. Further experimentation should be encouraged:

- What happens if an object that floats is held under water and then released?
- What happens if a floating object such as wood is weighted down with nonfloating objects such as stones?

Observing Grains of Sand

A magnifying glass will encourage children to examine and compare different types of sand. Older children might enjoy using a simple microscope. They can compare how sand under the microscope differs from sand viewed with the naked eye. A clear marble can also serve as a magnifying glass. Alternatively, a water lens can be constructed using a clear plastic bottle filled with water.

Here are some questions to guide children in this observation:

- What does the sand look like?
- How does the sand feel?
- What things do you see when you look through the microscope? Under water?
- Is the sand you look at with the microscope different from the sand on the table?

Comparing Different Types of Sand

Fine-grain sand, coarse-grain sand, and dirt all have different properties. Fine-grain sand is best for molding. Dirt grains are small, but water does not go through them easily. However, the substances in dirt—such as twigs and stones—strengthen constructions. Have children experiment with each type of sand, first dry sand and then wet sand that they can mold and build with. Encourage children to talk about their observations by asking questions such as the following:

- Which pile of sand got "wettest"?
- Which pile of sand was easiest to build with?
- Which pile of sand felt best to touch?
- Which pile of sand would you want to use for making a castle?
- Which pile of sand would you like to have in the sand tub?

Other areas of the curriculum that can be easily linked to sand and water play are the house corner, storytelling in the library area, art, and music. Here are activities you might wish to try with children if you want to support their learning in these areas:

Using Sand and Water in Dramatic Play

As children play with both sand and water, ideas for dramatic play naturally develop. For example, children like to wash dishes, bathe dolls, and do laundry in the water basin. Teachers can thus readily use the water area as an extension of activities conducted in the house corner. Similarly, sand play lends itself well to explorations of fantasy. The traditional sand castle, for example, can be used to spur children's storytelling or help them deal with fears. As they build their castles, children can tell stories of scary dragons and brave knights. Using sand and water for dramatic play is especially effective because these substances are soothing to children. Emotions and/or problems experienced and dealt with in the comfort of this area become less threatening to children.

Using Sand and Water in Art

Most young children enjoy using their bodies in art activities. One sand-related activity that includes this feature is making casts. To cast a mold, ask children to add water to a small, individual tub of sand. Then have the children press one of their hands into the wet sand. Using Plaster of Paris, assist the children in filling the hand prints with plaster. After 40 to 50 minutes, the plaster will feel cool and hard to the touch. The children can then carefully lift their molds out of the sand. The casts can be painted, decorated, or left as they are. Children can use this same technique to cast molds of their feet or of objects such as shells or keys. As children work at this activity, you might wish to ask them questions such as these:

- How did it feel when you put your hand in the wet sand?
- What did you do to make sure that all of your fingers made a print in the sand?
- How can we tell when the plaster is hard?
- How does the plaster hand look like your real hand? How does it look different?
- How can you tell your handprint from someone else's?
- What other body parts could we make casts of?

Using Sand and Water with Music

Children can use water play to determine the unique sounds that pots, pans, and plastic containers make when they are sprayed with water. Help the children select pots and pans that can be taken outside and leaned against a wall or tree. Using squirt bottles, have the children blast the "instruments" with a steady stream of water to make "music." Younger preschool and kindergarten children will enjoy making sounds and copying their timbre and vibration. Older preschool children might like to try to create musical tones and rhythms to accompany songs such as "Twinkle, Twinkle, Little Star."

The activities presented here are just a sampling of the many activities and experiments teachers can introduce into the sand and water area to engage children's interest. Depending on the developmental capabilities and interests of the children, you'll want to supplement this list with ideas of your own.

V. Sharing Sand and Water Play with Parents

When parents watch their child empty a pail of sand in a playground sandbox or play with water during a bath, they are not always aware that their child is learning about science and math concepts, refining motor skills, and trying out social skills. Parents may even complain when their children come home with sand in their hair. These problems can often be avoided when teachers take time to help parents appreciate the opportunities for learning that sand and water play provide.

Conducting Workshops on Sand and Water Play

One of the most effective means of helping parents learn about sand and water play is to hold workshops where parents can learn firsthand what goes on in their children's classroom. In an introductory workshop on sand and water, parents can play directly with the sand and water tubs, using available props. As parents sift sand and measure quantities of water, they can generate a list of all the science and math concepts children might be learning from the materials.

You can then share with parents how you use this interest area to stimulate children's socio-emotional, cognitive, and physical growth. By trying out selected planned learning activities, parents can discover for themselves how tracking objects in sand develops fine motor skills or how adding soap flakes to water illustrates an important principle of science. It's important to emphasize why you value sand and water play as a crucial part of the preschool and kindergarten curriculum.

Another subject you might wish to focus on is how props enhance children's learning in the sand and water area. Start the workshop by instructing parents to play at the sand and water tub without props. How long does it take before they become bored? To pique interest, invite them to select any of the classroom props they see. After about 10 minutes, ask the group to discuss which props they selected and why. Which props worked best with water? Which with sand? What concepts do they think their children might learn from using these props?

As a follow-up activity, have parents work in groups to find props that would enable them to:

- blow bubbles of a variety of shapes and sizes,
- create a dramatic play scene, and
- illustrate how children could learn math concepts.

Involving Parents in the Classroom

When parents visit the classroom and observe children conducting scientific experiments at the water tub and casting molds in the sand tub, they often experience a new respect for sand and water play. If you urge parents to serve as volunteers in the sand and water area, they can introduce children to new props, lead science experiments, or just be close at hand to encourage children as they play.

For those parents who aren't able to help out in the classroom, you might ask their assistance in collecting some additional and unusual props that would add a new dimension to the children's play. By finding some way to involve parents in their children's play with sand and water, you can help them appreciate the important role that these materials play in the curriculum.

A Letter to Parents on Sand and Water Play

What We Do and Why

Although you're probably used to your children splashing in the bathtub and digging in a sandbox at the playground, you may be surprised to know that the sand and water area is an important part of our classroom. This is because sand and water aren't just fun—they're also a natural setting for learning.

When children pour water into measuring cups, they gain a foundation for mathematical thinking. When they drop corks, stones, feathers, and marbles into a tub of water, they observe scientifically which objects float and which sink. When they comb sand into patterns, they learn about both math and art.

We encourage children to experiment with these materials and as they do, we ask questions that encourage them to think about what they are discovering:

*   "Why do you think the wet sand won't turn the wheel?"
*   "How did the water change when we added the soap flakes?"
*   "Does the sand feel different when it's wet?"
*   "How many of these measuring cups of water will it take to fill this quart pitcher?"

What You Can Do at Home

In addition to your child's everyday experiences with sand and water at home, you may want to find some places in your home where your child can play regularly with sand and water in the same ways we do at school. If you choose to do this, be prepared for some messes. Spills and stray sand are natural byproducts of children's enthusiastic play!

Here are some thoughts on setting up for sand and water play at home:

*   Water play can be set up at the bathroom or kitchen sink. A large towel should be laid on the floor. If the sink is high for the child, a stool or stand can be provided. Outdoors, a small pool, tub, or old baby bath can be used.
*   A dishpan can be used as a miniature sand box. Your child could use this sandbox on a table, on the floor, or even resting on the lap. Collect small items for the miniature sand box such as shells, plastic animals, coffee scoops, etc.
*   If a sandbox is not available outdoors, a dirt hole can be dug for sand play. Indoors, a plastic tub can be filled with sawdust or aluminum pie crust beads.

Giving children an opportunity to play with sand and water on a regular basis helps them develop their minds and bodies in a relaxing and enjoyable way.

LIBRARY

I. Why the Library Is Important

The library can be an oasis in the classroom—a place to get away from more active interest areas, relax in a soft environment, and enjoy the wonderful world of literature. When children are read to regularly and encouraged to look through books on their own, to listen to story tapes, and to make up their own stories, they develop the motivation and skills to read and write.

The library may include a writing center and a listening center with tapes, flannel boards, and puppets. These media, along with storytelling by teachers and children, promote literacy skills (reading, writing, and communication). At the same time, the library area facilitates children's progress in other areas of growth and development. In the library, children:

- expand their imaginations and creativity;

- learn about the importance of print as a means of communication;

- gain information and adjust to new experiences by reading and listening to stories on such topics as the birth of a sibling, moving, going to a new school, or visiting the dentist or doctor;

- learn to deal with difficult events, such as being hospitalized, the death of a family member, the death of a pet, divorce, and sibling rivalry;

- acquire knowledge of science, math, history, health and safety, and famous people;

- learn about social responsibilities, such as how to be a good friend, how to care for the environment, share and take turns, and how to behave in specific social situations; and

- become familiar with different literary genres, including stories, poems, rhymes, folk and fairy tales, and biographies.

Exposure to books and storytelling helps children understand that their feelings, fears, questions, and problems are not unique to them. Acquiring a love for books is one of the most powerful incentives for children to become readers.

Objectives for Children's Learning

The following is a list of sample objectives to help you determine the learning possibilities in your library area. The objectives you choose will depend on the ages and interests of the children in your classroom.

Objectives for Socio-Emotional Development

- Develop concern for others (demonstrating empathy after hearing a story about people with disabilities or people who have suffered from prejudice).

- Try out different roles (play-acting characters from a story).

- Share time and materials with others (inviting another child to join in listening to a tape).

- Enhance self-esteem (making a book composed of photos of themselves and their families).

Objectives for Cognitive Development

- Develop an understanding of symbols (relating the picture of a boy to the written word "boy").

- Increase vocabulary (learning the names of animals in a book on Africa).

- Predict events (telling what's going to happen next in a story being read aloud).

- Recognize objects, colors and shapes (pointing to objects on a flannel board and describing their attributes).

- Understand sequence (opening up a book and turning the pages in order).

- Apply knowledge to new situations (making up a nonsense rhyme after hearing poems of this type on a tape).

- Develop storytelling abilities (dictating stories to a teacher or creating a story with scribbles or invented spellings).

Objectives for Physical Development

- Develop small muscle skills (writing with a marker).

- Strengthen eye muscles (following pictures and words in a book as it is being read out loud).

- Coordinate eye and hand movements (placing objects on a flannel board).

- Refine visual discrimination skills (finding an object or person in a complex illustration such as Waldo in the *Where's Waldo?* books).

Teachers can use the library area to accomplish a wide range of learning objectives. Not all the objectives indicated here are appropriate for any one child; you can individualize by selecting objectives that best match the developmental levels of the children in your group.

II. Arranging the Environment

The library area in the *Creative Curriculum* includes space for looking at books, listening to records and tapes, and writing. In some classrooms these different activities are located together; in others, writing tools may be incorporated into the art area and records and tapes may be part of a music area. Regardless of their location, the crucial factor is how teachers choose to arrange the space and materials. As in other areas, arrangement of the library area plays a major role in facilitating children's learning.

Creating Space

The key to establishing an effective library area is to make it an inviting place where children will want to spend time. The library area should be situated in an area that is not well-traveled and is near other quiet classroom activity areas, such as art and table toys, so that children are free to relax and concentrate. A successful library area conveys the message that exciting things can happen in a quiet atmosphere.

Furnish the area with soft chairs and pillows. Relaxing furniture lets children know that this is a comfortable place to be. A rug on the floor, a big beanbag cushion, a rocking chair, or even a mattress covered with an attractive piece of fabric creates a warm, cozy environment.

Include a table and chairs in the area. Some children prefer to look at books or write while sitting at a table. A brightly colored tablecloth or a plant on the table can add warmth.

Decorate the walls. Book jackets, photos of children and adults reading, and children's artwork can all make this area more inviting. Charts and signs help create a print-rich environment.

Light the area well. Children shouldn't have to strain their eyes. Natural light, if possible, is always best; a standing lamp or an overhead fixture can provide additional lighting if necessary.

Selecting Materials

The library area can be one of the most popular places in the classroom when teachers carefully select materials to include. Take time to think about what books, tapes, and writing materials are most appropriate for the children in your classroom.

Selecting Books

There are many wonderful and appropriate books written especially for young children. How do you go about choosing books from the many available titles? It's important to begin with the interests, life experiences, and skills of the children. Young children's attention is centered on themselves, their families, their homes, and their friends. They like stories about characters they can identify with.

Appropriate books for young preschoolers have the following characteristics:

- a simple plot about familiar experiences;
- colorful and bold illustrations that are clear, realistic, and filled with detail;
- illustrations drawn from the child's point of view;
- lots of repetition in the story; and
- rich language (rhymes, nonsense words, and repetition).

Older preschoolers and kindergarteners like books with a story line. Their attention span is longer, and they appreciate humor and fantasy. Books that are appropriate for them have these characteristics:

- a plot that can be followed;

- a story with humor or perhaps a surprise ending;

- imaginative accounts of things they know can't happen;

- stories that extend their understanding of the world around them;

- colorful illustrations with lots of details; and

- stories about faraway places and other cultures with elements similar to their own experiences.

Books for all children should challenge prejudice, bias, and stereotyping and convey positive messages to children about differences of all kinds. This means that the books you select should show the following:

- men and women in a variety of roles, displaying the ability to make decisions, solve problems, care for family members, and work outside the home;

- a variety of family configurations (e.g., a father and child, two children and a grandmother, etc.);

- illustrations that portray people realistically (e.g., mothers who wear clothing other than aprons and people of various ethnic origins portrayed realistically, not stereotypically);

- people of all ethnic backgrounds who can be assertive, solve problems, make decisions, take on a variety of family roles, and display a wide range of emotions; and

- adults and children with disabilities who participate in all aspects of life, including mainstreamed schooling, an active family life, and participation in sports and other recreational activities.

We have included a bibliography of recommended children's books at the end of this module. You can use this list to build and augment your own selection of books for your classroom.

It isn't necessary to gather the entire inventory of books at the start of the year. Some teachers find that when they regularly rotate books, children have the feeling of seeing new books or they are reminded of old favorites not seen for awhile. Moreover, as new interests emerge, appropriate books can be added. For example, if a child must go to the hospital for a tonsillectomy or is upset by the birth of a sibling, books on these topics can be added to the library at appropriate times.

You can also include materials that encourage children to tell their own stories and dramatize stories they have heard. Props such as flannel boards and puppets elicit storytelling and enhance the area.

Equipping the Listening Center

If possible, the listening center should include two or three small cassette players and a variety of tapes for children to select. Headphones allow children to listen to tapes without disturbing others.

The same general guidelines noted for books also apply to selecting story tapes. The best tapes are:

- short, because children's attention spans are limited;

- lively in their presentation, because nothing is more boring than a dry, monotonous voice;

- technically well-produced, without static and hisses;

- anti-bias in content; and

- narrated by both men and women.

In selecting story tapes, begin with stories that are familiar to children or that accompany books you have in the classroom. You can make tapes yourself, selecting books that the children particularly love and know well. As you record the story, you might wish to include sound effects or put in cues to let children know when to turn the page while reading along with the tape.

In addition to story tapes, you may want to include music tapes in the listening area. (Recommended records and tapes can be found in the Music and Movement module.) If you regularly add to and rotate the materials in the listening center, you will find that this area has a dynamic character.

Equipping the Writing Center

An effective writing center invites children to explore the world of print. The following is a list of suggested materials to include in this area:

- *Writing tools*

    thick pencils—black lead and colored
    magic markers—thick and thin, water-based
    chalk and chalkboards
    wooden "pencils" and magic slates
    crayons
    lap pads

- *Printing tools*

    letter and design stencils
    alphabet letter stamps and ink pad

- *Paper*

    computer printout paper
    magazines
    index cards
    envelopes and stationery
    unlined and lined paper
    construction paper
    carbon paper
    small blank books

- *Other tools*

    hole punch
    stapler
    scissors
    paper clips
    pencil sharpener

Displaying Materials

How the materials in the library are displayed is directly linked to how often and how effectively they will be used. Books should be in good repair and attractively arranged on shelves in such a way that children will be drawn to them. They need to be free-standing, with their covers in view so children can pick out titles readily by themselves.

Tapes and writing materials can be stored on shelves or grouped in storage containers such as bins, cans, folders, and boxes. By drawing pictures of objects contained inside a folder or box, you let children know exactly where particular items are stored.

Older preschoolers and kindergartners often like to see the written word as well as a picture of the object on a label. By adding words to labels, you can help children increase their sight vocabularies while they seek out and clean up library materials.

Caring for Materials

Keeping the library area in good condition sends children the message that its contents are valued. If books are torn and marked up, pencils have no points, and markers are dried out, children soon receive the idea that this is not a very important place to be. It's a good idea to check periodically to see that all books, tapes, and equipment are in good repair. Torn materials, nonfunctional cassette players, and worn-out supplies should all be replaced as soon as possible.

You can also solicit the children's help in caring for library materials. Books in particular should be checked routinely and mended with the children's help. Older preschoolers and kindergartners can be especially helpful in taping torn pages and erasing pencil marks in books. To facilitate this effort, a "book repair kit" can be kept in the library area. A cigar box works well to house the repair items, which might include the following:

- transparent tape to repair torn pages,
- cloth tape to repair the spines of books,
- gum erasers to remove pencil marks,
- correction fluid to cover ink and crayon marks, and
- a pair of scissors.

The presence of a book repair kit in the library and its use by teachers and children conveys the message that books are to be respected and cared for by everyone in the classroom.

Assessing the Effectiveness of the Area

Every day, you can observe how children as a group use the library. With this information, you can determine how effectively this area is meeting the objectives you've set for it. Here are some questions to ask yourself as you make your observations:

- How frequently do children choose the library area?
- Do girls choose this area as frequently as boys?
- Is one type of activity (e.g., tapes or books) more popular than the others?
- Are children able to use the area independently?
- Do children tend to read the same books and listen to the same tapes day after day?
- Do children like to play here alone, with a friend, or with an adult present?
- Do children clean up and take responsibility for this area?

Based on your observations, you may wish to add new materials or change your approach to storing materials. If your observations uncover no problems, you can take pride in the fact that the library is meeting children's needs well.

III. Observing and Promoting Children's Learning

By observing what children do in the library, talking with them about what they are doing, reacting to their accomplishments and discoveries, and asking open-ended questions, teachers promote children's learning. The process begins with knowing how children's play with library-related materials develops.

How Children Use Library Materials

In their use of the library, children go through developmental stages similar to those in other areas. Awareness is the first stage in young children's use of library materials. Being read to, observing parents and teachers write, and seeing books (and other forms of print) in the environment spark children's curiosity about reading and writing. The stages of development after awareness differ somewhat for reading and writing.

Developmental Stages in Using Books

Exploring Books. Copying their parents and older children, young children like to "play" at reading. They also ask to have books read to them. This frequently means reading the same picture book over and over again at one sitting. Often it's adults who tire—long before the child—of hearing the same story read many times. Children enjoy these repetitions because they love to anticipate what happens next and feel powerful knowing the answer.

Understanding Sequence. Children gradually recognize that stories have a beginning, middle, and end. After repeated readings of picture books, children proudly retell the story. Adults are often amazed at a child's ability to recite a story nearly verbatim. Details are especially fascinating to children at this stage.

Recognizing that Written Words are Symbols. Children gradually start to relate the stories contained in books to both the pictures and the words on the page. They realize that printed words function differently from pictures and that words stand for ideas and thoughts.

Matching Words with the Printed Text. At this stage, young children like to run their fingers along the text or point to individual words as a book is being read. These behaviors indicate that they are beginning to understand that printed letters represent specific words.

Recognizing Printed Words. Now children take an active interest in the text and demonstrate curiosity about the meaning of words. They may ask questions such as these: "What does this say?" or "Where does it say that?" During this stage, children develop what is known as sight vocabulary. They may notice words from a favorite book in real-life settings and excitedly point them out.

Developmental Stages in Writing

Young children love to use pencils, pens, crayons, and other writing implements to imitate adult writing. These early attempts at writing mark the first developmental stage. Although writing at this stage looks more like scribbling than anything else, it takes on definite form. In the child's mind, beginning attempts at writing are quite different from beginning attempts at drawing. The illustration below shows how a child distinguished between the picture she was drawing and what she wanted to write.

In the second stage of development, scribbles gradually transform into little marks. Many times, a recognizable letter will suddenly emerge from a row of little marks. With practice, though, recognizable letters begin to outnumber unrecognizable marks.

By the end of preschool years and early in kindergarten, children's writing generally shows increased organization. Children learn that letters are not just randomly placed on a page. Many children begin to use invented spelling in their writing.

Observing Individual Children

Children using the library materials tend to be quiet, so there is a temptation for busy teachers to turn their attention to more active and noisy areas of the room where children demand their immediate assistance. Yet the library area offers so many opportunities for learning that it's important to make time during every work period to periodically visit the area and talk with children.

You can gain many insights into children's language development and emerging literacy skills by observing them in the library area. An appropriate starting point for such observations is to look for the stages of development described earlier. In observing a child's use of the library area, you might ask yourself questions such as the following:

- How often does the child choose to play in the library?
- What materials does the child use? Books? tapes? writing tools?
- Does the child request that the teacher read books to him or her?
- Does the child show a preference for certain topics and books?
- Does the child talk about the story, pretend to read it, and point out words in the text?
- Does the child "read" to other children?
- Does the child use puppets or the flannel board to retell a story?
- Does the child make letters or signs for a purpose?
- Does the child draw a picture first and then add scribbles, marks, or invented spellings?
- For how long a time is the child able to listen to tapes?
- Is the child able to use the equipment independently?
- Is the child able to follow a story from a familiar book?

Questions such as these can provide a picture of each child's interests and skills in activities related to library activities. Your assessment can then be used to plan specific activities to extend each child's learning and growth.

Interacting with Children

When you work with children in the library area you can:

- promote emerging literacy skills,
- help children become aware of what they are learning,
- promote language development, and
- convey the message that children's play in the library area is important and valued.

Reading Books to Children

When you take time to look at and read a book with one child or a small group, you can more effectively individualize your approach. Sometimes you may select a book knowing that it's a child's favorite or because of its rich language. Books can also be chosen to teach something about a special topic of interest or to address a concern that a child has expressed.

Reading to a young preschooler:

- Have the child sit comfortably beside you or in your lap.

- Look at and discuss the book's cover.

- Ask questions as you read: "What's happening in this picture?" or "Why do you think the little girl was sad?" or "What do you think will happen next?" or "Did anything like this ever happen to you?" Give the child time to respond. If there's no response, try asking the question another way: "What happened to the little girl's dog?" If there's still no response, answer the question yourself in a matter-of-fact tone of voice.

- Give feedback to the child's verbal and nonverbal cues. For example, if a child points to a glass of juice being knocked over, you might respond: "Uh-oh. The glass is about to spill."

- Encourage the child to anticipate the storyline: "What do you think will happen next?"

- Relate what is happening in the story to the child's own life: "The little boy in this story has a new baby brother just like you do, Tiffany."

Reading to an older preschooler or kindergarten child, you might add the following strategies:

- Point out words in the text as you read. Encourage the child to point to the words, too.

- Discuss the completed story with the child. Ask the child for opinions about characters, feelings, and ideas.

- Ask the child if he or she would like to read the book to you or to another child.

Another way to reinforce children's use of the book area is to comment on their independent choices and actions.

- *Note a child's preferences:* "This must be your favorite book. You've picked it out every morning this week. Tell me what you like best."

- *Comment on a picture in a book* that a child is leafing through: "Look at how many insects are hiding in the grass in that picture."

- *Reinforce how the child handles books:* "I like the way you are turning the pages so carefully. You really know how to take care of our books."

You might also ask questions that encourage children to do the following:

- *Remember and retell a story:* "Can you tell me what you remember about the story?"

- *Think critically:* "What would you do if you were Andrew?" or "Why do you think Peter's mother said 'No'?"

- *Come up with new ideas and solutions:* "That glue on her shoes really slowed her down, didn't it? What else could they have done to make her go slower?"

- *Explore feelings:* "Have you ever felt like Francis?" or "I bet you know just how Ira felt about sleeping at a friend's house. Have you ever stayed overnight at a friend's house?"

Storytelling is another way to inspire an interest in books. When told in an animated way and with props, storytelling can fascinate children as much as their favorite picture books. Children can also be encouraged to retell stories they know or to make up stories. In this way, they gain a greater understanding of the relationship of the written and spoken word.

Listening to Tapes with Children

To promote children's learning in the listening center, take the time to join one or two children in listening to a taped story. For some children, you may need to turn the pages of the book to keep up with the recorded voice. Other children may be able to do this on their own. Sometimes children like to listen to a story or music tape with their eyes closed so they can imagine their own pictures.

Some children may be reluctant to select a story or music tape on their own, or they may be unsure about how to operate the tape recorder. Sometimes the assistance of another child is all that's needed. Once children learn to operate the equipment, they can usually play in this area quite independently.

Promoting Children's Writing

An attractive writing center filled with interesting materials will appeal to many children. Young children like to experiment with rubber letters and a variety of writing tools, especially when these materials are readily available. You can encourage children to write by maintaining an inviting environment and showing an interest in what children do. Try the following approaches:

- *Comment on the child's work:* "I see you've been working very hard on your writing. Would you like to read me what you've written?"

- *Describe what you see:* "You made a whole row of A's and then a row of M's."

- *Help a child use the equipment:* "Let me help you find an easy way to make sure that the marker caps are on tightly."

- *Ask questions that help a child solve a problem:* "That pencil isn't writing very well. What could you do to make it work better?"

A teacher's genuine interest and involvement in the library area can go a long way in reinforcing children's budding interests in writing and reading.

IV. Extending and Integrating Children's Learning

One of the easiest ways to extend and enrich children's experiences in the library is by regularly adding new books, new tapes, and new writing materials. An environment that changes slightly but frequently will motivate children to explore and try something new.

Your community library is a good source for new books. If it is conveniently located, you can take small groups of children to the library to exchange books on a regular basis.

One simple way to make new story tapes is to enlist the help of parents who particularly like reading stories. A variety of tapes can then be made of the children's favorites.

Special Activities

The primary way in which teachers extend children's learning in the library area is by reading stories every day and using storytelling to nurture a love for literature.

Story Time

Learning to listen to a story in a group is an important goal for young children. Younger preschoolers may be able to listen only for five minutes in a group. As children grow older, a well-narrated story can hold their attention for 15 minutes or more.

In reading books to a group of children, teachers can use several techniques to make this an especially enjoyable and enriching experience. Taking time to become familiar with a story before you share it with children will make a big difference. Reviewing the book ahead of time will provide answers to important questions such as the following:

- How long will it take to read the book, and can the children sit still for that length of time?

- Are there places where the children can join in (for example, repeated phrases, questions posed in the book)?

- Are any of the concepts or ideas in the book likely to be unfamiliar to the children?

- Is there anything special about the illustrations that the children might notice (for example, tiny details, hidden surprises)?

- Are sound effects (for example, animal noises, sirens, etc.) part of the story, and how can they enhance the experience?

Once you are familiar with the story, you can design an approach for gaining the children's attention. Children will be more likely to listen to a story if they have a reason to be interested. Here are some suggestions.

- *Tie the theme of the book to something the children have recently experienced.*

    "Today it seemed like everyone was angry. Paula was angry at Gina on the playground because she wanted her swing. Mark was angry because he couldn't find his shoes. So I thought I'd read a book about being angry. It's called *Boy Was I Mad.*"

- ***Show the cover of the book or the first illustration*** and ask questions to gain their attention.

   "What do you see happening in this picture?"

- ***Share an object that is an important part of the story*** and discuss its relevance.

   "Here's a nice round stone I found on the playground. Do you think it's possible to make soup from a stone? Let's see what happens in this book called *Stone Soup*."

A low chair makes it possible for the children to see you and the book and is more comfortable for you. Children can be seated in a semi-circle or in a group at your feet.

In reading the story, try these techniques:

- Hold the book to one side so the children can see the pictures as the story is read.
- Speak clearly to suit the story, varying the tempo.
- Be dramatic— change your voice for different characters.
- If some children are having difficulty listening, ask questions to get their attention: "What do you think will happen next?"
- Invite children to join in whenever possible with refrains and responses.

After reading the story:

- Discuss something in the book and ask the children to share their own experiences. "Have you ever felt like Andrew did? Did people not listen to you when you had something to say to them?"

- Provide props and puppets so children dramatize the story as a group.

- Make flannel board cut-outs of favorite stories so children can retell the story themselves. Books such as *The Little Red Hen* and *Caps for Sale* readily lend themselves to flannel board activity.

- Always keep books that have been read at story time out on the shelves so the children can look through them again and again.

By sharing books in a supportive and comfortable setting, you can help children learn to love books as they develop the skills they need to read.

Storytelling

Storytelling experiences open up a new world for many children, especially those who need more eye-to-eye contact and a more animated style to keep their attention. Encouraging children to tell stories themselves builds important skills for reading.

Some teachers try to do this by showing children an interesting picture or a book without words and asking children to tell a story about the pictures. Often the child talks about the pictures but doesn't really tell a story. Another approach is to encourage children to tell an original story or to retell one they know. This technique often leads children to begin with the ever-familiar "once upon a time...."

Some children need encouragement to tell stories. Puppets can be helpful because the child talks through an object. Flannel board figures also can be used. You can ask questions to elicit a child's ideas, such as the following:

- "Who is in your story?"
- "What happened first?"
- "Then what happened?"
- "How did he react to that?"
- "What happened at the end?"

By asking specific questions, you can lead the child through the sequence of a story, giving the child a framework on which to build the story.

Integrating the Library with Other Curriculum Areas

The library is the hub of the classroom's focus on literacy. It is also an area that can be readily coordinated with other classroom projects and activities.

The books you select can relate to all the other activities in the classroom. There are books about building (blocks), books about what people in other countries eat (cooking), books about weather (outdoor science), books about museums (art), and books about make-believe (house corner). Children's books also cover virtually every skill and activity that is acquired in preschool and kindergarten classrooms—from bathroom habits or learning about numbers to learning how to share. The wonderful thing about children's books is that you can almost always find a book that will reinforce what you are trying to do with or for children.

Books don't have to remain only in the library area. Block builders can take a book on skyscrapers to the block area for inspiration. Cooks can take a children's recipe book to the cooking area for use there. Books and other print materials should always be included in the house corner. And any book can be taken outdoors for a special treat.

Like reading, writing need not be confined to the library area. Children can be exposed to the written word in meaningful ways in all areas of the room. Children's experiences in the art area, for example, are directly related to developing their writing skills.

Here are several other suggestions for weaving writing activities into the rest of the classroom:

- Place props in the house corner that expose children to writing, such as stationery, shopping lists and pencils, and magazines and newspapers.
- Invite children to make signs for their buildings in the block corner.
- When children have worked out a solution to a problem, suggest that it be written down.
- Develop a group story about a shared experience, such as a trip or a visitor to the classroom.
- Make signs and labels for the classroom that children can copy and/or illustrate, and encourage children to do so.
- Write a group thank-you letter to a visitor.
- Prepare shopping lists with the children for a planned cooking activity.

Activities such as these demonstrate to children the importance of print as a means of communicating ideas, messages, and feelings.

IV. Sharing the Library with Parents

A basic principle of the *Creative Curriculum* is that parent participation enhances the learning process. When teachers actively seek the support of parents, children always benefit.

Conducting Workshops on the Library

Although many topics related to the library area would make successful workshop sessions, some of the following may hold particular interest for parents:

- emerging literacy (what is it and what parents can do),
- promoting children's language development,
- assembling a home library,
- using the local public library,
- using books and tapes to support reading readiness, and
- supporting America 2000's goal for readiness.

On many of these topics, such as emerging literacy, some teachers like to have expert advice to back them up. You might also want to consult some of the references included in the Appendix to reinforce your position.

A workshop is a good place to explain why your program emphasizes literacy but shuns the use of workbooks. Many parents firmly believe that workbooks are essential to learning to read and write. They like to see worksheets as proof that their children are learning the alphabet and numbers.

Teachers have a responsibility to convey to parents that the most effective way to help children become readers is to cultivate a love for books and stories in the early years. In a workshop you can help parents appreciate how their children's experiences in the library contribute to overall development. For example, you might explain how children can refine their fine muscle skills, develop eye-hand coordination, and learn directionality through the use of library materials. You can also show parents how library materials can be used to develop social skills and cope with fears, problems, and prejudices. The varied benefits of books and other library materials can be demonstrated for parents.

Involving Parents in the Classroom

Many parents will enjoy the opportunity to read to children or participate in storytelling. Others may initially be reluctant; however, with some coaxing and preparation, you may be able to generate widespread support for this activity. Having parents tell stories that reflect the diversity of their backgrounds is especially enriching for the children.

Parents who don't wish or aren't able to help out in the classroom might be willing to tape record stories of their children's favorite books, help children make their own books, or accompany the children on a trip to the public library.

On the following page is a letter that you might wish to send to parents outlining what goes on in the library area of your classroom.

A Letter to Parents on the Library

What We Do and Why

The library area is an essential part of our program and of your child's life. It's where children gain the foundations for reading and writing. It's also a place where children can relax and enjoy the wonderful word of children's literature.

We encourage children to use the library on their own. We invite them to look at books, to listen to taped stories, and to scribble and "write" throughout the day. We also work with children one-on-one and in small groups. Sometimes children dictate stories to us, which we record in "books."

Every day we read stories to the children. We read books to introduce new ideas, to develop pre-reading skills, to help children deal with problems, and mostly to develop a love for books. Here are some of the things we do with children as we read:

- We look at pictures together and ask children questions: "What is that silly cat doing?"
- We encourage children to predict what will happen next: "What do you suppose will happen now?"
- We encourage children to repeat words, rhymes, and phrases they've memorized.

What You Can Do at Home

If you're interested in setting up a home library for your child, here are some suggestions:

- Designate a place in the house where your child can independently read, write, look at magazines, and listen to tapes.
- Decorate the chosen area with pictures (preferably homemade by your child) and plants.
- Add pillows and soft furniture to this area so your child feels relaxed and happy here.
- If bookshelves are not available, cover sturdy diaper boxes (large size) with contact paper and use as bookcases, or use wooden or plastic crates as bookshelves.

If you'd like some guidance on choosing books or tapes for your home library, please come see us. We have an excellent bibliography of recommended children's books that we'd be delighted to share. You can draw on the resources of your local public library to keep your child's home library well-stocked.

Books, tapes, and writing materials are wonderful ways to help children learn. When you take time to read to your child every day, you are doing the very best thing to help your child grow up to be a successful reader.

VII. Recommended Children's Books

Books on Self-Concept

Alexander and the Wind-Up Mouse (Leo Lionni)
Black Is Beautiful (Ann McGovern)
Dandelion and Corduroy (Don Freeman)
Flossie and the Fox (Patricia McKissack)
Harry the Dirty Dog (Gene Zion)
I'm the King of the Castle (Shiego Watambe)
Just Me (Marie Ets)
Leo the Late Bloomer and *The Littlest Rabbit* (Robert Kraus)
My Mama Needs Me (Mildred Walker)
Sylvester and the Magic Pebble (William Steig)
The Boy Who Didn't Believe in Spring (Lucille Clifton)
The Carrot Seed (Ruth Krauss)
The Little Engine That Could (Watty Piper)
Titch (Pat Hutchins)
Tony's Hard Work Day (Alan Arkin)
Umbrella and Crow Boy (Taro Yashima)
When Will I Read? (Miriam Cohen)
You Look Ridiculous (Bernard Waber)

Books About Daily and Family Life

Bedtime for Frances (Russell Hoban)
Betsy and the Doctor and *This Is Betsy* (Gunilla Wolde)
Goodnight Moon (Margaret Wise Brown)
How Do I Put It On? (Shiego Watanabe)
I Know a Lady (Charlotte Zolotow)
I'm Telling You Now (Judy Delton)
Ira Sleeps Over (Bernard Waber)
Jesse Bear, What Will You Wear? (Nancy Carlstrom)
Just Like Me (Ruth McKay)
Little Rabbit's Loose Tooth (Lucy Bates)
My Book (Ron Morris)
My Doctor, My Dentist, and *My Nursery School* (Harlow Rockwell)
The Do-Something Day (Joe Lasken)
The Blanket and *The School* (John Burmingham)
The Philharmonic Gets Dressed (Karla Kushin)
The Way to Start a Day (Byrd Baylor)
What Can I Do? (Norma Simon)

Books on First Experiences, Fears, and Adjusting to New Situations

Betsy's First Day at Nursery School (Gunilla Wolde)
Georgie and the Noisy Ghost (Robert Bright)
Gila Monsters Meet You at the Airport (Marjorie Sharmat)
Goodbye House (Frank Asch)
I'll Protect You from the Jungle Beasts and *Sabrina* (Martha Alexander)
I'm Lost and *Mommy Don't Go* (Elizabeth Crary)
Lost in the Museum (Miriam Cohen)
*My Mama Says There Aren't Any Zombies, Ghosts, Vampires, Creatures, Demons,
   Monsters, Fiends, Goblins or Things* (Judith Viorst)
Moving Day (Tobi Tobias)
My Mother and I (Aileen Fisher)
Shawn Goes to School (Petronella Breinburg)
Shy Charles (Rosemary Wells)
The Night When Mother Was Away and *The Storm Book* (Charlotte Zolotow)
There's a Nightmare in My Closet (Mercer Mayer)
Where the Wild Things Are (Maurice Sendak)
The Bundle Book (Ruth Krauss)
The Runaway Bunny (Margaret Wise Brown)
The Three Robbers (Tomi Ungerer)
The Two Friends (Grete Mannheim)
Your Turn, Doctor (Carla Perez and Deborah Robinson)

Books About Cooperation/Love/Feelings

Abby (Jeannette Caines)
A Letter to Amy and *Peter's Chair* (Ezra J. Keats)
Always Room for One More (Sorche Nic Leodhas)
Ask Mr. Bear (Marjorie Flack)
Best Friends and *Be My Valentine* (Miriam Cohen)
Best Friends for Frances (Russell Hoban)
Do You Want to Be My Friend? (Eric Carle)
Ernest and Celestine (G. Vincent)
Grown-Ups Cry Too (N Hazen)
May I Bring a Friend? (Beatrice Schenk de Regniers)
Hold My Hand and *My Friend John* (Charlotte Zolotow)
I Love My Mother (Paul Zindel)
I Sure Am Glad to See You, Blackboard Bear (Martha Alexander)
Ooh La La (Max in Love) (Maira Kalma)
On Mother's Lap (Ann Herbert Scott)
Play with Me (Marie Ets)
The Biggest Bear (Lynd Ward)
The Giving Tree (Shel Silverstein)

The Little Bear (Else Holmelund Minarik)
The Rag Coat (Lauren Mills)
Zeila, Zorek, and Zodiak (B. Pelt)

Books on Anger, Jealousy, and Sibling Rivalry

A Baby Sister for Frances (Russell Hoban)
Amanda the Panda and The Redhead (Susan Terris)
Boy Was I Mad (Kathryn Hitte)
Don't Touch My Poem (Patricia Lakin)
Don't Wake My Baby (Jonathan Franklin)
I'll Fix Anthony and *Alexander and the Terrible, Horrible, No Good, Very Bad Day* (Judith Viorst)
I Love My Sister (Most of the Time) (Elaine Eldman)
I Was So Mad (Norma Simon)
No Fighting No Biting (Else Holmelund Minarik)
Nobody Asked Me If I Wanted a Baby Sister and *My Mean Old Mother Will Be Sorry,*
  Blackboard Bear (Martha Alexander)
Noisy Nora (Rosemary Wells)
Let's Be Enemies (Janice Udry)
Secrets of the Small Brother (Richard Margolis)
She Come Bringing Me That Little Baby Girl (Eloise Greenfield)
The Hating Book, The Unfriendly Book, and *The Quarreling Book* (Charlotte Zolotow)
The Small Big Bad Pony (Irina Hale)
The Temper Tantrum Book (Edna Preston and Rainey Bennett)
Tough Eddie (Elizabeth Winthrop)

Books About Divorce and Separation

A Father Like That (Charlotte Zolotow)
All Kinds of Families (Norma Simon)
Benji; Emily and the Klunky Baby; and *The Next Door Dog* (Joan Lexau)
Daddy (Jeannett Caines)
Daddy Doesn't Live Here Anymore (Betty Boldgehald)
Dinosaurs Divorce: A Guide for Changing Families (Marc Brown and Laurene Krasny)
Do I Have a Daddy? (Jeanne Lindsay)
Everett Anderson's Year and *Some of the Days of Everett Anderson* (Lucille Clifton)
I Love My Mother (Paul Zindel)
Lucky Wilma (Wendy Kindred)
Mommy and Daddy Are Divorced (Patricia Perry and Marietta Lynch)
Mushy Eggs (Florence Adams)
My Dad Lives in a Downtown Hotel (Peggy Mann)
My Special Best Words and *Stevie* (John Steptoe)
She's Not My Real Mother (Judith Vigna)
Two Homes to Live In (Barbara Hazen)

Two Places to Sleep (Joan Schuchman)
Where Is Daddy? The Story of a Divorce (Beth Coff)

Books on Hospitalization

A Hospital Story (Sara Stein)
*A Visit to the Sesame Street Hospital (*Deborah Hautzig*)*
Curious George Goes to the Hospital (Hans Augusto Rey and Margaret Rey)
Danny Goes to the Hospital (James Collier)
Elizabeth Gets Well (Alfons Weber)
Eric Needs Stitches (Barbara Marino)
Gregory's Stitches (Judith Vigna)
Jenny Is in the Hospital (Seymour Reit)
Just Awful (Alma Whitney)
Madeline (Ludwig Bemmelmans)
My Doctor and *My Dentist* (Harlow Rockwell)
The Emergency Room (Anne and Harlow Rockwell)
Tracy (Nancy Mack)

Books on Old Age and Aging

Annie and the Old One (Miska Miles)
Grandfather and I and *Grandmother and I* (Helen Buckley)
Grandma Is Someone Special (Susan Goldman)
Grandpa (Barbara Borack)
Grandpa and Bo (Kevin Henkes)
Grandpa and Me (Patricia Gauch)
Granpa (John Burmingham)
I Love Gran (Ruth Sonneborn)
Kevin's Grandma (Barbara Williams)
Mandy's Grandmother (Liesel Moak Skorpen)
Mary Jo's Grandmother (Janice Mary Udry)
The Patchwork Quilt (Valerie Flourney)
Through Granpa's Eyes (Russell Hoban)
When You Were Just a Little Girl (B.G. Hennessy)

Books on Death

About Dying: An Open Family Book for Parents and Children Together (Sara Stein)
Everett Anderson's Goodbye (Lucille Clifton)
Frog and the Birdsand (Max Veithuijs)
Go Tell Aunt Rhody and *The Two of Them* (Aliki)
I Had a Friend Named Peter (Janice Cohn)
I'll Always Love You (Hans Wilheim)
I'll Miss You Mr. Hooper (Norma Stiles)
My Grandson Lew (Charlotte Zolotow)
My Grandpa Died Today (Joan Fassler)

Nana Upstairs and Nana Downstairs (Tomie DePaola)
Some of the Pieces (Melissa Madenski*)*
The Tenth Good Thing About Barney (Judith Viorst)
The Dead Tree (Alvin Tresselt)
The Old Dog (Sara Abbott)
The Accident (Carol Carrick)
The Old Bullfrog (Bernice Freschet)
When Violet Died (Mildred Kantrowitz)

Books on Mainstreaming and People with Disabilities

A Button in Her Ear and *A Cane in Her Hand* (A. Litchfield*)*
About Handicaps (Sara Stein)
Anna's Silent World and *Don't Feel Sorry for Paul* (BernardWolf)
Apt. 3 (Ezra Jack Keats)
Don't Forget Tom (Hanne Larsen)
Grandma's Wheelchair (L. Henriod)
He's My Brother (Joe Lasker)
I Have a Sister, My Sister Is Deaf (Jeanne Whitehouse Peterson)
Janet at School (Paul White)
Lisa and Her Soundless World (Edna S. Levine)
See You Tomorrow, Charles (Miriam Cohen)
My Friend Janet (Lucille Clifton)
My Friend Leslie: The Story of a Handicapped Child (Maxine Rosenberg)
One Little Girl; Howie Helps Himself; The Boy with a Problem, and *Don't Worry Dear*
   (Joan Fassler)
Our Brother Has Down's Syndrome (Jasmine Shelly and Tara Cairo)
Our Teacher's in a Wheelchair (M.E. Powers)
The Balancing Girl (Bernice Rabe)

Books About People of Different Backgrounds and Different Lands

Anancy and Mr. Dry-Bone (Fione French)
Arrow to the Sun (Gerald McDermott)
Ashanti to Zulu (Margaret Musgrove)
Ba-Nam (Jeanne Lee)
Barto Takes the Subway (Barbara Brenner)
Bringing Rain to Kapiti Plain: A Nandi Tale and *Why Mosquitoes Buzz in People's Ears*
   (Verna Aardema)
Dancing Teepees (Virginia Driving Hawk Sneve)
Gilberto and the Wind (Marie Ets)
Grandma's Hat (Rosemary Kahn)
Island Winter (Charles Martin)
Issun Boshi: An Old Tale of Japan (Momoko Ishil)
It Could Always Be Worse (Margot Zemach)
It Happened in Pinsk (Arthur Yorinks)
Jambo Means Hello and Moja Means One (Muriel Feelings)
King Island Christmas (Jean Rogers)

Mama, Do You Love Me? (Barbara M. Joose)
The Five Chinese Brothers (Claire Bishop)
The Jolly Mon (Jimmy Buffet and Savannah Buffet)
The Mitten (Alvin Tressalt)
The Mountains of Tibet (Frane Lessac)
The Rooster Who Understood Japanese (Yoshiko Uchida)
The Story About Ping (Marjorie Flack)
Tikki Tikki Tembo (Arlene Mosel)
When Clay Sings, Hawk, I'm Your Brother and *They Put On Masks* (Byrd Baylor)
Where the Buffaloes Begin (Olaf Baker)
Umbrella (Taro Tashima)

Books of Poetry and Rhymes

A Basket Full of White Eggs (Brian Swann)
Birds and the Beasts Were There and *Humorous Poetry for Children* (William Cole)
Birthday Candles Burning Bright and *A Treasury of Birthday Poetry* (Sara and John Preston)
Catch Me and Kiss Me and Say It Again and *Father Fox's Pennyrhymes* (Clyde Watson)
A Child's Garden of Verses (Robert Louis Stevenson)
Give a Guess (Mary Mullen)
Going Barefoot (Aileen Fishers)
Jelly Belly (Dennis Lee)
Jingle Jangle (Zhena Gay)
Lend Me Your Wings (John Agard)
Mama, Papa, and Baby Joe (Niki Daly)
Nonsense Book (Edward Lear)
Now We Are Six and *When We Were Very Young* (A.A. Milne)
On the Farm (Lee Bennett Hopkins)
Prefabulous Animilies (James Reeves)
Rainbow in the Sky (Louis Untermeyer)
The Real Mother Goose (Blanche Wright)
Tyrannasaurus Was a Beast (Jack Prelutsky)
When the Dark Comes Dancing: A Bedtime Poetry Book (Nancy Larrick)

Books That Encourage Participation

The Changing City (Jorg Muller)
Each Peach Pear Plum: An "I Spy" Story (Janet and Allen Ahlberg)
Handtalk: An ABC of Finger Spelling and Sign Language (Remy Charlip and Mary Miller)
Fred Is That You? (Mavis Smith)
Have You Seen the Crocodile? (Coline West)
Have You Seen My Duckling? (Nancy Tafuri)
Mary Wore Her Red Dress, and Henry Wore His Green Sneakers (Merle Pee)
One Little Teddy Bear (Mark Burgess)
Read to Me, I'll Read to You (John Ciardi)
Where's Spot? (Eric Hill)

Where's the Bunny? (Ruth Carroll)
Where's Waldo? and *Find Waldo Now?* (Martin Handford)

Books That Convey Anti-Bias Themes

All Kinds of Families and *Why Am I Different* (Norma Simon)
Amos and Boris (William Steig)
Bizzy Bones and *Uncle Ezra* (J.B. Martin)
Cornelius, Frederick, The Biggest House in the World, and *Fish Is Fish* (Leo Lionini)
Elliott's Extraordinary Cookbook (Joan Sandin)
Frog in Love (Max Velthuijs)
Girls Can Be Anything (N. Klein)
Mothers Can Do Anything (Joe Lasker)
My Best Friend Martha Rodriguez (O. Macmillan and Dan Freeman)
My Daddy Is a Nurse (M. Wandro)
My Mom Travels a Lot (Caroline Bauer)
My Mother the Mail Carrier (I. Maurey)
My Special Best Words (John Steptoe)
One Morning in Maine and *Blueberries for Sale* (Robert McCloskey)
Straight Hair, Curly Hair (A. Goldin)
Tell Me a Mitzi (Lore Segal)
The Hunter and the Animals (Tomi de Paola)
The Man Who Kept House (Kathleen and Michael Hague)
UFO Diary (Satoshi Krtamura)
What Is a Girl? What Is a Boy? (S. Waxman*)*
Why Does That Man Have Such a Big Nose? (M.B Quigley)
William's Doll (Charlotte Zolotow)

Fairy Tales and Fables

A Hundred Fables (Jean de La Fontaine)
American Myths and Legends (Charles M. Skinner)
Arabian Nights and *The Blue Fairy Book* (Andrew Lang, editor)
Celtic Fairy Tales, The Fables of Aesop, and *English Fairy Tales* (Joseph Jacobs, editor)
French Legends, Tales and Fairy Stories (Barbara Leonie Picard)
Grimm's Household Tales (Margaret Hunt, translator)
Old Italian Tales (Domenico Vittorini)
Old Peter's Russian Tales (Arthur Ransone, editor)
Popular Tales from the Norse and *Tales from the Fjeld* (Peter Christian Asbjornsen and Jorgen Moe)
Scottish Folk-Tales and Legends (Barbara Ker Wilson)
Tales from a Finnish Tupa (James C. Bowman and Margery Bianco)
The Jack Tales (Richard C. Chase, editor)
The Oak Tree FairyBook (Clifton Johnson, editor)

MUSIC AND MOVEMENT

I. Why Music and Movement Are Important

Music naturally delights and moves children. Whether the music is a lively dance tune or a gentle lullaby, even babies feel its force—both emotionally and physically. An infant only two months old will stop squirming at the sound of music, entranced by what she hears. A baby of ten months will rock her body and wave her arms to a tune on the radio. Toddlers will happily clap, rock, or sway to music. They may also sing along, and though they may not get the words or the melody right, they love to make music. Preschool and kindergarten children move in time to music and often make up little dances to dramatize songs or events and to express emotions.

Throughout the early childhood years, children are learning to do new things with their bodies. Young children are also learning that movement can communicate messages and represent actions. A thumbs-up sign means everything's okay; bringing an imaginary spoon to the mouth indicates eating. Young children are able to perform and recognize pantomimed actions such as ironing, stirring, swimming, or playing the piano.

Most young children usually are quite at home with movement. They begin to learn about the world by acting on objects and people, and they "think with their bodies" well before they think with words. This is why body movement is not only fun for young children but also a good opportunity for them to solve problems. When you ask questions that call for verbal responses ("Can you think of some other ways that Pooh could get up to the honey tree?" or "What did we do to make applesauce yesterday?"), some children may have difficulty responding in words. But when questions call for movement ("What are some different ways you can think of to get from this side of the mat to the other?"), children aren't limited by their verbal abilities. Movement problems challenge children in different ways and help teachers learn about the problem solving and creative abilities of less verbal children.

Singing or chanting can help make routine activities and transitions, such as gathering children into a circle for a group activity, smoother and more enjoyable. And music helps to set a mood. Quiet, soothing music calms and relaxes children, while a lively marching tune rouses them for an energetic clean-up time. Music and movement are also social activities that help children feel part of the group.

As children grow in their appreciation of the beauty of music and dance, they acquire a gift that will bring them great pleasure. Music brings another dimension of beauty into our lives. An early childhood program that includes time for music and movement provides an outlet for children's energy and high spirits and benefits their development in a number of ways.

Objectives for Children's Learning

Children's experiences with music and movement can contribute to their socio-emotional, cognitive, and physical development in a variety of ways. The following are some objectives that you might set for movement and music activities.

Objectives for Socio-Emotional Development

- Participate in a group (singing or dancing with other children).

- Develop social skills by playing cooperative musical games (simple games such as "Ring Around the Rosy," or those requiring more cooperation such as "Farmer in the Dell").

- Express anger, fear, joy, and other emotions through music and movement (creating a happy dance to celebrate snow).

- Recognize that music and dance express moods and feelings.

- Enhance self-concept by sharing the music and dance of each child's culture (teaching the group a familiar song from home).

Objectives for Cognitive Development

- Refine listening skills by noticing changes in tempo or pitch (adapting one's dancing or clapping to shifts in tempo or beat).

- Increase awareness of different movements or body positions (folding legs like a child in a picture book).

- Develop creativity and imagination by responding to problems in movement or music (creating thunder sounds with instruments).

- Learn new words and concepts through songs and movement (learning body parts by singing "Head, Shoulders, Knees, and Toes").

- Explore cause and effect (experimenting with musical instruments and other devices for creating sounds).

Objectives for Physical Development

- Explore the many ways in which a body can move (finding different ways to get to the other side of a line without stepping on it).

- Develop large motor skills (moving to music and participating in other creative movement activities).

- Improve balance, coordination, and rhythm through dancing and other movement activities (playing "Follow the Leader").

- Improve small motor skills (learning finger plays and playing musical instruments).

This entire list of objectives probably won't be appropriate for any particular child or group of children. However, it provides a framework that you can use in planning an effective and enjoyable program of music and movement for the children in your care.

II. Arranging the Environment

The block area, the house corner, the sand and water area—each of these distinct areas of the classroom is set up to give children opportunities to play with special materials assembled there. By comparison, music and movement may be enjoyed just about anywhere in the classroom, outdoors, or even on a field trip.

From the time children arrive, when they may be greeted with a song or chant, many teachers find music an effective way of easing children through transitions and routines: coming to sit down for snack, calming down for rest or naptime, cleaning up the room, or putting on clothes to go outside. Music and movement are naturals for times when the whole group is gathered. And children individually and in small groups—on their own or with a teacher—can enjoy music or movement activities.

Music spontaneously enters into many activity areas as children create their own songs or chants to go with their actions pounding clay or pushing a truck. While movement and music aren't tied to one location, there are some points to consider in planning a physical environment that will set the stage for a rich array of music and movement experiences for children.

Creating Space

It isn't necessary to have a permanent dance-and-movement area in the classroom. However, you may want occasionally to set up a special area—a place with plenty of space, musical instruments, a tape recorder, and a variety of props that lend themselves to movement.

Props might include scarves and streamers, hoops, capes that swirl, wrist-bells, maracas, and other instruments. A full-length mirror allows children to see themselves in movement. Most children are

intrigued by seeing their shadows as they dance, which you can arrange by placing a strong light source (such as a bright lamp or a projector) in a dim room. Tumbling mats on the floor invite children to explore other kind of movements.

If it's feasible to set up a movement area within your classroom, you may find this particularly welcome on rainy days when children need a place for physical activity. And when the weather is good, the outdoor area is wonderful for music and movement activities.

Selecting Materials

The listening center, typically located in the library corner and including story and music tapes, should be comfortable and inviting. To foster children's awareness of various types of music and their own preferences, try to provide access to music during times of the day when children are free to select their own activities. To make this possible, you need to ensure that the listening center includes:

- easy-to-operate tape recorders and earphones;
- shelf space to make tapes accessible to children;
- labels to identify tapes (e.g., pictures of children dancing, marching, resting, etc., to match the music; or colors or symbols to identify types of music such as bluegrass, classical, or rap); and
- a variety of tapes, including music that is:

    fast and lively or slow and soothing so that children can choose music to fit their mood,

    diverse in style and tradition (such as folk, classical, country, jazz, rock, reggae, bluegrass, and ragtime), and

    representative of the children's cultures.

If you change the materials in the center regularly, children know that new discoveries await them when they come to listen.

Instruments

Should the musical instruments be near the listening area? You might think so until you try it! The listening area, typically located in the library corner, is designed for quiet reading and listening, and having the musical instruments nearby tends to make noise. You may choose instead to put out instruments during free play from time to time.

Some teachers like to take instruments outdoors. With lots of space and no noise limitations, children enjoy using instruments to try out various sounds and to stage parades, circuses, and shows.

Many instruments can be made or purchased at reasonable cost by teachers or parents. Among the instruments most appropriate for young children are these:

drums	tambourines
rhythm sticks	triangles
cymbals	maracas, shakers, rattles
kazoos	bells/bell bands

Each of these instruments has many versions, and different forms are found in different cultures. You might invite children's parents to bring in less familiar instruments and introduce them to the children.

Of the simple instruments listed here, you may want to purchase triangles and bells along with a xylophone or other instrument on which a melody may be played. Percussion instruments, such as drums, rhythm sticks, and bells, are commonly used with young children because they are relatively constant in pitch and not difficult to play. They're also easy to make. For example, drums can be made from oatmeal boxes, cymbals can be made using tin pie plates, and rattles can be made by filling containers with macaroni, rice, or buttons. Below are instructions for making your own musical instruments.[1]

Drums and Sticks

Materials for drums:

Large oatmeal box
40" shoestring
Rubber inner tube
Paint
Scissors

Directions for drums:

Cut the oatmeal box in half and paint it. Cut two round drum covers from the rubber inner tube, each 4" in diameter. Use scissors or a hole punch to make 10 to 12 small holes around the edges of both drum covers. When the paint is dry, place one piece of inner tube on each end of the oatmeal box and lace the holes with the shoestring.

---

[1] Based on Tapp Associates, *Learning Experiences for Young Children* (Atlanta, GA: Tapp Associates).

Materials for drumsticks:

> 2 dowels (10" to 12")
> 2 wooden beads with holes
> Glue (nontoxic)
> Scissors

Directions for drumsticks:

> Sharpen the ends of both dowels to fit the holes in the wooden beads. Make sure the pointed ends are hammered in tightly after you apply the glue.

Bell Band

Materials:

> 6" of elastic, 1" wide
> Small bells
> Needle and thread
> Velcro (optional)

Directions:

> Sew the elastic to make a small circle, or attach velcro to the ends of the elastic strip. Sew several bells on the outside of the band.

Kazoo

Materials:

> Empty toilet paper tube
> Contact paper or paint and brush
> Rubber band
> Scissors
> Wax paper (2" by 2")

Directions:

> Cover the paper tube with contact paper or paint. Punch three holes in the tube with scissors. Cut a small square of wax paper and fit it tightly over the end of the tube. Secure it with a rubber band.

Maraca

Materials:

> Several bottle caps
> Construction paper, colorful contact
>   paper, tin foil, or paint
> 6 to 10 pieces of 12" ribbon or paper
>   (1/2" wide)
> Paper towel roll
> Piece of lightweight cardboard
> Tape

Directions:

Decorate the paper towel roll with colorful paper, contact paper, tin foil, or paint. Put several bottle caps inside the roll. Cut out two small cardboard circles to fit the ends of the roll and tape them securely. Tape several colorful streamers, ribbons, or paper on one end of the roll.

Sand Blocks

Materials:

2 small boxes with tops (about 2" by 2" by 4")	Measuring tape or string
2 pieces of elastic (6" long and 1/2" wide)	Tape
	Scissors
Paint, construction paper, tin foil, or colorful contact paper	Thread and needle
	Paste or household cement
6" by 6" piece of sandpaper	Ruler

Directions:

Make two slits slightly larger than the width of the elastic where indicated on the top of the box.

Measure across the widest part of the child's hand. Measure across the box from one slit to the other.

Add these two measurements together, adding 1". Cut a piece of elastic this length for each box. Thread the elastic through the slits in the tops and sew the ends together. Tape tops on the boxes. Cover the boxes with paper, tin foil, colorful contact paper, or paint.

Cut a piece of sandpaper to fit the opposite side of the box. Glue the sandpaper to the box using paste or household cement. (White glue will melt the sandpaper.) Allow to dry.

Shaker

Materials:

Empty oatmeal box
Clothespin (nonclipping type)
Small plastic medicine bottle cap
    (1" to 2" in diameter)
Bells or buttons
Scissors
Glue or paste (nontoxic)
Tape
Paint (nontoxic)
Paintbrush
12" by 12" piece of construction paper,
    colorful cloth, or contact paper

Directions:

Cover an oatmeal or salt box with material, construction paper, or contact paper. Cut a hole in one end of the box large enough to fit a clothespin.

Put several buttons or bells inside the box. Cut a hole the same size as the clothespin in the plastic bottle cap. Glue the plastic cap over the hole in the box, making sure the holes line up. Allow to dry. Paint the clothespin. Insert the clothespin through the holes in the cap and the box. Leave enough of the clothespin sticking out of the box for a handle (about 2"). Glue the clothespin in place and allow to dry. Tape around the bottom of the clothespin and plastic cap for more support.

Tambourine

Materials:

2 paper plates
Yarn and needle
Bottle caps
Magic markers

Directions:

Punch holes along the edges of both plates. Sew the plates together with yarn and a plastic needle. Place the bottle caps between the two plates before finishing. Decorate with magic markers.

Assessing the Effectiveness of the Area

On a regular basis, you will be observing children's use of the music and movement area. Your observations will help you plan what changes to make to the area. For instance, if you observe that few children know how to use the earphones, you might decide to plan practice sessions with several children at a time. You may choose to move the lively dance tapes to another area where children

can dance to the music without disturbing others. Or you may discover that several musical instruments need to be repaired or replaced.

Here are some questions to consider as you observe in the music and movement area.

- How often is the listening area used for listening to music? Are children aware of this option? Do I need to make it more clear or make this area more accessible?

- Which children tend to select musical tapes and why?

- Do children use the area by themselves or with others?

- Are children able to find tapes and put them away independently?

- Are children able to operate the tape recorder and earphones on their own? Do they need more instruction and/or practice?

- What kinds of musical tapes are selected often, rarely, or never? Is there enough variety?

- Are all instruments in working order, or do they need to be repaired?

- Is there a sufficient selection of musical instruments? Do children fight over the instruments? Should I add more?

By periodically observing children's use of the listening area, you will be able to make needed changes.

III. Observing and Promoting Children's Learning

As a teacher, you play an active role in selecting music for children's enjoyment, and introducing songs, action games, and other music-and-movement activities. But your primary role, as in other areas of the *Creative Curriculum*, is to facilitate children's development by observing them, talking to them about what they are doing, reacting to and reinforcing their explorations, and asking open-ended questions. Knowing children's basic patterns of development in music and movement will help you do these things more effectively.

How Children Engage in Music and Movement Activities

There are many different ways in which children engage in music and movement activities. How they do so depends a lot on their stage of development and their experiences.

Listening. From infancy, children attend to music and are able to recognize snatches of familiar tunes. A child's musical attention span generally increases with age. Children also get better at noticing variations in musical selections, such as changes in tempo (fast-slow), pitch (high-low), and volume (loud-soft). Older children begin to be able to listen to their own singing or playing in order to match or correct tones.

Singing. At first, children are able to sing along with others but not always in time or in tune. Next, they are able to match tones as they sing with others. Then comes the ability to sing alone and, finally, to sing in tune.

Movement to music. At first, children move to their own beat rather than the beat of the music. It is especially difficult for young children to follow a slow tempo. By the age of three or four, they typically can "keep time" to a regular beat. Then they begin to be able to adjust their body movements to accompaniment that involves contrasts such as slow and fast or light and heavy.

Playing instruments. In the first stage, children manipulate and experiment with instruments. They become aware of differences in sound in relation to how an instrument is played, and they learn to recognize the sounds of various instruments. In the second stage, children use instruments to accompany their movements—as in beating sticks while marching—but they may not match the rhythm to their steps. Next, most children can play a simple percussion or rhythm instrument, responding accurately to the tempo of another instrument or a recording.

Imitating/representing movement. Infants can imitate simple movements they see you do, such as smiling or opening their mouths. By the second year, children can reproduce actions they've seen days before. It's more difficult for them to represent the movements of objects. For instance, it is harder for a child to represent the motion of a seesaw, windshield wipers, or a falling feather than to reproduce the motion of someone kicking a ball or washing his or her hands. A challenge for older children is to communicate words or concepts through movement ("show me angry faces" or "how do you pick up something heavy?").

Observing Individual Children

As you observe the children in your group when they engage in music and movement, you'll learn more about each child so that you can promote individual growth and development. Here are some questions to guide your individual observations:

- Does the child join in singing and finger plays with the group? If showing little active participation, does the child seem to enjoy listening and watching?

- Does the child enjoy moving to music? Does the child need more encouragement?

- Does the child move differently to different kinds of music? Does the child move in time to the beat?

- Is the child able to perceive and describe variations in music, such as differences in tempo, pitch, and volume?

- Is the child able to imitate the movements of others? To reproduce movements seen previously?

- What new physical skills and kinds of movement is the child in the process of acquiring or refining? What can I plan to enable the child to practice these new skills?

- Does the child come up with original ideas in response to open-ended questions relating to movement?

- In playing an instrument, does the child respond to the beat and tempo of the music?

These kinds of observations will provide a basic picture of children's interests and skills in relation to music and movement. To document each child's growth and development, you can use the Child Development and Learning Checklist in Appendix A. Having a good sense of each child's development with respect to music and movement—a sense acquired through regular observation—helps you respond to each child's interests, abilities, and needs.

Interacting with Children

Picking up on children's spontaneous involvement in music and movement is one of the best ways to reinforce their explorations, problem solving, and creativity in music and movement. Such interactions, besides validating their actions, increase children's awareness of what they are doing. They begin to see themselves as people who can make and enjoy music and movement.

Describing What Children Are Doing

As you interact with children, begin with where they are. Sometimes you may simply describe what you see the child doing. Suppose, for example, that you hear a child making up her own song as she squishes the clay through her fingers. You might comment, "That clay makes you think of a song," and then sing along with her. A response such as this makes the child more aware of her actions and how much you value what she is doing.

Your descriptions of what you see or hear also expand children's music and movement vocabulary. When listening to music or exploring movement with children, you can introduce words such as "smooth," "jerky," "gliding," or "bouncy." You can help children make connections between music and movement: "The way you're moving is called 'gliding'—do you think the music sounds like

257

gliding?" Movement often helps children notice musical qualities better than words can. For example, hearing higher and lower notes played, children can stand up high on tiptoes and stoop down low.

Asking Open-Ended Questions

Asking children open-ended questions about what they are doing or perceiving helps you discover where each child's interest is directed at the moment. One child playing a xylophone might be focusing on "how each color sounds," while another may be experimenting with volume or pretending he is playing the piano like his father. When you find out what the child is interested in, your questions and comments are more likely to elicit a positive response.

Here are some open-ended questions you might ask:

- "How does it sound?"
- "Have you ever heard that before?"
- "Does it sound the same when you hit each drum (or each note on the xylophone)?"
- "How is she moving?" "Are they moving the same way?"
- "What would happen if...?"
- "Tell me about what you're doing."
- "What else could you do...?"
- "Are you making music that's loud or soft?" "How would you make the drum sound soft?"

Open-ended questions are good for getting children to think about what they are doing. However, it's important to be sensitive to what a child is experiencing before you jump in and ask a lot of questions. Sometimes the best approach is to not say anything because it's obvious that the child is enjoying freely exploring alone.

Joining in Music and Movement Activities

Another way to enrich a child's experience with moving to music is simply to join in when the child is dancing—children love to have adults follow their lead—and then add a variation. For instance, Carlos was bouncing his body to a lively song. The teacher bounced with him for a while and then began moving her head from side to side along with the beat. Soon Carlos was moving his head from side to side and rotating his body as he bounced. Without saying a word, the teacher sparked the child's desire to explore new possibilities for movement.

As you interact with children, take care not to interrupt the spontaneity of children's movement and musical expression. When you see that children are caught up in dancing, for instance, it's better to stand back and not ask a lot of questions. Sometimes questions and comments are well-timed just after the child finishes dancing, or perhaps between tapes. ("You were dancing a special way to that music. I wonder if this next tape will make you want to dance the same way or differently.")

Enjoying Music Together

Music experiences don't always have to include movement. Sometimes you may want to listen to music by itself and enjoy a quiet time with the children. You might have the children listening for certain sounds, such as the sound of a drum or bells. Or, suggest closing their eyes and listening to see what the noise makes them think of.

Music should be reserved for certain times of the day. It should not be played as background noise throughout a work time as children will tune it out. Rather, experiences in music should teach children that music is to be enjoyed, appreciated, and noticed.

IV. Extending and Integrating Children's Learning

You can extend and enrich children's music and movement experiences by frequently adding new recordings in the listening center and new musical instruments to be explored. Use the public library to rent tapes, make tapes from records, and encourage parents to help build the classroom tape collection.

One teacher started a "sound table" with a few small boxes and an assortment of objects such as buttons and paper clips and suggested that the children add to the collection. The children brought objects they found elsewhere in the room (beads, small blocks) and outdoors (rocks, wood chips, gravel). From time to time the teacher added new materials, including rice, marbles, tiny bells, and boxes of varied sizes, from band-aid boxes to coffee cans. Encouraged to try different combinations of boxes and objects, the children became more aware of sound and more interested in exploring the sound-making possibilities of the instruments. They used some of the sound boxes (with the tops glued or taped shut) to accompany their songs and as sound effects for stories and dramatic play.

Group Singing and Movement Activities

Singing and moving together is enjoyable for children and helps everyone feel a part of the group. Even shy children tend to feel a little more at home when singing with the group. Group singing and action games also help children learn to cooperate with a group, including learning to sing when the group is singing and be quiet when everyone is quiet.

Here are some types of songs and related activities that are popular with young children:

Simple songs with lots of repetition (a repeated line or refrain). Children's affection for songs such as "Yellow Submarine," "Old McDonald Had a Farm," and "Skip to My Lou" is partly based on the easy, repetitive refrains of these songs. Even if children cannot remember the verses, they can always join in on the refrain.

Songs with finger play. "Wheels on the Bus," "Where Is Thumbkin?" and "Eensy Weensy Spider" are a few of the many songs with finger movements that children love. Some children may participate by moving their hands and fingers before they actually sing.

Singing games and action songs. Games such as "Farmer in the Dell," "Go In and Out the Window," "Hokey-Pokey," and "You Sing a Song" combine music, movement, and group cooperation. Music-and-movement games do not have to use standard movements and lyrics. You can encourage children to make up new verses to familiar songs ("this is the way we swing our arms") and invent games that call for originality. For instance, set up a series of Hula Hoops on the floor and challenge the children each to move through them in a different way. A simple chant ("Jenny is spinning, spinning, spinning") adds to the fun.

Songs with funny sounds or silly lyrics. Nursery rhymes have lots of funny sounds, like "higgledy, piggledy," "hey-diddle-diddle," and "rub-a-dub-dub." Many folk songs have silly lyrics. Children like songs that play around with familiar words, particularly with their own names ("Annie, Annie, Bo-Bannie").

Songs and dances of different cultures. You may already know some songs and dances you can teach to children. Better still, invite parents to come into the classroom to share with the children the songs, music, and instruments of their culture.

Movement games without music. Older children can play charade-style games such as "What Animal Am I?" or "What Am I Doing?" Usually they will be more proficient at guessing than at acting out, but both sides of the game encourage children to attend closely to aspects of movement.

Integrating Music and Movement with Other Curriculum Areas

Both music and movement have natural connections with other activities that young children enjoy. Here are a few of the many possibilities for tapping these connections and creating an integrated curriculum.

The Music of Words

Language itself, made up of sounds and rhythms, shares many of the qualities of music. Poetry is closely akin to music, and much of the poetry that children love is especially rich in word sounds and word invention. Writers such as Edward Lear, Laura E. Richards, A.A. Milne, and Dr. Seuss—not to mention the Mother Goose nursery rhymes—are delightful resources in sound and word play. Richards, for instance, plays with words as a child does—mixing up "elephant" and "telephone" to get "telephant" and "elephone"—and her nonsensical humor sends children into laughter.

A great many children's books are rhythmic and full of rhymes, repetition, and other musical sounds. Such books are meant to be read or chanted aloud, and they offer many opportunities for children to join in. Children's librarians can direct you to these books and suggest those that children like best. Of the hundreds of authors of highly "musical" books, here are some names to look for:

Verna Aardema	Mary Mullen
John Agard	Merle Peek
Nancy White Carlstrom	Charlotte Pomerantz
William Cole	Jack Prelutsky
Bruce Degen	Sara and John Preston
Zhena Gay	James Reeves
Nancy Larrick	Dr. Seuss
Edward Lear	George Shannon
Dennis Lee	Robert Louis Stevenson
Margaret Mahy	Brian Swann
Bill Martin	Louis Untermeyer
A.A. Milne	Nadine Bernard Westcott

Some teachers like to use music or sound effects in conjunction with reading to children or enacting a story with puppets. Background music can accompany the moods of the story. Or the music may be chosen to evoke characters or events in a story—a rainstorm, a swan skimming along the water, a heavy-footed giant, or a delicate fairy. For these purposes you can make special tapes, use existing tapes at one or two key points in a story,[2] or use instruments to create the desired effects (drumming for the giant and tinkling a tiny bell for the fairy).

Books/Videotapes

You can use the pictures in books to stimulate children's awareness and exploration of what the body can do. For instance, noticing the body position of a pictured character, you might ask the children "Can you do this?" and then describe the position: "You're stretching your arms up high" or "You're sitting cross-legged." Children find this match-the-picture game challenging and fun.

Videotapes, though only used sparingly in the *Creative Curriculum*, can be effective in enlivening children's participation in music and movement. The delights of dancing and singing, as conveyed by good musical videotapes, are contagious. Videos that present the music and dance of various cultural groups are a wonderful way of expanding the range of multicultural experiences in your classroom. Tapes can also help teachers who are not comfortable doing music and movement activities to build their confidence and their repertoire of songs and games.

Here are a few of the videotapes that you and the children in your class can enjoy together:

Babysongs, More Babysongs, Even More Baby Songs, and *Turn on the Music* feature Hap Palmer songs in live action and either animation or clay animation (Hi-Tops Videos, 30-32 minutes).

Kids Sing Along features live-action, contemporary versions of favorite children's songs (Good Housekeeping, 30 minutes).

---

[2] William Painter offers a wealth of such possibilities in *Musical Story Hours: Using Music with Storytelling and Puppetry* (Hamden, CT: Library Professional Publications, 1989). Here is one: Just at the point in *Harriet and the Roller-Coaster* where Harriet and her friend get on the roller coaster to begin their wild ride, suddenly start Rimsky-Korsakov's "The Flight of the Bumble Bee" (or other frenetic music) to add a real punch to the story.

Kidsongs produces live-action videos, including *What I Want to Be, A Day at the Circus,* and *I'd Like to Teach the World to Sing* [international songs] (Viewmaster Video, 25 minutes).

Mister Rogers: Music and Feelings explores moods of music, with cellist Yo Yo Ma and Ella Jenkins (65 minutes). Also *Mister Rogers: Musical Stories* (59 minutes).

Raffi videos present his live concerts and show children in the audience singing and dancing along (Shoreline, 45 minutes).

See, Sing & Play includes familiar games, finger plays, and sing-alongs with partial animation (Golden Music Video, 30 minutes).

Sesame Street has many music/movement videos with segments from the show, including *Monster Hits, Sing Yourself Silly, Sing Along,* and *Dance Along* (Sesame Songs Home Videos, 30 minutes).

Tickle Tune Typhoon's Let's Be Friends features songs and dance from a diverse cast of "differently abled" musicians (Tickle Tune Typhoon Productions, 50 minutes).

Art Activities

From time to time you may want to try playing music in the art area and seeing how this affects the way children draw or paint. It's best not to stress "drawing to music" or to give the children any special instructions about how to do so. An occasional descriptive comment or question may be in order though ("What happened to your painting when the music got very fast?").

Movement is especially prominent in some art activities, such as finger painting or drawing in sand. Try asking questions to focus a child's attention on movement: "How is your hand moving when you're making those wiggly lines? Can you do it again?"

Dramatic Play

While you shouldn't interrupt with a string of questions that pull children out of a make-believe play scenario, an occasional comment or question during dramatic play can increase children's awareness of how movement communicates to others. For instance, when a child is performing the action of ironing, you might say, "What are you ironing, Keisha (or 'Mommy')? Your arm is going back and forth to iron your baby's dress." Songs and chants can also focus on a child's actions ("This is the way we iron our clothes...").

When the older children are acting out a story such as "The Three Billy Goats Gruff," you can ask movement-related questions ("How would the Big Billy Goat walk over the bridge?" "How is that different from the Little Billy Goat?" "Can you show us how the goat butted the troll with his head?"). In such an activity, avoid performing the characters' actions for the children to imitate. Instead, it's useful to ask questions to encourage the children to think about the actions, characters, and cause-effect relationships in the story. Remember that the goal isn't the accuracy with which the story is acted out but the thinking, creativity, and imagination that the activity stimulates in the children.

V. Sharing Music and Movement with Parents

When parents and children enjoy music and movement experiences together, they can share hours of pleasure and creativity, and children's development and learning are enhanced. To help parents appreciate the rich potential for increasing children's learning and enjoyment of music and movement, you can incorporate these activities in parent workshops, involve parents in the classroom, and share ideas in a letter.

Conducting Workshops on Music and Movement

Singing and movement games can be great icebreakers at parent meetings and workshops. You may choose to include these activities in other parent workshops and meetings rather than dedicating a session to music and movement. Or you may decide to plan a special music-and-movement workshop with some of the following kinds of activities:

- Lead the group in singing some songs that are the children's favorites and ask the parents why they think these are so popular. Ask parents to suggest other songs that their children like or that they themselves remember liking when they were children.

- Ask for a volunteer who knows a finger play and will teach it to the group. Then ask: "Would this finger play be hard for young children to learn to do?" "Why or why not?" "Does anyone know an easier finger play? A harder one?" Teach the parents finger plays at different developmental levels and discuss why children enjoy them.

- Challenge parents with movement problems that call for problem solving and creativity ("Move sideways and see what different things you can do with your feet as you go").

- Hold a workshop where parents make simple instruments for their children to use at home (using the directions provided in this module).

Involving Parents in the Classroom

Some parents have special abilities and experiences with music and movement that they would probably enjoy sharing with the children. A parent who plays an instrument, for instance, can show it to the children and demonstrate how it is played. Parents might be willing to share the songs, dances, and instruments of their culture or make tapes of the music they enjoy. It's a good idea to provide parents with blank or recycled tapes for this purpose.

Parents can also help in videotaping the children dancing, singing, jumping, doing finger plays, and engaging in other kinds of movement. (A parent or staff member may have a videocamera to lend; if not, a video store may be willing to donate a day of rental time during a slow week). Seeing themselves on tape intrigues children and enhances their self-image and awareness of what their bodies can do.

On the next page is a letter that you can send to parents to let them know about the kinds of music and movement activities that take place in your classroom—and why.

A Letter to Parents on Music and Movement

What We Do and Why

We do a lot of singing and creative movement in our program. Singing and moving to music give the children a chance to move freely, practice new skills, and feel good about what their bodies can do. The children love our daily time for singing together, and it helps them develop the ability to cooperate in a group. Here are some of the things we do to encourage a love for music and movement:

- Sometimes we take a tape recorder outside and play jazz or folk music, and the children dance and act out the songs.

- We give the children colored scarves and paper streamers to use as they move to the music.

- We play musical instruments, some of which are homemade.

- We use chants to help us get through the daily routines, such as clean-up time.

- We have a comfortable listening center with a wide variety of tapes for children to listen to on their own.

What You Can Do at Home

You don't have to be musical to enjoy music with your child. Taking a few minutes to sit together and listen to music can provide a welcome break for both of you. Also, the music you share with your child doesn't have to be only "kid's music." It can be rap, reggae, country, jazz, classical, or any music you like. Here are some ideas for enjoying music and movement with your child:

- Children love a song or chant about what they are doing at the moment, especially when it uses their name. While pushing your child on a swing, you might chant, "Swing high, swing low, this is the way that Julie goes." The child likes this because it is about her and what she is doing, and the rhythm matches her movements.

- Songs and finger plays help keep children involved at tough times, such as during car or bus trips, while waiting in line, or while grocery shopping.

- Chanting or singing also helps at times when your child needs to switch gears and start picking up toys, getting ready to go outside, undressing for a bath, and so on. You might try a chant such as, "water is filling up the tub, up the tub, up the tub..." or "pickin' up a toy and put it on the shelf..." (to the tune of "This Is The Way We Wash Our Clothes").

- Musical instruments can easily be made or improvised at home. You (or your child) may already have discovered that cooking pots and lids make wonderful instruments. We have directions for making a variety of musical instruments from household objects such as empty oatmeal containers, paper plates, and buttons. We'd be delighted to share these ideas with you—just ask us!

VI. Recommended Resources for Music and Movement

Records and Tapes

Children's Songs and Folk Music

American Folk Songs for Children; Stories and Songs for Children; Birds, Beasts, Bugs and Little Fishes; and *Precious Friends* (Pete Seeger)

And One and Two; Ella Jenkins' Nursery Rhymes; Country Games and Rhythms for the Little Ones; I Know the Color of the Rainbow; This a Way, That a Way; and *You'll Sing a Song and I'll Sing a Song* (Ella Jenkins)

Baby Beluga; Singable Songs for the Very Young; Rise and Shine; and *One Light, One Sun* (Raffi) (song books are also available)

Children's Greatest Hits; Activity and Game Songs; and *Music for Ones and Twos* (Tom Glazer)

Comets, Cats, and Rainbows (Paul Strausman)

Family Hug, The Flyers, and *Step into the Light* (The Flyers)

Free to Be You and Me (Marlo Thomas)

Little White Duck and *Other Children's Favorites* (Burl Ives)

Mr. Rogers: Let's Be Together Today (Fred Rogers)

One, Two, Three, Four, Live (Sharon, Lois and B. Bram)

Sesame Street: Let Your Feelings Show; Sesame Street: The Anniversary Album; and *Sesame Street Gold: The Best of Sesame Street* (Sesame Street Records)

Sing Along with Bob and *Songs and Games for Toddlers* (Bob McGrath)

Shake Sugaree (Taj Mahal)

The Cat Came Back and *Fred Penner's Place* (Fred Penner)

Finger Play

Let's Play Fingerplays (Tom Glazer)

Wee Sing Silly Songs and *Wee Sing Nursery Rhymes and Lullabies* (Wee Sing Tapes)

Exercise and Movement

Activities for Individualization in Movement and Music (Rosemary Hallum)

Animal Walks, Bean Bag Activities, and *Folk Dance Fun* (Kimbo Records)

Creative Movement and Rhythmic Exploration; Feelin' Free; Movin'; and *Homemade Band* (Hap Palmer)

Exercise! (Sesame Street Records)

Play Your Instruments and Make a Pretty Sound (Ella Jenkins)

Music for Twos and Threes (Tom Glazer)

Quiet Music

Lullaby Magic, Morning Music (Discovery Music)
Earth Mother Lullabies from Around the World (Pamela Ballingham)

Classical Recordings

Bach, Brahms, Beethoven, Chopin, and Mozart, plus traditional children's favorites:

Amahl and the Night Visitors (Menotti)
An American in Paris (Gershwin)
The Children's Prayer from Hansel and Gretel (Humperdinck)
Introduction to the Orchestra (Britten)
La Mer (Debussy)
Peter and the Wolf (Prokofiev)
Pictures at an Exhibition (Moussorky)
The Planets (Holst)
Toreador Song from Carmen (Bizet)

Songbooks/Finger Play Books

Bertail, Inez. *Complete Nursery Songbook* (New York: Lothrop, Lee & Shepard, 1947).

> 160 nursery rhymes put to song with simple piano arrangement.

Cromwell, Liz, and Hibner, Dixie. *Finger Frolics.* (Princeton, NJ: Partner Press, 1983).

> Collection of finger plays under the categories of seasons, holidays and the world around us (animals, circus and zoo, community helpers, Indians, safety, soldiers and sailors, transportation); country; nursery rhymes; and activity verses.

Glazer, Tom. *Do Your Ears Hang Low?* (Garden City, NY: Doubleday, 1980).

> Fifty familiar and unfamiliar musical fingerplays for piano and guitar.

Glazer, Tom. *Eye Winker, Tom Tinker, Chin Chopper* (Garden City, NY: Doubleday, 1973).

> A songbook containing 50 well-known children's songs with piano arrangement and guitar chords as well as finger play directions. All are action songs and game songs.

Glazer, Tom. *Music for Ones and Twos* (Garden City, NY: Doubleday, 1983).

> Short, simple, familiar and unfamiliar songs for very young children dealing with subjects such as senses, toys, playing, and sleeping, along with some familiar finger plays and game songs.

Glazer, Tom. Tom Glazer's *Treasury of Songs for Children* (Garden City, NY: Doubleday, 1988)

Revised and updated with new illustrations, a book with a wide variety of song types, music arranged for piano with guitar chords, and historical information about each of the 130 songs.

Grayson, Marion F. *Let's Do Fingerplays* (Bridgeport, CT: Robert B. Luce, 1962).

Large collection of familiar and unfamiliar finger plays in categories such as the family, things that go, animals, and holidays and special occasions.

Hart, Jane. *Singing Bee! A Collection of Favorite Children's Songs* (New York: Lothrop, Lee & Shepard, 1982).

Over 125 lullabies, Mother Goose rhymes, finger plays, games, folk songs, rounds, and holiday songs with piano accompaniment and guitar chords.

The Reader's Digest Children's Songbook (Pleasantville, NY: Reader's Digest Association, 1985).

131 family favorites with piano arrangements.

Seeger, Ruth Crawford. *American Folk Songs for Children* (Garden City, NY: Doubleday, 1948).

Over 90 favorite folk songs, including ballads, work songs, chants, spirituals, and blues. The introductory chapter explains how to sing the songs, improvise on the words, and use the songs at home and at school. Most of the songs are easily adaptable for young children and can be used for finger plays and game songs.

Winn, Marie. *The Fireside Book of Fun and Game Songs* (New York: Simon and Schuster, 1974).

A collection of group sing-along songs divided into categories, from tongue-twisters and action songs to nonsense and gruesome songs. The songs are geared for preschoolers through elementary school children; you'll need to find the age-appropriate songs.

COOKING

I. Why Cooking Is Important

Cooking enables children to experience the world of food firsthand. They learn not only how food is prepared but how it contributes to their health and well-being. Cooking offers children opportunities to experiment with food, to be creative, and to prepare nutritional snacks. It could be considered a "survival skill" that is basic to the education of all boys and girls.

Cooking can be one of the most satisfying activities in the classroom. Not only is food preparation enjoyable, it's also a true laboratory for learning. As children melt cheese, they learn about science. As they measure a cup of milk for a pudding recipe, they learn about measurement and volume. As they stir peanut butter, knead biscuit dough, and peel carrots, they develop physical skills and increase their vocabularies. Making hummus teaches children about good nutrition and cultural preferences. When they make zucchini muffins for their morning snack, children see a task through to completion and can take pride in their accomplishment. Cooking appeals to children's senses and provides a wealth of learning opportunities.

On of the most appealing aspects of cooking for children is that it is one of the few activities in which they are allowed to do the same things that adults do. In the block corner they make pretend roads and bridges. In the house corner they imagine they are parents, teachers, and doctors. In cooking, they have an opportunity to behave just as grown-ups do—a rare treat for children.

Making the Decision to Include Cooking

Many early childhood teachers feel that food experiences are a natural part of their program and they include cooking as an activity choice on a regular basis. Others put off cooking experiences until they feel the children are familiar with the classroom routines, able to select activities, and work independently. Because supervision is essential to ensuring children's safety, you may want to consider scheduling cooking experiences on days when a volunteer is available to provide an extra hand in the classroom. The most important factors in making the decision to include cooking in your program are your own level of comfort and your ability to make the time required to plan and prepare for cooking.

Some programs have neither the space, the facilities, the staff, nor the resources to set up a separate interest area for cooking. If your program is one of these, read this module with an eye toward what you *can* do, and what you feel comfortable about trying. You can effectively incorporate the spirit of this module into your program, no matter how limited your resources. You'll find suggestions for activities you can do on an ongoing, informal basis without having to set up a complete interest area.

Keep in mind that children's health and safety is a primary concern. Prior to beginning any cooking program it's important to know about children's food allergies, as well as the beliefs and preferences of the families in your program. Consult children's records and parents for this information. Review the suggestions in this module when you have time and pick out one or two ideas that you feel ready to try. Your success in implementing a cooking experience or establishing a cooking area, and the children's enthusiasm for this activity choice, may inspire you to become even more ambitious.

Objectives for Children's Learning

When thinking about cooking, your primary goal may be to teach children an important self-help skill or to lay a foundation for good nutrition habits. But cooking is a wonderful activity for helping children grow in all areas—socio-emotionally, cognitively, and physically. As you select objectives to work on with the children in your classroom, consider these offered below:

Objectives for Socio-Emotional Development

- Work cooperatively in small groups (making bread).
- Develop self-help skills (preparing snacks for oneself).
- Complete a task (preparing a recipe from start to finish, including clean-up).
- Develop independence (following a recipe by referring to picture signs without adult supervision).
- Show consideration (sharing and waiting one's turn when working with others).
- Develop pride in oneself and one's heritage (preparing and serving a family recipe).

Objectives for Cognitive Development

- Learn about nutrition (preparing a healthy snack).
- Solve problems (determining how high to fill a muffin tin to allow for rising batter).
- Develop beginning reading skills (relating recipe picture cards to written directions).
- Gain a foundation for math concepts such as sequencing and measurement (filling a quart pitcher with four cups of water).
- Learn about the scientific properties of food (turning cream into butter by vigorously shaking the cream).
- Express creativity (making nontraditionally shaped pretzels out of pretzel dough).

Objectives for Physical Development

- Develop fine muscle control (chopping celery, stirring batter, and squeezing lemons).
- Enhance eye-hand coordination (cracking an egg).
- Learn directionality (using a wire whisk).

This list is just a sampling of the many ways in which cooking can be used to promote children's growth in all areas of development. You'll want to add to this list individual objectives that you've set for children in your classroom, based on their particular needs and interests.

II. Arranging the Environment

As stated earlier, cooking objectives can be achieved whether or not you have a designated cooking area. This section discusses how you can set up a cooking area in your classroom when you have the facilities and resources to do so. Following this are some suggestions for creating temporary space for cooking in your classroom on the days when you wish to offer this activity choice.

Creating Space

If your program has the space and resources for a cooking area, you'll want to select a space that is near a sink and has access to electrical outlets. The cooking area is best placed in a noisy area of the room, as it generates lots of team discussion as well as the natural sounds of cooking. If you have room next to the sand and water area, this would be a good choice, as both learning centers can share a common sink. A sample layout for the cooking area is shown below.

As this illustration shows, the area is defined by open shelving. Kitchen utensils and supplies are arranged on the shelves. A counter at the children's elbow level has been built against the back wall to make use of the electrical outlets. A pegboard on which measuring cups, spoons, and potholders are hung is within the children's reach. In the center of the area are child-sized chairs and a table, which serve as both a work station and an eating area. Clean-up materials are stored near the sink. Aprons hang on a hook at the children's height.

Selecting Materials

In setting up the cooking area, you needn't try to recreate a kitchen in the classroom. Your aim is to provide children with cooking experiences—not to spend a lot of money equipping the area. Instead of a conventional oven, you can use a toaster oven, electric wok, electric frying pan, or electric Dutch oven. A refrigerator, although nice to have, isn't necessary; you can store perishables in a cooler or in the school's refrigerator (if one is available).

The following inventory is offered to inspire your thinking. You are can add and subtract items from this list to reflect your preferences and resources:

Measuring

> plastic measuring spoons
> plastic measuring cups
> 4- and 8-cup pyrex measuring cups
> pitchers

Baking/cooking

> plastic mixing bowls of various sizes
> rolling pin
> spatulas
> cookie cutters
> cookie sheet
> muffin tin
> cake pans (round or square)
> griddle
> saucepans with lids
> biscuit cutter
> pastry brush

Gadgets/Appliances

> hullers
> graters
> grinders
> manual juicer
> vegetable peelers
> corers
> ice-cream freezer

Utensils

> wooden spoons
> funnel
> wire whisk
> egg beater
> potato masher or ricer
> tongs
> colander
> manual sifter or strainer
> knives (plastic in activity area, sharp ones out of children's reach)
> can openers
> ladle
> large slotted spoon
> scissors or cooking shears

Accessories

> cutting board
> candy thermometer
> cheesecloth
> pastry bag with coupler and tips
> trivets
> potholders

In assembling materials, try to select ones made of rubber or unbreakable plastic. Accidents are bound to happen, so you'll want to protect children from being hurt by broken bowls, glasses, or utensils. In some cases, pyrex utensils are recommended, as they allow children to see what's going on during the cooking process. Similarly, some cooking activities involve the use of sharp objects such as knives, grinders, graters, or corers. Use of any sharp utensils should always be under close adult supervision. However, we encourage you to allow children to use real kitchen equipment as they may become frustrated trying to make "toy" utensils work.

Displaying and Storing Materials

The key to making the cooking area both functional and attractive is to store and display equipment and supplies neatly and in such a way that children can get at them independently. Bowls, pots and pans, and pyrex measuring cups can be stored on open shelving at the children's eye level. It's a good idea to group items by function, such as mixing, baking, rolling dough, and so on. Just as blocks and props are labeled, you can trace outlines of these items on colored contact paper and then place the labels on the appropriate locations on the shelf.

Small items such as cheesecloth or a pastry bag and tips can be placed in cardboard boxes or large juice cans stored on the shelves. To identify the contents of these bins, you can either draw, photograph, or cut out magazine pictures of the items and paste the pictures on the outside of their storage containers.

Utensils such as wooden spoons or spatulas can be stored in a large food can covered with contact paper or coated wallpaper and placed on a counter. Often-used items such as measuring cups, spoons, and potholders can be hung on hooks near the area where actual cooking will take place. Another approach is to place these items in hanging baskets within the children's reach.

Smocks or aprons made of old shirts or oilcloth can be hung from a children's coat tree or on a pegboard hook placed near the entrance to the activity area. Clean-up supplies such as a dishpan and drainer, sponges, paper towels, and mops should be stored on or near the sink area, accessible to children.

Sharp items such as knives, cheese slicers, and graters should be stored out of the children's reach. Cleaners and cleaning solvents should also be locked away.

To further ensure children's health and safety in the cooking area, consider posting picture signs. For example, next to the sink area you might post a sign showing dirty hands to remind children to wash their hands before beginning to cook.

Assessing the Effectiveness of the Area

By observing the children at work, you can tell how well the area is supporting their cooking efforts. You'll want to look at traffic patterns, the use of utensils, who chooses to use the area, and how children work together. Here are some questions to guide your observations:

- How often is the cooking area chosen by children during child-selected play? What can I do to make the area more inviting?

- Do children use the cooking area individually or only with other children? What activities can I introduce for children to do by themselves?

- Do boys choose to cook as frequently as girls? Are there recipes or activities that would be especially inviting for boys?

- Are children able to understand and follow the recipe cards? Are the pictures clear?

- Is sharing a problem? Is there enough equipment for children to work cooperatively?

- Are children able to clean up after themselves? Are shelves and containers clearly labeled? Are cleaning supplies handy?

Ongoing assessments are an effective way of ensuring that children have positive cooking experiences. If you note problems, you can try making changes to the environment or your approach to cooking activities.

Creating a Temporary Cooking Area

If you don't have the space or facilities for a permanent cooking area, you might want to consider temporarily converting another interest area into a cooking site. If the art area has a nearby sink, this might be a good choice, as children can use the art table as a work station. Another choice might be the sand and water area if it has tables and a nearby sink.

To set up for cooking with a minimum of disturbance to the existing area, consider a portable cooking box. In this box you could include basic kitchen utensils—perhaps several wooden spoons, spatulas, a vegetable peeler, measuring cups and spoons, and plastic knives. If an electrical outlet is nearby, you could also place an electric wok in the cooking box or a saucepan and an electric burner. You might want to have several portable cooking boxes: one for baking; one for making soups, pudding, and other saucepan-based activities; and one for cooking activities that don't require baking or heating. Then, when a cooking activity is planned, you need only grab the appropriate box and take it to the temporary cooking area.

If you are in a classroom with no sink facilities, you can still offer cooking activities that don't require the washing of food. If this describes your classroom situation, you can choose any table in the classroom for your temporary cooking site. Again, it's a good idea to have a portable cooking box with plates, plastic ware, knives, a cutting board, and other utensils that lend themselves to nonmessy cooking activities such as preparing a snack or tasting experiences.

With a little planning, cooking experiences can be incorporated successfully into every early childhood classroom.

III. Observing and Promoting Children's Learning

Cooking provides wonderful opportunities for working one-on-one with children and for leading group projects. Perhaps most important, it is an activity in which children can work and learn independently. No matter what type of cooking activity you select, you'll want to make sure that it is appropriate for the children's developmental levels. To do this, it's helpful to know how children learn as they try out cooking activities.

How Children Learn Through Cooking

Children's interactions with food and cooking begin with explorations. In this beginning stage, known as **functional play,** they use all their senses to find out what food is like. Feeling the texture of a kiwi's skin, smelling bread as it bakes, watching cheese melt in a grilled-cheese sandwich, hearing popcorn kernels pop, and tasting the tartness of unsweetened lemonade give children an understanding of food's properties. By tasting and observing how food reacts to being cooked, sliced, and mashed, they learn about food in its raw and cooked states.

Once children have a feel for what food is like, they experiment with it. In this stage they want to see what happens to dough that has been kneaded and then punched down. Using a cookie cutter to cut shapes in dough, they are able to see what happens to those shapes when baked. During this experimentation phase, also known as **constructive play,** children's actions are purposeful. They want to see how food reacts to their manipulations. Many children delight in creating finished products that can be admired and eaten.

Children who cook also have an opportunity to experience **play with rules.** Cooking with recipes demands that children follow directions, carry out activities in a pre-set sequence, and behave according to rules. These are play behaviors that will serve children well throughout their lives.

Observing Individual Children

By observing each child participating in cooking activities, you can plan an approach that will enhance the experience. As you observe each child, look to see which learning objectives have been achieved. For example, what fine motor skills has the child developed? Can the child unscrew the lid off a jar? Turn the handle of an egg beater? Stir batter with a wooden spoon? It's helpful to jot down your observations so that you can maintain a record of the skills you see children working on. As you make your observations of individual children, take a few moments to think about such questions as these:

- Does the child choose independent or group activities? Is this because of the types of activities available or because of the child's preferences? What could I do to promote more independence or more cooperative efforts?

- Which cooking activities hold the child's interest?

- Does the child need help in learning new skills?

- Does the child choose a particular job or wait to be assigned a task? How can I encourage this child to be more independent? What can I do to encourage a shy child?

- Can the child follow a recipe card?
- Does the child do the same activities day after day? What other activities could I introduce?

These questions will give you insight into the kinds of things children choose to do as well as the ways in which they do them. Anecdotal information will also prove helpful in planning for each child's learning.

Interacting with Children

Your awareness of the learning potential in cooking activities enables you to promote children's growth and development. One of the best ways of doing this is to engage children in conversation. Thoughtful dialogue will accomplish the important goals of:

- conveying to children that their activities are important,
- developing critical thinking skills, and
- increasing vocabulary and communication skills.

Talking with children about their cooking activities is something you can do even if you don't have a cooking area in your classroom but plan activities on an occasional basis. As a starting point, describe for children what you see them doing:

- "You've put all the strawberry stems together in one bowl. That will make clean-up very easy."
- "You're working very hard to mix the peanut butter and corn syrup together, Tony. The peanut butter balls are going to come out nice and smooth."
- "You've been over to the tasting table twice this morning. I noticed that you especially liked cutting and tasting the banana."

When you describe what they've done, children review their actions in their own minds. This helps develop self-awareness. Next, you can encourage children to observe aloud what they've been doing. Questions such as these help children think about and articulate their actions:

- "Kwasi, you really like punching that bread dough. How does it feel to you?"
- "Juanita, I see you've taken the potato masher off the shelf. What will you be doing with it?"
- "Joanna, you and Shantelle have been at the tasting table for a while. What have you discovered?"

Once you have helped children reflect on the types of things they've been doing, you can facilitate their learning further by encouraging them to think about their activities in new ways. In this step you are posing questions for children to analyze and solve. Here are some examples of questions to extend children's learning:

- "Patrick, is there something we could do to this cookie dough to make it less sticky?"
- "Valikia, what did you do to the cream to turn it into butter?"

- "Look at all the cheese balls we made. How many different sizes are there?"
- "What did you like best about making trail mix, Linda?"

Introducing Cooking Skills to Children

Children can learn basic techniques that help them feel confident as cooks. To introduce these techniques, you can show children one at a time or in small groups how a particular activity is done. Provide the children with repeated opportunities to practice the skill in your presence. As you do this, you can question them about the process: "How can you tell when all of the potato is peeled?" Questioning helps children become more aware of their actions.

Here are some techniques to consider, along with some ideas for introducing them to children of specific ages.

Techniques for All Children

- *Melting:* Place cheese-covered bread under the broiler of a toaster oven to make grilled-cheese sandwiches.
- *Dipping:* Hold fresh or dried fruits by one end and lower halfway into melted chocolate; place fruits on a cookie sheet lined with waxed paper and allow chocolate to harden.
- *Scrubbing:* Wash carrots in a bowl of water prior to peeling.
- *Measuring dry ingredients:* Fill a measuring cup with one cup of flour and level off with a knife.
- *Kneading:* Punch down bread dough.
- *Pouring:* Fill a pitcher with water for making iced tea.
- *Stirring:* Mix yogurt into fruit salad.
- *Measuring liquids:* Fill a four-cup pyrex measuring cup with one cup of milk.
- *Shaking:* Make butter from cream by vigorously shaking a jar of cream.
- *Spreading:* Cover bread with cream cheese.
- *Rolling with hands:* Form meat balls or cheese balls from mixed ingredients.
- *Forming shapes:* Use cookie cutters, biscuit shapers, and melon ballers with dough or melons.
- *Squeezing:* Make lemonade with a hand juicer using fresh lemons.
- *Basting:* Use a baster to pour excess french toast batter over bread.
- *Rolling with rolling pin:* Roll out dough.
- *Peeling with fingers:* Remove the shell from a hard-boiled egg.
- *Cracking:* Break an egg against the lip of a pyrex measuring cup.

Techniques for Older Preschool and Kindergarten Children

- *Hulling:* Use huller to pull stems from strawberries.
- *Grinding:* Make peanut butter using a hand grinder to grind peanuts.

- *Beating:* Whip heavy cream or turn egg whites into meringue.
- *Peeling with vegetable peeler:* Remove skin from potato or carrot.
- *Grating:* Use a grater to prepare cheese for nachos.
- *Pitting:* Use a pitter to remove cherry pits for making jelly.
- *Coring:* Use a corer to remove an apple or pear core while making baked fruit.

These techniques are just a sampling of the many ways in which children can naturally develop skills through cooking.

IV. Extending and Integrating Children's Learning

You can enhance children's learning through cooking by planning special activities. This section begins with sample activities that can be done in either a permanent or temporary cooking area. Following this are enrichment activities that require cooking equipment and facilities more likely to be found in an established cooking area.

In introducing these activities, teachers need to find a balance between supervising the activity for safety reasons and taking a "background" role. It is a good rule with cooking—as well as all learning—that the more the teacher does, the less children learn. Your role in cooking experiences should be to introduce cooking techniques, exercise safety, and facilitate children's independent actions.

Special Activities for All Early Childhood Programs

To help children try out and master various cooking techniques, you can set out foods that require only minimal preparation for children to prepare independently for snacks. To make this activity one that children can do on their own, you might try creating picture cards that illustrate the sequence of actions involved. For example, for the task of preparing a bowl of strawberries for a snack, picture cards would illustrate two actions: (1) rinsing the berries in a colander and (2) hulling the green stems.

To have children prepare carrots, you could place carrots in a bowl along with picture instruction cards that show three actions: (1) carrots being washed, (2) the ends being cut, and (3) the carrots being scraped with a vegetable peeler.

Older preschoolers and kindergarten children who want to prepare strawberries or carrots for their snack can (individually or in pairs) get out the needed equipment, wash their hands, prepare the snack, wash their hands again, eat, and clean-up.

Snacks that can be prepared by most young children include:

- celery sticks stuffed with cream cheese or peanut butter
- lettuce "roll-ups" stuffed with peanut butter
- bologna and cheese roll-ups
- peanut butter-covered crackers
- yogurt mixed with fruit
- banana sandwiches
- pineapple tidbits
- peanut butter-covered apple slices
- trail mix
- cottage cheese and raisins
- freshly squeezed orange juice

Tasting Centers

You can encourage children to explore unfamiliar and interesting nonperishable foods by setting up a "tasting center." Depending on the children's backgrounds, the definition of "unfamiliar" will vary from group to group. You may wish to try fennel, crystallized ginger, or star fruit. Familiar foods can also be paired with unfamiliar ones for children to compare and contrast: Brussel sprouts with cabbage, for example, or green peas with black-eyed peas.

To extend children's learning in the tasting center, try asking questions such as these:

- "In what ways are bananas and plantains alike? In what ways are they different?"
- "Do the Brussel sprouts smell like cabbage?"
- "How did the ginger taste?"
- "Does the fennel smell like anything else you've ever eaten?"
- "How does a sliced kiwi look different from an unsliced one?"
- "Which food did you most enjoy tasting today?"

Recipes for One

Older preschoolers and kindergarten children often enjoy being able to cook by themselves. If you select recipes that children can follow independently, you can set up this activity in any area of the classroom. Look for recipes that make use of foods that don't spoil quickly and that can be prepared without electrical equipment.

Here are some suggestions for setting up this activity:

- Using 5" x 8" index cards or pieces of tagboard, make up recipe cards for the selected recipe. Depending on the ages of the children in your group, you can make cards that are strictly picture-based or add simple text. No matter how you choose to do recipe cards, it's always a good idea to laminate the finished cards or cover them with clear contact paper. Spills are inevitable and if this activity is successful, you'll want to use the recipe cards again.
- Make sure that all needed equipment and ingredients are accessible to the children.

- Discuss the recipe cards with the children. Ask questions to make sure they understand what needs to be done when.
- Let the children know you are available to assist, answer questions, or lend support.

Encourage children to eat their prepared recipes at snack or lunch time. As children work on these recipes, you might wish to ask questions such as these to help them reflect on what they are doing:

- "What happened to the raisins when you soaked them in water?"
- "How did you know when the carrot was all peeled?"
- "How does the juicer keep the lemon's seeds from falling into the juice?"
- "How could you make a triangle out of this square of cheese?"
- "Which part of the recipe did you like doing the best?"

Here are some recipes for one that you might wish to put on recipe cards:

Cucumber Boat

Food:

Half a cucumber, sliced lengthwise
Cottage cheese (1/3 cup)
Raisins (1 T)
Sunflower seeds (1 T)
Cheese (1 slice)

Equipment:

Vegetable peeler
Cutting board
Plastic knife
Teaspoon
Measuring cups

Measuring spoons
Bowl
Wooden spoon
Toothpick

Method:

1. Peel cucumber.
2. Using teaspoon, scoop out seeds.
3. Mix together cottage cheese, raisins, and sunflower seeds in bowl, using wooden spoon.
4. Spoon cottage cheese mixture into seeded cucumber.
5. Using knife and cutting board, cut out a triangle of cheese. Attach to toothpick.
6. Secure toothpick to end of cucumber boat.

Waldorf Salad

Food:

Apple (1)
Celery (1 stalk)
Raisins (10 or so)
Walnuts (2 or so)
Mayonnaise (1 T)

Equipment:

Cutting board
Mixing bowl
Plastic knife (serrated)
Nutcracker
Wooden spoon

Method:

1. Slice apple and cut into bite-size pieces. Place in mixing bowl.
2. Slice celery and cut into bite-size pieces. Place in mixing bowl.
3. Add raisins to bowl.
4. Crack walnuts. Remove shells. Break up pieces. Place in bowl.
5. Add mayonnaise.
6. Stir all ingredients together.

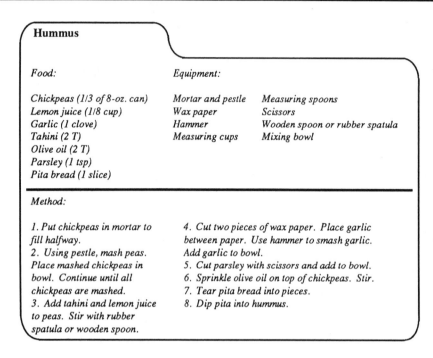

Hummus

Food:

Chickpeas (1/3 of 8-oz. can)
Lemon juice (1/8 cup)
Garlic (1 clove)
Tahini (2 T)
Olive oil (2 T)
Parsley (1 tsp)
Pita bread (1 slice)

Equipment:

Mortar and pestle   Measuring spoons
Wax paper   Scissors
Hammer   Wooden spoon or rubber spatula
Measuring cups   Mixing bowl

Method:

1. Put chickpeas in mortar to fill halfway.
2. Using pestle, mash peas. Place mashed chickpeas in bowl. Continue until all chickpeas are mashed.
3. Add tahini and lemon juice to peas. Stir with rubber spatula or wooden spoon.
4. Cut two pieces of wax paper. Place garlic between paper. Use hammer to smash garlic. Add garlic to bowl.
5. Cut parsley with scissors and add to bowl.
6. Sprinkle olive oil on top of chickpeas. Stir.
7. Tear pita bread into pieces.
8. Dip pita into hummus.

Recipes for Group Projects

Group recipes that don't require electrical equipment can be done in any area of the classroom at any time of the year. Group recipes are most effective when limited to three or four children at a time. Some three-year-olds may have difficulty doing advanced tasks, so it's important to match activities to the children's skills. In a mixed-age group, the older children can assist the younger ones. Group recipes (such as making "solar tea" or growing alfalfa sprouts) lend themselves to circle-time projects that can be done by children of all ages.

Here are some suggestions for introducing group recipes:

• Prepare recipe cards ahead of time.

- Make sure all needed equipment and ingredients are at hand.

- Go over the entire recipe aloud, reading and discussing each card.

- Ask for volunteers to do each step in the recipe. For example, for the recipe to make peanut butter, children could volunteer to either shell, grind, or stir the peanuts, place them in the bowl, add the oil, or spread the finished product at the end.

- As children are working, ask questions that will help them reflect on the process: "Why do we use a vegetable peeler to peel the apples instead of using our fingers, like we do to peel a hard-boiled egg?" "What did you add to the applesauce that made it turn brown?"

- As the culminating step in the cooking process, have the children serve and eat their handiwork. Make this eating session an experience in savoring the children's talents.

- Invite all children to participate in the clean-up process. Children can take turns washing and drying utensils, mopping counters, wiping the eating area, and putting supplies away.

Here are two group projects and one group recipe you might like to use:

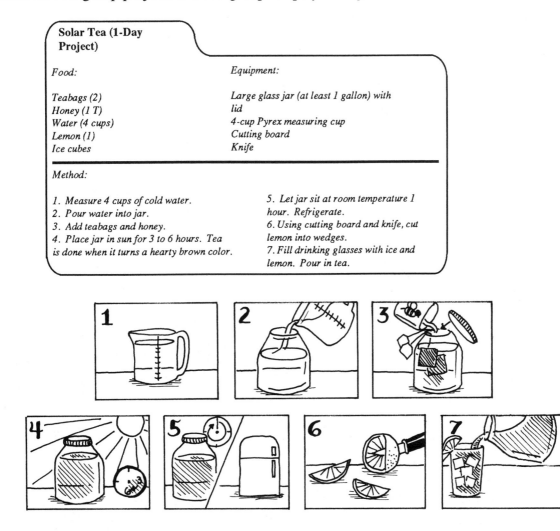

Solar Tea (1-Day Project)

Food:

Teabags (2)
Honey (1 T)
Water (4 cups)
Lemon (1)
Ice cubes

Equipment:

Large glass jar (at least 1 gallon) with lid
4-cup Pyrex measuring cup
Cutting board
Knife

Method:

1. Measure 4 cups of cold water.
2. Pour water into jar.
3. Add teabags and honey.
4. Place jar in sun for 3 to 6 hours. Tea is done when it turns a hearty brown color.
5. Let jar sit at room temperature 1 hour. Refrigerate.
6. Using cutting board and knife, cut lemon into wedges.
7. Fill drinking glasses with ice and lemon. Pour in tea.

Sprouts (1-Week Project)

Food:

Alfalfa seeds (1 T)
Water

Equipment:

32-oz. jar
Cheesecloth
Rubber band

Method:

1. *Place seeds in jar.*
2. *Cover with warm water.*
3. *Let seeds soak for 24 hours in warm, dark place.*
4. *Cover the top of jar with cheesecloth. Secure with rubber band.*
5. *Pour out water. Rinse and drain twice.*
6. *Repeat for 5 days.*
7. *On last day, place sprouts in window to turn green.*
8. *Store in refrigerator.*

Peanut Butter

Food:

Peanuts (1 lb.)
Peanut oil (2 T)

Equipment:

Handgrinder (on which a cardboard collar has been placed to make it safer)
Bowl
Measuring spoons
Wooden spoon

Method:

1. *Secure grinder to table or counter. Place bowl near grinder's spout. Shell peanuts.*
2. *Place handful of peanuts in grinder.*
3. *Gradually add oil so grinder turns smoothly.*
4. *Grind all peanuts.*
5. *Stir ground peanuts in bowl with spoon.*

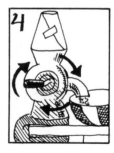

Field Trips

Children are often curious about food: Where does food come from? How does it get from the farm to our school? Because children learn best from first-hand experiences, you can make the answers to these questions come alive by taking children on a field trip to food-related sites such as these:

- bakery
- bee colony (apiary)
- bottling plant
- cafeteria or restaurant
- cannery
- dairy
- farm
- grocery store
- hatchery
- mill
- orchard

Although not all of these sites will be within traveling distance, you may be able to locate two or three sites that would enrich children's understanding of how food is harvested, processed, and made available to the public. By arranging in advance for a tour of these facilities, you can broaden children's understanding of the world of food. Moreover, field trips are a way of extending cooking activities even if your program is unable to support a cooking area.

Special Activities for Programs with Cooking Areas

Whenever children cook with electrical equipment, a more controlled environment and close supervision is needed. If you don't have a cooking area but do have an art or sand and water area with nearby outlets, you may be able to conduct the activities noted here. (Using the prop-like cooking boxes described earlier will make these activities go more smoothly.)

Introducing Children to New Recipes

To keep cooking interesting, you will want to periodically add new recipes for children to make on their own and as part of the group. Keep familiar ones around, however, as children often like to repeat old favorites.

What recipes should you pick? Your choices will probably depend on these factors:

- the ages and developmental levels of the children (can they successfully use corers, graters, peelers, juicers, etc.?);
- the appliances you have and whether adequate supervision can be arranged;
- the children's food interests (can a recipe be tied to a book or field trip?); and
- cost considerations (making use of seasonal fruits and vegetables is a cost-effective approach).

In selecting recipes, try to find ones that involve making something from scratch. This provides for a more satisfying experience—one in which children can learn about food and not simply make a finished product.

If you need assistance in locating recipes, begin by asking the children's parents for ideas. Parents can be a rich resource for new recipes. By inviting them to share recipes from home, you foster a home-school connection and provide opportunities for multicultural experiences. Many home recipes can be simplified.

If you'd like to obtain a specific recipe but can't locate one that would be appropriate for classroom use, you might ask your county U.S. Department of Agriculture Extension Agent for some ideas. These trained home economists are a wonderful free resource for recipes and safety tips.

There are a number of excellent cookbooks prepared especially for children that will give you cooking ideas and suggestions. Here are several you might wish to consult:

- Ault, R. *Kids Are Natural Cooks.* Boston: Houghton Mifflin, 1974.
- *Better Homes and Gardens Step-by-Step Kids' Cookbook.* Des Moines, IA: Meredith, 1984.
- *Betty Crocker's Cookbook for Boys and Girls.* New York: Western, 1986.
- Coyle, R. *My First Cookbook.* New York: Workman, 1985.
- de Brunhoff, L. *Babar Learns to Cook.* Westminster, MD: Random House, 1974.
- Ellison, V.H. *The Pooh Cookbook.* New York: E.P. Dutton, 1984.
- Ferreira, N.J. *Learning Through Cooking: A Cooking Program for Children Two to Ten.* Saratoga, CA: R&E, 1986.
- Veitch, B., and Harms, T. *Cook and Learn—Pictorial Single Portion Recipes: A Child's Cook Book.* Menlo Park, CA: Addison-Wesley, 1981.

Some recipes you might like to start out with are given below:

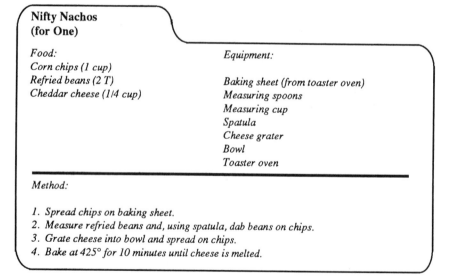

**Nifty Nachos
(for One)**

Food:
Corn chips (1 cup)
Refried beans (2 T)
Cheddar cheese (1/4 cup)

Equipment:

Baking sheet (from toaster oven)
Measuring spoons
Measuring cup
Spatula
Cheese grater
Bowl
Toaster oven

Method:

1. Spread chips on baking sheet.
2. Measure refried beans and, using spatula, dab beans on chips.
3. Grate cheese into bowl and spread on chips.
4. Bake at 425° for 10 minutes until cheese is melted.

Muffin Meatloaf (for One)

Food:

Ground beef (1/4 lb.)
Stale bread (1 slice)
Ketchup (2 T)
Egg (1)
Salt, pepper, garlic powder

Equipment:

Muffin tin
Mixing bowl
Wooden spoon
Toaster oven
Paper towel

Method:

1. Preheat toaster oven to 350°.
2. Crumble meat and add to bowl.
3. Crumble stale bread and add to bowl.
4. Break egg into bowl. Mix together with meat and bread.

5. Add ketchup and two shakes each of salt, pepper, add garlic powder to bowl.
6. Dab some ketchup on a paper towel and coat one of the muffin holes with ketchup.
7. Fill muffin hole and bake for 25 minutes or until meat is browned.

Tropical Gelatin Jigglers (Group Project)

Food:

Pineapple juice (2-1/2 cups)
Strawberry-banana gelatin (2 pkgs.)
Crushed pineapple (1 8-oz. can)

Equipment:

Saucepan
Mixing bowl
Wooden spoon

13" x 9" pan
Cookie sheet
Cookie cutters
Electric burner

Method:

1. Empty gelatin into bowl.
2. Pour pineapple juice into a saucepan and bring to a boil.
3. Add juice to gelatin. Stir until dissolved.
4. Stir in crushed pineapple.
5. Pour into 13" x 9" pan.
6. Chill in refrigerator until firm (about 3 hours).

7. Fill cookie sheet with warm water.
8. Dip gelatin pan in warm water for 15 seconds.
9. Press cookie cutter patterns into gelatin.
10. Using clean fingers, remove shapes from pan and place on serving tray.

A Bucket of Biscuits (Group Project)

Food:

Self-rising flour (2 cups)
Solid shortening (4 T)
Buttermilk (2/3 cup)

Equipment:

Measuring cups
Measuring spoons
Mixing bowl
Fork

Wax paper
2" biscuit cutter
Baking sheet

Method:

1. Preheat toaster oven to 450°.
2. Add flour to bowl.
3. Add shortening to flour, 1 T at a time, using fork to mix in shortening.
4. Add milk. Stir with fork.
5. Turn dough onto sheet of wax paper.
6. Knead dough 8 to 10 minutes.

7. Flatten dough.
8. Using biscuit cutter, cut out approximately 16 biscuits.
9. Place biscuits one inch apart on baking sheet. Bake 10 to 12 minutes or until golden.

Variations in Cooking Approaches

You can further enrich children's cooking experiences by providing some variations in approach. Here are two ideas:

- Have the children prepare a meal or snack from start to finish. This includes planning a menu, assembling ingredients, preparing and serving the food, eating the meal family-style, and cleaning up. To make this exercise "complete," children might even grow some of the ingredients, such as the alfalfa sprouts, which can be used in salads, stir-fries, or sandwiches.

- Have the children experiment with finding different uses for the same food. For example, at Halloween children might use one large pumpkin to make pumpkin soup, pumpkin bread, pumpkin stew, and pumpkin pie. The seeds can even be soaked in salt water and then baked in a toaster oven until dried for a tasty snack.

Integrating Cooking with Other Curriculum Areas

Cooking activities can be linked to activities you are working on with children in other interest areas. In fact, you can probably find a natural tie-in with nearly every other activity going on in the classroom. Some examples follow; as always, you'll want to consider the needs and interests of your children.

Health and Nutrition

Every cooking activity can be a lesson in good eating habits. When you set out fruits and vegetables for children to prepare and eat, you send children the message that these foods are important. Similarly, when you encourage children to eat fruits instead of sweets, they learn that fruits are better for them.

As you cook with children, you can discuss nutrition concepts such as these:

- People need to have a balanced diet every day.
- The best way to get a balanced diet is to eat a wide variety of foods.
- Foods from every ethnic background can be healthy to eat.

With older preschoolers and kindergarten children, you can begin to teach actual nutrition principles. If appropriate for the children in your group, you might want to discuss these ideas during cooking:

- Berries and citrus fruits have vitamin C, which is good for our gums and fights infections.
- Milk, cheese, and yogurt have vitamin D and calcium, which are good for growing bones and teeth.
- While we need some sugar, salt, and fats in our diets, large amounts are unhealthy.

Cooking activities also serve the important function of letting children take an active role in their own nutrition decisions. When children decide to prepare a healthy recipe, they take personal responsibility for their own well-being. This active role can set the stage for a lifetime of healthy eating habits.

Science and Math

The cooking area is a natural laboratory for science. Children can observe the physical changes that materials undergo—as when ice cream freezes, yeast proofs, or eggs are fried. With older preschoolers or kindergarten children, you can discuss how making solar tea uses the sun's energy. Absorption can be observed when beans or dried fruit are soaked in water or rice is simmered. Even watching mold grow on perishable foods as they spoil is a lesson in science.

Planting seeds such as radishes, peas, and cucumbers that can be grown for cooking activities enables children of all ages to see science in action. Sweet potatoes or avocado seeds can be suspended in jars of water until they root and give off branches. Later, they can be planted in the classroom as a reminder that some plants are not only beautiful to look at but often serve as food sources, too.

Math concepts are incorporated into nearly every cooking activity. Cups of flour need to be measured, as do teaspoons of vanilla. Older children can gain a beginning understanding of equivalency as they add four cups of water to a quart pitcher of lemonade. They can also learn about volume when they whip air into egg whites.

Emerging Literacy

As young preschoolers "read" picture recipe cards, they learn to associate the pictures with actions. Older preschoolers and kindergarten children who use picture cards with written descriptions may begin to recognize some letters and words, to follow the sequence of the pictures and words, and to understand that reading involves left-right directionality. By interacting with the printed word in this natural way, children build a foundation for literacy.

Literature and music can be extended naturally into cooking activities. Some of the children's favorite books, songs, and poems focus on food. By preparing these foods as a class project, you can personalize these stories and songs. Little Miss Muffet, for example, talks of curds and whey. By making cottage cheese from milk and vinegar, children can see the curds separate from whey and actually picture what Miss Muffet was snacking on. Other books, songs, and stories you might wish to use as cooking tie-ins include these:

- Berenstein, J. *Little Bear's Pancake Party*. New York: Lothrop, Lee, & Shepard, 1966.
- Brown, M. *Stone Soup*. New York: Charles Scribner's, 1947.
- DePaola, T. *Pancakes for Breakfast*. New York: Harcourt Brace, 1978.
- Dr. Seuss. *Green Eggs And Ham*. New York: Beginner Books, 1960.
- Hoban, R. *Bread and Jam for Frances*. New York: Harper & Row, 1964.
- *"Kinds of Food" Learning Basic Skills Through Music*. Freeport, NY: Hap Palmer Record Library Educational Activities.
- McClosky, R. *Blueberries for Sal*. New York: Viking, 1948.

- *"Popping Corn" Songs for Our Small World.* Minneapolis, MN: Schmidt Music Center.

- Scheer, J. *Rain Makes Applesauce.* New York: Holiday House, 1970.

- Sendak, M. *Chicken Soup with Rice.* New York: Harper & Row, 1962.

- Van Woerkom, D. *The Queen Who Couldn't Bake Gingerbread.* New York: Knopf, 1975.

- Winslow, M. *Mud Pies and Other Recipes.* New York: Macmillan, 1961.

Social Studies

With the help of parents, you can extend cooking activities by using recipes that are family favorites. A simple walk to the store to purchase the ingredients for snack offers rich opportunities to informally discuss people's work and services in the neighborhood.

Other natural linkages are with reading books at circle time, visiting museums, or taking field trips. For example, after a visit to a Caribbean festival, children could make coconut bread, roti, callalou, and tamarind candies for a festival of their own. Some background calypso music or steel drum sounds would transport the flavor of the Caribbean to the classroom.

V. Sharing Cooking with Parents

The bridge between the classroom and the home is easily spanned by cooking activities. Because cooking is an activity that already takes place in children's homes, a built-in mechanism exists for reinforcing classroom cooking activities, and parents can be included easily.

Conducting Workshops on Cooking

Many successful parent meetings begin with a potluck supper. You might invite parents to bring a special dish that reflects their cultural background and a copy of the recipe to share. Parents can take turns cooking for different meetings.

You might also plan a workshop just on cooking in which you invite parents to participate in cooking activities just as their children do. Set up cooking stations in the classroom complete with recipe cards and ingredients. Parents can choose the station they want and work in small groups. After 15 to 20 minutes, bring the parents together to discuss the experience. What activities did they do? What did they learn? What do they think children learn from cooking experiences?

You might also invite a representative from the local U.S. Department of Agriculture Extension Service or the National Dairy Council to present a workshop on nutrition. These experts can give parents creative ideas for preparing nutritious meals and snacks at home.

Involving Parents in the Classroom

One of the best ways of helping children develop a positive self-concept is to make them feel good about themselves, their heritage, and their families. When the children's parents participate in classroom activities, children feel proud that you have included their family members in their school life. And when you focus on a recipe that is typical of their heritage, you also help children feel good about who they are.

Because this activity can have so many positive benefits, we suggest that you regularly invite parents to your classroom to lead children in a special cooking activity. Ask parents ahead of time for a favorite family recipe so that you can obtain all the needed ingredients in advance. Several days prior to the scheduled session, meet with the parent to make picture recipe cards for the session. Together, discuss how you can best introduce and conduct the session so that it will be successful. If your program does not have a permanent cooking area, decide what area of the room would be best to use.

Be sure to share the information in this module on introducing new recipes. Let the parent familiarize himself or herself with the cooking area and equipment ahead of time—and be close at hand to support the parent during the cooking activity. With advance planning, everyone's self-concept will be enhanced!

The letter that follows can be sent to parents to let them know about cooking activities that take place in your classroom.

A Letter to Parents on Cooking

What We Do and Why

Cooking is an important part of our curriculum. When they cook, children have an opportunity to learn about food, to be creative, and to prepare their own nutritional snacks. Lots of discoveries happen during cooking. When children see dough rise, they learn about science; when they measure flour, they learn about math. Following picture recipe cards, they learn skills that will prepare them for reading. And when we make and eat Mexican tacos, Chinese vegetables, or African peanut stew, the children learn to appreciate other peoples and cultures.

Cooking offers a special treat for children—it allows them to do things adults do. With all the adult things children aren't allowed to do, it's very rewarding for them to be encouraged to cook "just like grown-ups."

When children cook in the classroom, we talk a lot about what they are doing:

- measuring flour,
- mixing tuna with mayonnaise,
- cracking eggs,
- whipping egg whites,
- grating cheese, and
- peeling potatoes.

As we talk, children learn new words. They also learn to think about what they're doing. They describe what happens when water is added to dry ingredients. They solve problems, such as how much batter should be placed in a muffin tin to allow for the ingredients to rise. They also learn to make healthy eating choices.

What You Can Do at Home

It takes a little more time on your part to involve children in home meal preparations. But if you think about all the things your child will gain from the experience, it becomes well worth the effort. Here are some things you might point out and discuss with your child as you cook together:

- where different utensils are found in the kitchen (and should be returned);
- the names of various foods;
- how various foods look, smell, feel, and taste;
- how many teaspoons or cups of particular ingredients are used;
- why some foods need to be kept in the refrigerator or freezer;
- how heat changes food;
- why a variety of foods are served at each meal; and
- how foods are arranged on plates to make them look appealing.

We welcome any family recipes you would like to share with us. And, we would be delighted for you to come in at any time to participate in a cooking activity.

COMPUTERS

I. Why Computers Are Important

Having a computer area is both innovative and controversial. Some early childhood educators feel that computers are not developmentally appropriate for young children. They would prefer to see children building with blocks, exploring manipulatives, engaged in art activities and dramatic play. Other teachers fear that children working alone at computers can become isolated and fail to develop social skills.

These are, of course, valid concerns. The *Creative Curriculum* shares the belief that blocks, table toys, books, sand and water, art, dramatic play, and the outdoors should be the core curriculum for all early childhood programs. Yet, we also believe that having these activities doesn't mean that a preschool or kindergarten classroom can't also have computers. In fact, research shows that computers can provide highly effective learning opportunities for children. The developmental appropriateness of computers is directly tied to *how* they are used. It would be inappropriate for a teacher to seat a child alone at a computer to work on "drill and practice" exercises. If, however, a teacher has two children working together on a computer program that encourages them to engage in open-ended explorations, the experience is more likely to be appropriate and rewarding. Douglas Clements, in an article in *Young Children*, states, "Computers are no more dangerous than books or pencils—all could be used to push a child to read too soon. However, they can also be used to provide developmentally appropriate experiences." [1]

Social development can be promoted through the use of computers if early childhood programs set up the computer area as any other interest center within the classroom, arranged so that children can work in pairs or small groups. Turn-taking, sharing, and peer tutoring are typical behaviors that teachers observe with this arrangement.

Including computers as an interest area in the classroom may also be an important step in ensuring equal opportunities for all children. Many children today have access to and are familiar with home computers. Many others, however, have no exposure to computers at home and are therefore at a disadvantage. Because there is little doubt that society's needs for a computer-literate population will only increase over time, including computers in your classroom may be an important step in ensuring that all children have equal opportunities to become comfortable with this technology.

Finally, computers offer a different kind of learning experience for children. We know that children, like adults, have individual learning styles and preferences. Including computers in the classroom provides opportunities for children to learn in a variety of ways at a pace that meets their individual needs.

Making the Decision to Include Computers

Increasingly, early childhood programs are acquiring computers and teachers are being asked to include them in their program. After careful consideration, we decided to add computers as an enrichment module in the *Creative Curriculum* in order to show how they can be appropriately incorporated into an early childhood program. For older preschoolers and kindergarten children who have the eye and hand coordination and attention span to sit at a computer for 10-20 minutes, computers can be an exciting enhancement to the curriculum.

---

[1] D.H. Clements. "Computers and Young Children: A Review of Research." *Young Children*, 43, 1, 1987, p. 44.

As noted earlier, many teachers are apprehensive about using computers because they are so often misused. However, when computers are offered as another interest area in the classroom, they are more likely to be used appropriately than when children are assigned to work for a specific time period in a computer lab. We also believe that software programs themselves can contribute to the misuse of computers. Many provide little more than a workbook on a computer screen. We have therefore included a list of recommended software programs and publishers to help you get started, and a checklist that you can use in assessing software to determine if it is developmentally appropriate.

Your own level of comfort with computers is another important factor in your decision to include them in your classroom. If you use and appreciate the value of computers, you are more likely to succeed in making this an effective interest area. If you are not familiar with how computers work and what programs are available, you may want to seek out training opportunities in your school or community before starting up a computer area. Computer user groups often sponsor workshops and some will arrange for private lessons. Another option is to set up a "buddy" system with another teacher. The two of you can help each other refine your computer skills, select appropriate software, and support each other in making the computer area an exciting, innovative place for the children you teach.

Objectives for Children's Learning

Children will be more likely to benefit from computer play when teachers set learning objectives that match their developmental levels and interests. By thoughtfully considering the needs of each child in your program, you can help children grow in many ways. The following is a list of objectives you may want to consider.

Objectives for Socio-Emotional Development

- Work cooperatively with others (working in pairs at the computer).
- Take responsibility for one's own work (directing the flow of a program).
- Develop perseverance (seeing a program or task through to completion).
- Take pride in one's accomplishments (making a printout of completed work).

Objectives for Cognitive Development

- Identify and sort objects by attributes such as color, shape, and size (using programs that develop classification skills).
- Learn sequencing and order (using programs that focus on size and patterning).
- Develop early reading skills (relating word labels to graphics).
- Understand cause and effect (seeing what happens when keys are pressed and feedback is given during a program).
- Extend creativity (using programs that encourage free explorations or simple graphics-creation programs).

COMPUTERS

Objectives for Physical Development

- Develop small muscle skills (putting a disk in the disk drive, clicking a computer mouse, using the keyboard).

- Refine eye and hand coordination (moving the cursor to a desired place on the screen).

- Improve visual skills (tracking movement on the screen).

These objectives are just some of the skills and knowledge children can develop when computers are

II. Arranging the Environment

Successful experiences with computers are tied to how the computer is integrated into the classroom. How you set up the computer area and the types of software you select make a crucial difference in whether children's experiences are successful or frustrating.

Creating Space

In deciding where to locate the computer area, ask yourself the following questions:

- Where can the computer be placed to be out of the line of traffic?
- Where can children concentrate and talk quietly?
- What other activity areas would be good to have close by—or far away?
- Where are there sufficient electrical outlets to support the equipment?
- Where are room dividers low enough for adults and other children to view computer activities?

If possible, locate the computer in a quiet part of the classroom, perhaps near the library. You'll want to avoid locating the computer too close to art, sand and water, or cooking activities because food, water, and paint can be harmful to the equipment. Low bookcases or other shelving can be used to define the space. The computer area should be out of the line of direct traffic but readily accessible. Good lighting is important, but try to avoid lighting that will cause glare on the computer screens. Equipment is best placed against a wall or partition to prevent children from tripping over wires or fiddling with the electrical outlets. This arrangement also allows children to view printouts of their work, which can be displayed on the wall facing them.

In selecting furnishings for the computer area, you'll need:

- a child-sized table or desks for the computers,
- two child-sized chairs per computer, and
- a table, stand, or shelf for a printer.

The setup illustrated here encourages group interaction. Typically, with this type of arrangement children share ideas, discuss what's going on, and help each other. The two-station approach also avoids long waits for the computer.

As with all learning centers, you'll want to promote independent use of the computer area. This means that children need to be able to get to the computers, the printer, and the software disks on their own.

Selecting Hardware

Computer hardware refers to the physical equipment itself. Hardware serves three major functions: (1) to get instructions (known as input) into the computer, (2) to process the received information, and (3) to display the results (known as output) to the user. A typical hardware setup is shown here:

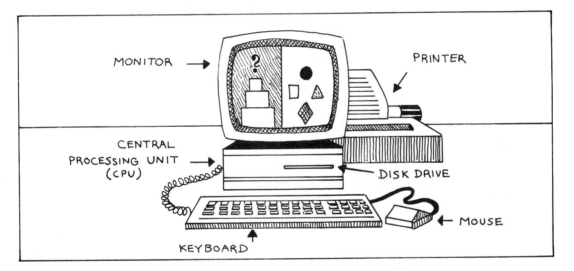

- *Central Processing Unit.* The CPU is the "brains" of a computer. Other hardware must be connected to the CPU in order to work.

- *Keyboard.* The keyboard allows you to type instructions to the CPU. Children need to learn only a few keys to run a program. These usually include return, delete, escape, the directional arrows, and adjust-number keys.

- *Mouse.* The mouse (a commonly available, hand-held hardware attachment) can be used to pass instructions to the computer in programs that are written to accept this kind of input. For many younger children, the larger-size mouse is easier to use than a keyboard.

- *Disk Drive.* The disk drive is the place where a disk containing a software program is inserted. At this time, two sizes of disks are generally available: 3-1/2" and 5-1/4".

- *Monitor.* The monitor is the TV-like screen that allows you to see what is going on with the program being used.

- *Printer.* The printer enables you to make a paper copy of your work on the computer.

One important consideration in selecting computer hardware is the availability of appropriate software; not all software runs on all computers. In general, early childhood software has been developed for use on three types of computers:

- Apple II series (primarily the Apple IIe and IIgs)/Macintosh II LC. (Note: In 1991, Apple introduced the Macintosh II LC. This "School Mac" runs with Macintosh software plus software developed for the Apple IIe with the addition of a board inserted into the CPU.)

- Commodore 64/128 series.

- IBM and IBM-compatible machines manufactured by Tandy, Zenith, and Epson, among others.

Currently about 85 percent of the available software for preschoolers and kindergarten children runs on the Apple II series or Macintosh II LC. Approximately one-third of the software is available in a Commodore version. Slightly less than one-third is available in an IBM or IBM-compatible version. Although much of this available software is not of the quality that would warrant its use in your classroom, you should be aware of the overall availability of software for each brand of computer.

Whatever model you select, the following is a suggested list of hardware plus a "wish list" for enhancing this area.

Basic System Hardware

- Two computers (of the same make), each with standard memory and one floppy disk drive. (Note: if your program cannot afford two computers, start with one.)

- Color monitors (color enhances the operation of many programs.)

- Standard keyboards.

- A mouse for each computer.

- A shared printer with color capability. (Note: Dot-matrix color printers are relatively inexpensive.)

- A T-switch for the printer, which allows two or more computers to use the same printer.

- A surge protector and cables.

Wish List Hardware

- Voice production equipment for computers. (Note: It is possible to produce both human-quality and synthesized speech, depending on the type selected.)

- Alternative input devices, such as a joystick, Power Pad, Touch Screen, or Koala Pad.

- Additional floppy disk drive or hard drive.

Finding Resources

The start-up costs for a computer area can be high. In addition to purchasing the equipment, you may also have to take additional precautions for security reasons, such as added insurance and locks for the door.

What can you do if you want to have a computer area but lack the resources? Many programs begin by actively seeking donations from local businesses. In some communities grocery store chains have created partnerships with schools. Parents and teachers are encouraged to save grocery sales receipts that can be exchanged for a new computer when a certain dollar amount is reached.

It's also helpful to check classified ads, yard sales, and charity auctions for possible equipment. Older computers can sometimes be found at bargain prices. These older models are outdated for business purposes but can make excellent additions to a classroom computer area.

You might also consider sharing a computer area with another classroom. Under this arrangement, the two classrooms share the costs of equipping the computer area and then rotate the area between their classrooms every six to eight weeks.

Ideally, the computer area includes two computers so that the opportunities for social interactions are maximized. However, if you have resources for only one computer, you can still set up an effective interest area. Work with what you have and modify this module's suggestions as necessary to accommodate your budget.

Selecting Software

Software is what makes the hardware useful. The programmed instructions contained on the software disks allow the user to play games, type stories, create art, and make music.

Your choices of software will be among the most important decisions you make in using a computer. A current review of software lists nearly 450 programs that are marketed as "appropriate" for the preschool classroom. Actually, about half of these programs are inappropriate. To find out which programs are truly appropriate, begin by consulting the experts. The following publications rate software annually:

1. *Survey of Early Childhood Software* by Warren Buckleitner, published by the High/ Scope Educational Research Foundation.

2. *Only the Best, Preschool-Grade 12* by Shirley Boss Neill and George W. Neill, published by R.R. Bowker.

3. *The Educational Software Selection* (TESS), published by EPIE Institute.

You can use these documents to find descriptions of available software that have been recognized by experts for excellence. In addition, you can consult the list of recommended software products at the end of this module for further guidance.

Learning How to Review Software

While expert opinions are a good starting point, you can learn how to review software yourself. New software programs are being written for young children constantly. Take a few moments to preview every software program you are considering. Most software publishers have a preview policy that allows you to do this. In addition, many school districts have resource centers where you can preview software. In assessing a particular program, check for the following features:

- *Age-Appropriateness.* To be developmentally appropriate, software should match children's skill levels. (Many software programs for preschoolers and kindergarteners on the market require cognitive abilities such as abstract thinking that are beyond the developmental levels of that age group.)

- *Child Control.* Look for software that children can use independently. (Some programs are highly structured and provide little opportunity for children to make choices.) A good program encourages children to skip around, decide what activities they want to do, and explore freely.

- *Fast Pacing.* Children respond positively to software that is fast-paced. (If children have to wait a long time for the program to load or for graphics to appear, they tend to lose interest.)

- *Concrete Representations.* Software that is "icon-driven" uses pictures to represent ideas or directions. Icon-driven software helps children who think concretely to work independently.

- *Clear Instructions.* Look for software with "help" screens that make use of graphics and are designed for nonreaders.

- *Open-Endedness.* Good software will actively engage children in exploration. The goal of children's computer play should be to learn from the process rather than to come up with a product or correct answers. The better software products allow children to be creative and solve problems.

- *Flexibility.* Because preschool and kindergarten children are at different developmental levels, the better software products will allow you and the child to set varying difficulty levels and to control features such as the speed of the program and the sound level.

If the software programs you are considering include the features highlighted above, you can feel confident that they are developmentally appropriate and suitable for use in your classroom. The checklist that follows provides you with a tool for reviewing and selecting software.

CHECKLIST FOR SELECTING DEVELOPMENTALLY APPROPRIATE SOFTWARE

	Item	Yes	No
1.	Program has age-appropriate content and approach		
2.	Child can use independently		
3.	Child can control movement through the program		
4.	Child can exit the program at any time		
5.	Program is reasonably fast-paced		
6.	There is always something on the screen for the child to view		
7.	Program is icon-driven (pictures used to represent words or ideas)		
8.	Instructions are clear		
9.	Instructions and program movement don't depend on reading skill		
10.	Program is process-oriented		
11.	Program offers open-ended exploration and choices		
12.	Program can be set at varying levels of difficulty		

Other Considerations in Selecting Software

In addition to the developmental appropriateness of the software, there are a few other considerations that will influence your choices. For example, you might want to know what teacher-support materials are available and if the programs have recordkeeping functions for tracking student progress, time on task, and so on. It may also be important to you for the children to have alternatives to using the keyboard, such as a joystick or mouse.

The critical consideration in selecting software is that it should meet the goals and objectives of the curriculum. Keep in mind that different software programs have different purposes. Some are intended to allow open-ended explorations. Others are intended to provide the child with tools that encourage the creative process. Still others are intended to help children acquire specific skills and concepts. Some of these take a direct teaching approach, while others provide a learning environment where children can practice developmental learning tasks. We encourage you to make selections that reflect what will best meet the children's learning needs and styles. Start with five to ten programs that are appropriate and add to your collection over time.

Displaying Materials

The layout of the equipment should be planned so that children can use the computers independently and so that social interaction is fostered. Children need to be able to comfortably work at the computer, use the keyboard or mouse, and reach the printer on their own. This means the use of child-sized furnishings and shelving at the child's eye level. In addition, if more than one computer station is being used, it's helpful to position the monitors close to one another to encourage social interaction between the children at both work stations.

Software should be kept where children can get at it independently. Because they won't be able to read the names off the disk labels, draw picture labels to help children identify the program disks. Drawing programs might have crayons on the outside; shape-recognition programs could feature circles, squares, and triangles. You don't need to be artistic in making labels; it's more important that you devise an icon-based (pictorial) system that will allow the children to recognize the content of each disk without having to ask for your assistance.

To store the disks, you might wish to use the plastic disk boxes made for storage, which can be purchased at any computer store. Or you might wish to make your own boxes, which could be organized according to functional topics such as drawing, shapes, color, size, gardening, time, and so on. Again, pictures and written labels can be placed on the outside of these boxes.

Other related computer supplies, such as printing paper, printer ribbons, or cartridges, should be controlled by the teacher and stored in the office or on a high shelf in the building.

Caring for Software and Hardware

The computer area should be located away from water, food, paint, and things that may become magnetized (scissors, knives, and staples). Children need to be aware that bringing food and water into the computer area is potentially harmful to the equipment and therefore not allowed.

Hands should always be clean when handling disks. Nothing will damage a disk faster than peanut-butter smudges! Heat is another potential hazard. Storing disks near a heating vent will cause them to warp. Also, the CPU itself should be located in a fairly cool area so that the hard drive won't be exposed to a lot of heat.

The best and easiest way to care for software is to make back-up copies of the program disks for routine use and to store the original disks in an office or storage closet. With continued use, most disks (especially the 5-1/4" floppies) eventually develop problems. By making and using back-up copies, you will always have a copy of the program available.

Assessing the Effectiveness of the Area

On an informal, ongoing basis, you'll want to observe the computer area to see how effectively it is being used. You can tell if changes need to be made to the environment or if new or different software should be added by asking yourself questions such as these:

- (If your program has two computer stations) do children working on one computer interact with children at the other computer?
- Do children prefer using a keyboard, mouse, or joystick (if all are available)?
- Do children talk about what they're doing and what they see?
- How long do children stay at the computer at one time?
- Are children getting software and using it without adult assistance?
- Do children ask to have their printouts displayed?
- Do girls use the computer area as much as boys?
- Is the computer area in great demand?

If children aren't actively talking with one another or sharing ideas, perhaps chairs need to be moved closer together. If children continually need adult assistance, they may be working on programs that are too advanced. If they don't help themselves to software, you may have to change the display area. On the other hand, if children appear active and happily engaged, the area is probably working as you have intended. By regularly assessing the computer area, you can ensure that the environment truly supports children's play with computers.

III. Observing and Promoting Children's Learning

The teacher's role in the *Creative Curriculum* is that of a facilitator. Through observation and thoughtful questioning, you can reinforce and promote children's involvement and learning in the computer area. It helps to be aware, as you observe, of how children typically use computers; in this way you can respond appropriately.

How Children Use a Computer

As with all learning, children use computers in developmental stages. The types of play you are likely to observe in your classroom are similar to those you've encountered in other interest areas.

During the first stage, which is **functional play** with computers, children investigate the computer under the supervision of an adult and later on their own. They see what happens to the screen when the "on" switch is flicked. They listen to the motor and see how the light flickers on the disk drive. They feel what it's like to press a key and to click a mouse. They learn how to put a disk in the disk drive. In this type of play, children explore the sights, sounds, and feel of the computer.

During **cause-and-effect play,** children become creative and thoughtful in their interactions. They look for answers to questions such as these: What happens when the disk is placed in the disk drive? What effect does clicking the mouse have? What happens on the screen if the return key is hit? By seeing that every action has an effect, children learn how to operate a program. Cause-and-effect play challenges children's thinking.

By learning to operate a program, children learn to follow directions, respond to feedback, and adjust and conform their actions. Such **games with rules** are embedded in most computer activities.

Introducing Children to Computers

It is essential to introduce children properly to computer hardware and software. By providing children with some initial directions for operating the equipment, you can give them the confidence to be able to use the area independently.

When you first introduce children to the area, encourage functional play with your guidance. As children explore the computer, you can comment on their actions, using simple and straightforward language. Then it's best to walk children through the use of a simple program that uses either a keyboard or a mouse and has a printout feature. (*Number Farm*, published by DLM, is a good beginning program that gives children hands-on practice in properly holding a disk, inserting it into the disk drive, moving keys or clicking a mouse, responding to feedback, and printing output.) As children work their way through the program, you can comment on the following:

- the need to hold a disk at the edges and not in its center,

- the location of various keys needed to operate the program,

- how a mouse can be used to move items on the screen,

- sounds to listen for that tell you that the printer is printing correctly, and

- how to tear off a printout.

It's probably best to introduce the computer to one or two children at a time or to a very small group.

Observing Individual Children

To support children's learning in the computer area, you'll want to observe the kinds of things they do so you can be sure that their experiences are positive. Try to observe specific children using the computer. As you watch these same children, think about the sample learning objectives presented at the beginning of this module as well as the individual objectives you've set for each child's growth and development. In addition, you might wish to consider these questions:

- Does the child take an active role in using the computer, or prefer to follow what other children are doing?

- Does the child use the computer independently or rely on adult assistance? Is the child unsure of how the computer works or is the program too advanced?

- Does the child try new software or continually repeat familiar programs?

- How long does the child stay engaged at the computer? Do I need to introduce more challenging programs or ones that are easier?

- How does the child respond to computer feedback? Can the child follow computer directions?

Based on your observations, you can design learning strategies that directly address each child's developmental needs.

Interacting with Children

One of the most important ways of encouraging children's computer play is to talk with them about their experiences. By so doing, you help children reflect on what they are doing and why. Your interactions can take place in separate stages, as discussed below.

Describing What Children Are Doing

As a first step, you can describe for the children what you see them doing. For example, you could discuss their:

- *interactions with the computer:* "When you pressed the return key, the screen changed," or "Clicking the mouse made the dollhouse light up."

- *use of the computer:* "You were able to put the disk in the right way the first time you tried."

- *reactions to feedback:* "You know just what to do to make the stars jump out of the hat."

- *social interactions:* "It didn't take very long for both of you to decide which program you wanted to use."

- *accomplishments:* "That's an interesting grouping you made of the animals at the farm. Let's print a copy of what you've done for all of us to look at."

Describing what they are doing lets children know you are interested in their play. By encouraging children to use the computer in their own ways, you allow them to be in control of their learning.

Encouraging Children to Talk About Their Actions

After children have heard you describe what they've done, they develop more confidence in their ability to use computers. The next step is to encourage children to put their actions into words by asking questions such as the following:

- "What happened when you pressed the escape key?"
- "How did you and Carly decide what program you would work on?"
- "What part of the program did you most enjoy using?"
- "Who was in charge of moving the mouse today?"
- "What printouts did you make?"
- "Kwasi was watching you and Cody use the computer. Did he help you boys work on the program?"
- "What did you work on after Talia left the computer station?"

When you ask questions like these, children see that you think their play experiences are valuable. Because you want to know more about what they're doing in the computer area, they realize this is an important place to be.

Asking Open-Ended Questions

Open-ended questions focused on what they are doing help children develop problem-solving skills. You can, for example, ask questions that encourage children to:

- *develop observation skills:* "What does the computer do when you put that disk into it?"
- *learn about cause and effect:* "What happens to the screen when you press the return key?"
- *make comparisons:* "Which program do you like best? Why is that?"
- *solve problems:* "How do we get back from the castle to the playroom?"
- *apply what they've learned:* "In the last program we clicked on the picture of the house if we wanted to return to the beginning of the program. What do you suppose we should click on here to get back to the beginning?"
- *learn to make predictions:* "What do you suppose will happen if I accidentally touch this escape key?"

Through your observations and conversations with children, you can promote each child's learning in the computer area.

IV. Extending and Integrating Children's Learning

The most natural way to extend children's learning in the computer area is to gradually introduce them to new software that will challenge them in different and exciting ways. If your budget permits, supplement your beginning inventory of five to ten programs with two or three new programs several times a year. By so doing, you add variety, interest, and increasing challenges for the children. At the same time, though, make sure that the children's favorites are always available to them. Many children find security in being able to go through a familiar program.

As you plan specific themes, you may want to look for software programs that address these topics. If, for example, you are planning a field trip to a farm, *Fun on the Farm* published by Polarware might be a suitable addition.

You can add software to your computer area in less expensive ways by critically previewing software that is in the public domain (and thus free to users) and programs known as "shareware," which offer users software for a minimal fee. Finally, if software has been purchased by your school or system, you can borrow from other classrooms or centers without breaking any copyright agreements. Keep in mind, however, that most commercial programs prohibit copying for distribution to others unless a special site license agreement is in place. Always read the terms of copying in the documentation that comes with the software, as restrictions vary from one publisher to another.

Integrating Computer Activities with Other Curriculum Areas

Although we know that it's important for children to use concrete materials in "hands-on" ways, many children enjoy recreating on the computer certain kinds of tasks they've tried while playing with table toys or engaging in art. You can use several strategies to help children practice these skills.

Mirroring

"Mirroring" is an instructional strategy that uses the computer to reinforce the exact same concepts teachers are working on with children in other interest areas. Mirroring is most often linked with manipulatives, although it can be readily used in conjunction with children's experiences with books and art, and with other curriculum areas.

You may be wondering if mirroring is necessary if children are already having these experiences through direct manipulation. The answer is that although mirroring isn't necessary, it's another option for reinforcement. The more ways a child is able to explore a concept, the more likely it is that the child will internalize that concept.

Mirroring also offers opportunities to extend children's learning. For example, children can use a computer program that mirrors attribute blocks to put blocks together into new shapes and designs. Familiar concepts are thus explored in new and exciting ways.

Several computer programs that have been specifically designed for use in mirroring include these:

- *Gertrude's Secrets*, published by The Learning Company (to mirror attribute blocks).

- *Building Perspective,* published by Sunburst (to mirror Cuisenaire Rods).

- *Electric Lines,* published by Sunburst (to mirror the geoboard).

312

- *Puzzle Tanks,* published by Sunburst (to mirror water play).
- *Moptown Parade* and *Moptown Hotel*, published by The Learning Company (to mirror people pieces).

Of course, you don't need to limit your mirroring to programs specifically designed for this purpose. As you become familiar with software, you'll be able to tell which programs would make good mirrors for activities in other interest areas of your classroom.

Language Development and Emerging Literacy

Computers offer another resource for helping children develop language. Here are some ways that you can use computers to help children develop emerging literacy skills.

- ***Linking words to pictures***. Just as picture books in the library corner can be used to help children attach written labels to objects, so too can computer programs be used to make this connection.
- ***Creating a story***. Some of the best programs on the market today allow you to work with children in creating their own stories in print. Just as you might write down a child's story to go with a picture the child has drawn, these programs allow you to capture the child's words on the computer. As you type letters on the screen, words appear in large font sizes. Some programs have the capability of "reading" printed words and sentences out loud. Children can then illustrate their stories.

Emerging Math Skills

You'll find programs available on key math concepts such as patterning, classification, seriation, one-to-one correspondence, counting and number relationships. Here is just a sampling of the many ways in which you can reinforce math learning in the computer area:

- ***Patterning***. Seeing how objects and eventually numbers relate builds a concrete understanding of math. Patterning software can provide children with practice in seeing relationships and predicting what comes next in a series. These software programs can readily be related to hands-on experiences with parquetry blocks or to music and movement exercises in which children snap patterns with their fingers and form patterns with their bodies.
- ***Classification***. Learning to identify and sort objects by their attributes is basic to both math and science. Classification activities go on in every interest area and can be reinforced in the computer area. Classification software encourages children to group objects by attributes such as size, color, and shape as well as to create groupings of their own design.
- ***Seriation***. During the preschool and kindergarten years, children learn to order an array of objects by size. Just as they arrange blocks from tallest to shortest in the block area, they can order objects on a computer.
- ***One-to-One Correspondence***. A preliminary step in understanding numbers is to learn how numbers correspond to real-life objects. When Matthew fits five pieces into the frame of a five-piece puzzle, he learns that the number of puzzle pieces corresponds to the space available for these pieces: in other words, there is a one-to-

one correspondence. Similarly, when Kisha passes out cups for juice to the four places at her table, she sees that she has used four cups. This concept is a difficult one for many young children to grasp because it involves moving from the concrete world of objects to the abstract world of numbers. A good computer program can help children make this transition.

- *Numerical Relationships*. Mastering concepts such as "more than," and "less than," and "the same as" is an important skill for understanding mathematics. Several software programs are specifically designed to give children practice learning these numerical relationships.

Art Experiences

The computer is also a medium for children to use for experimentation with color, shape, and design. Just as they would use crayons on paper or paint at an easel, children can use the "tools" available in a graphics program to create art. The better drawing programs, such as *Color Me!* (published by the Society for Visual Education), are icon-driven, which means that children can use the program independently.

The socio-emotional and creative benefits of drawing and painting can be gained as children select colors to fit their moods. Art programs can also be helpful in stimulating children's cognitive development, as they challenge the artist to figure out how to fill the screen, where to place objects, and in some cases how to use objects such as squares, circles, and triangles to make designs.

Using Computers with Children with Disabilities

Many special educators have found that the microcomputer is an effective learning tool for children with disabilities. Because it presents small bits of information in a planned sequence and offers repetition, individualized instruction, and immediate feedback, the computer is well-suited to special-needs children. Studies of children with developmental delays show that they enjoy and learn from computer experiences. Moreover, preschool and kindergarten children with attention-related problems seem to respond to computers in the same ways that children without disabilities do. Both groups of children can be happily engaged at computer activities for 15 to 30 minutes and more.

For children with mild developmental delays—the most common type of disability in young children—you don't have to alter your approach to the computer area. The benefit of the computer is its ability to respond to individual children's needs. This means that children with developmental delays can get the repetition and reinforcement they need simply by using the program as any other user would. You might consider pairing a child with developmental delays with a child who is not disabled; in this setting, the more skilled child will be able to encourage and boost the confidence of the other child. In cooperative learning experiences, both children can be enriched by their time at the computer.

For children who have vision-related or physical disabilities, there are any number of innovative adaptive devices that can be added to a computer station to make computers accessible. The chart that follows lists some of the more popular adaptive devices, the disability they address, and information on what they do.

COMPUTERS

COMPUTER ADAPTIVE DEVICES

Device	Problem Addressed	What Device Does
Large-size monitor	Vision impairment	Enlarges everything on the screen
Software magnification lenses	Vision impairment	Enlarges screen images
Speech synthesizer	Blindness/ severe vision impairment	When combined with speakers, can be used to read text on a screen
Voice-recognition system	Physical handicaps (lack of manual dexterity)	Accepts voice commands as input
Headpointer and mouth stick	Physical handicaps (lack of manual dexterity)	Provides an alternative for children with good head control
Keyguards	Physical handicaps (manual dexterity problems)	Prevents user from accidentally pushing wrong keys
Expanded keyboard	Physical handicaps (manual dexterity problems)	Provides more space for keys and can be positioned in an accessible location
Head-controlled mouse	Physical handicaps (lack of manual dexterity)	Mouse controlled by movements of the head

The foregoing list is just a sampling of the many exciting developments in this field. If you wish to make use of adaptive devices in your classroom or are interested in learning more about including children with disabilities in the computer area, there are several organizations you should know about:

- Foundation for Technology Access
  1307 Solano Avenue
  Albany, CA 94707

  A network of nonprofit resource centers that specialize in using computers to help people with disabilities.

- Center for Special Education Technology
  Council for Exceptional Children
  1920 Association Drive
  Reston, VA 22091

  A federally funded national exchange designed to promote the use of technology in special education.

- Trace Research and Development Center
  S-151 Waisman Center
  1500 Highland Avenue
  Madison, WI 53705

  A leader in the development of adaptive devices that maintains a database of every available adaptive product.

- Closing the Gap
  P.O. Box 68
  Henderson, MN 56044

  A national organization dedicated to providing training and disseminating information on adaptive computer technologies.

In this section we have explored some of the creative ways you can use computers to reinforce and extend children's learning, and to meet the individual needs of children.

V. Sharing Computers with Parents

Throughout the *Creative Curriculum*, we have emphasized the importance of reinforcing what children do in school with the messages they receive at home. When parents and teachers both support the use of computers, children learn that this is a valuable activity. In general, most parents are already convinced of the value of computer literacy. Therefore, you are likely to find parents are supportive of your work with children and computers.

Conducting Workshops on Computers

In planning a workshop for parents, consider what topics you feel are most important to cover. For example, you might want to let parents know how computer play supports children's growth in many areas, not just cognitive. You can show parents how you have arranged the computer area to make it a hub of social activity, sharing, and cooperative play. You might want to demonstrate that in using computers, children refine physical skills, improve their coordination, and learn to track objects visually.

The best approach is to plan a "hands-on" workshop in the computer area, where parents will be able to interact with computers in the same ways that children do. Some topics you might wish to cover could include:

- what computer literacy means at the preschool and kindergarten level,
- how to determine which software is appropriate for young children and why,
- how computers can help develop pre-math and pre-literacy skills,
- how computers support children's creativity, and
- what the adult's role should be.

To supplement this workshop, you might wish to reproduce (with permission) some of the articles cited in the Appendix. These will provide you with research-based support for your presentation.

Involving Parents in the Classroom

Another way to help parents understand your approach to using computers is to invite them to learn about computers along with their children. In the beginning of the school year, you might consider holding several Saturday or evening workshops to which parents could bring their children. Children and parents alike would then be introduced to computer basics—loading a program, using the keyboard and mouse, working through a program, care of the computer area, and so on. During these training sessions you might want to supplement your inventory with software that adults could use to develop their own skills. In this way, the computer area can help families—not just children— grow and develop.

Some of the benefits of involving parents in using computers with the children include the following:

- Parents who know nothing about computers can themselves learn computer literacy skills in a warm, nonthreatening environment.

- Parents who are familiar with computers can share their knowledge with the children.

- Parents gain a better appreciation of what their children are learning.

- Children gain a rare opportunity to do an "adult" activity alongside their parents.

- Children receive the message that the computer area is a valuable place to be because both their parents and teachers are working alongside them.

- Children have an added opportunity to spend time with their parents.

To involve parents in the classroom, make your computer area open to parents as much as possible. Let parents know that they are always free to visit and participate. If appropriate, encourage parents to serve as volunteers assisting children in using the computer.

The following letter to parents on computers may need to be adapted to suit your own program. It is offered here as a sample.

A Letter to Parents on Computers

What We Do and Why

In our program we have a special activity area where the children "play" with computers. While this may sound like a strange way of describing what children do with computers, this is in fact what goes on. The children experiment, using programs that help them develop in many exciting ways. Here are some of the things that children learn when they use computers:

- math skills and concepts such as counting and numerical relationships,
- beginning reading concepts,
- how to express creativity, and
- how to solve problems.

We encourage children to work at the computer in pairs. This helps them learn from each other and develops their social skills at the same time. While the children are working at the computer, we ask them questions such as these to help them think about what they're doing:

- "What made you decide to choose this program to work on?"

- "What do you suppose will happen if you press the escape key?"

- "How can you make the program move to something you've never played with before?"

- "What printouts did you decide to make today?"

By working with children in these ways, we not only encourage their growth and development but also help prepare them for a future in which they will need to know how to work with computers.

What You Can Do at Home

You may or may not have a computer in your home. It is certainly not necessary that you do have one in order for your child to benefit from the computer area. If you do have a home computer and would like to know some things that you can do with your child at home, please contact us. We will be glad to provide you with assistance, including how to judge which programs are appropriate for use with young children. We have some good information on this topic that we'd like to share with you.

You may be interested in visiting our program to observe how children use computers. If you'd like to volunteer to work with children in the computer area, we'd be delighted to have your help. Also, our program offers introductory instruction on using the computer for parents and children together. This can be an exciting opportunity for you to learn about computers side-by-side with your child.

VI. Recommended Software and Publishers

Here is a listing of some of the better software for preschool and kindergarten children. This listing is by no means complete; it is intended as a starting point for assembling a classroom inventory. Begin with a few programs and add gradually throughout the year.

Programs that Support Emergent Literacy

The Bald-Headed Chicken (D.C. Heath & Co.)
A Brand New View (D.C. Heath & Co.)
Cotton Tales (Mind Play)
Dr. Peet's Talk/Writer (Hartley Courseware)
FirstWriter (Houghton Mifflin Co.)
A Great Leap (D.C. Heath & Co.)
Just Around the Block (D.C. Heath & Co.)
Kermit's Electronic Storymaker (Joyce Hakansson Associates)
Keytalk (P.E.A.L. Software)
Kid Talk (First Byte, Inc.)
Magic Slate (Sunburst Communications)
Muppet Slate (Sunburst Communications)
Muppet Word Book (Sunburst Communications)
My Words (Hartley Communications)
Not Too Messy, Not Too Neat ((D.C. Heath & Co.)
Paint with Words (MECC)
The Puzzle Storybook (First Byte, Inc.)
Reading Magic Library: Floyd, The Bad Guy (Tom Snyder)
Reading Magic Library: Jack and the Beanstalk (Tom Snyder)
Talking Nouns I and II (Laureate Learning Systems)
Tiger's Tales (Sunburst Communications)
The Sleepy Brown Cow (D.C. Heath & Co.)
What Makes a Dinosaur Sore? (D.C. Heath & Co.)
Where Did My Toothbrush Go? (D.C. Heath & Co.)
Words & Concepts I, II, and III (Laureate Learning Systems)
1-2-3 Sequence Me (Sunburst Communications)

Programs That Support Emergent Mathematical Thinking

Balancing Bear (Sunburst Communications)
City Country Opposites (Random House Software)
Comparison Kitchen (DLM)
Conservation and Counting (Hartley Courseware)
Counting Critters 10 (MECC)
Curious George Goes Shopping; Curious George in Outer Space; Curious George Visits the Library (DLM)

Easy Street (Mind Play)
First Shapes (First Byte, Inc.)
Gertrude's Secrets (The Learning Company)
Grover's Animal Adventures (Hi Tech Expressions)
Inside Outside Shapes (Random House Software)
Learning About Numbers (C&C Software)
Learning with Fuzzywump (Sierra On-Line)
Make a Match (Springboard)
Match-on-a-Mac (Teach Yourself by Computer)
Math and Me (Davidson and Associates)
Math Rabbit (The Learning Company)
Muppetville (Sunburst Communications)
Number Farm (DLM)
Observation and Classification (Hartley Courseware)
Odd One Out (Sunburst Communications)
Patterns (MECC)
Patterns and Squares (Hartley Courseware)
Pockets Leads the Parade (World Book, Inc.)
Puzzle Master (Springboard)
Shape & Color Rodeo (DLM)
Size and Logic (Hartley Courseware)
Teddy and Iggy (Sunburst Communications)
Teddy's Playground (Sunburst Communications)
What's Next (Strawberry Hill Software)

Drawing Programs

Color Me! (Society for Visual Education)
The Extrateletactograph (DIL International)
Koala Pad Graphics Exhibitor (PTI/Koala Industries)
Magic Crayon (C&C Software)

Creative Exploration Programs

Fantastic Animals (Firebird Licenses, Inc.)
McGee (Lawrence Productions)
Mask Parade (Springboard)
Mr. and Mrs. Potato Head (Random House Software)
The Playroom (Broderbund)
Stickers (Springboard)

Utility Programs

The Print Shop (Broderbund)
SuperPrint! (Scholastic Software)

Addresses for the publishers referenced in this listing are as follows:

Broderbund Software
17 Paul Drive
San Mateo, CA 94903

C&C Software
5213 Kentford Circle
Wichita, KS 67220

Davidson and Associates, Inc.
6069 Grove Oak Place, #12
Rancho Palos Verdes, CA 90272

D.C. Heath & Co.
125 Spring Street
Lexington, MA 02173

DIL International
2025 Lavoisier Street, #180
Sainte-Foy, Quebec, CANADA G1V
1N6

DLM
One DLM Park
Allen, TX 75002

Firebird Licensees, Inc.
71 Franklin Turnpike
Waldwich, NJ 07463

First Byte, Inc.
333 East Spring Street, #302
Long Beach, CA 90806

Hartley Courseware
Box 419
Dimondale, MI 48821

Hi Tech Expressions
1700 N.W. 65th Avenue, #9
Plantation, FL 33313

Joyce Hakansson Associates, Inc.
2029 Durant
Berkeley, CA 94703

Laureate Learning Systems
110 East Spring Street
Winooski, VT 05404

Lawrence Productions
1800 S. 35th Street
Galesburg, MI 49053

The Learning Company
10493 Kaiser Drive
Fremont, CA 94555

Learning Technologies, Inc.
4255 LBJ Freeway, #131
Dallas, TX 75244

MECC (Minnesota Educational Copyrighting
Consortium)
3490 Lexington Avenue North
St. Paul, MN 55126

MindPlay
100 Conifer Hill Drive
Danvers, MA 01923

P.E.A.L. Software
5000 North Parkway
Calabasas Suite 105
Calabasas, CA 91302

Polarware, Inc.
1600 Keslinger Road
P.O. Box 311
Geneva, IL 60134

PTI/Koala Industries
269 Mount Herman Road
Scotts Valley, CA 95066

Random House Software
400 Harbor Road
Westminster, MD 21157

Scholastic Software
730 Broadway
New York, NY 10003

Society for Visual Education
1345 Deversey Parkway
Chicago, IL 60615

Sierra On-Line
Sierra On-Line Building
Coarsegold, CA 93614

Spinnaker Software Co.
One Kendall Square
Cambridge, MA 02139

Springboard Publications
7808 Creekridge Circle
Minneapolis, MN 55435

Sunburst Communications
39 Washington Avenue
Pleasantville, NY 10570

Tom Snyder Productions, Inc.
90 Sherman Street
Cambridge, MA 02140

World Book, Inc.
Merchandise Mart Plaza
Chicago, IL 60654

OUTDOORS

I. Why Outdoor Play Is Important

Outdoor play is fun for children and important for their growth and development. Children advance in all areas of development when adults carefully organize the outdoor environment and plan for its use.

Many different types of outdoor areas can provide rich settings for learning. The outdoor area may be an open grassy space or a blacktop area where children can engage in group games, ride wheeled toys, or run freely. Sandboxes and small playhouses are also common. There may be enough space for a picnic table. The natural landscape around most centers offers many new objects to observe and collect and textures to examine. Some programs have their own playgrounds with equipment specifically designed for young children; others may depend on nearby public playgrounds.

Because the outdoor environment is not defined by walls, it can be more than a single play area. Play and learning can take place as the group explores the local neighborhood and nearby parks, hills, ponds, streams, or lakes. Trips to forest preserves, nature centers, or farms also enhance children's outdoor experiences.

Opportunities to climb, run, jump, skip, hop, throw, catch, and use their "outside" voices provide children with a healthy release and break from the quieter activities of the classroom. Being outside allows children to stretch their muscles, breathe in fresh air, take in sunshine, and enjoy the freedom of space.

What goes on outdoors, however, is much more than physical activity. The special qualities of the outdoor environment set the stage for unique experiences. Science, for example, comes alive when nature is explored and observed firsthand. Children can watch plants grow and follow the change of seasons. As children see leaves change color, taste snow, touch the bark of a tree, hear crickets, or smell the air after a rain shower, they are using all their senses to learn about the world. Art, music, reading, dramatic play, constructive play, social play, and caring for pets can all take place outdoors.

Just as you design and organize the indoor space to ensure that children are exposed to activities and materials that support growth and development, so you must give careful thought to planning and using whatever outdoor space is available. Regardless of its size and shape, any outside area can become a setting for young children's learning.

Objectives for Children's Learning

The large spaces typical of outdoor environments are perfect for children to develop large muscle skills such as running and climbing. Using playground equipment also promotes upper and lower body strength, balance, and coordination.

In the *Creative Curriculum*, the outdoor environment is viewed as an extension of the indoor classroom. This means that the types of learning (socio-emotional, cognitive, and physical) that take place indoors also take place outdoors. The following objectives are intended as a starting point.

Objectives for Socio-Emotional Development

- Demonstrate social skills (pushing and being pushed on swings, helping care for a garden, participating in social play with peers).
- Take turns, negotiate compromises, and cooperate (using playground equipment, sharing art materials, playing group games).
- Express creativity (making art, sand, and woodworking creations, developing a new game).
- Enhance self-esteem (learning to use small and large muscles in competent ways).
- Increase independence (climbing a stepladder or going down a slide unassisted).
- Demonstrate pride in accomplishments (performing physical feats, caring for pets, growing plants from seeds).

Objectives for Cognitive Development

- Make decisions (choosing an outdoor activity).
- Plan and carry through ideas (playing games, building sand structures, doing woodwork, creating artwork, growing plants).
- Solve problems (making a tunnel through sand, getting from one place to another on playground equipment, connecting two pieces of wood).
- Reenact life experiences (playing ambulance driver, painting a fence with water, washing dolls or dishes).
- Identify cause and effect (making sand hold together by adding just the right amount of water, running through a sprinkler and getting wet).
- Learn about science (taking nature walks, observing growth in the garden, seeing outdoor animals in their habitat, noting seasonal changes).
- Develop an understanding of basic math concepts (counting jumps or hops, estimating distance, measuring the growth of plants).
- Increase vocabulary (conversing in the sandbox or at the woodworking table, acquiring new names for plants, animals, and objects found in nature).

Objectives for Physical Development

- Develop large muscle skills (climbing, swinging, jumping, skipping, running).
- Develop small muscle skills (playing with sand and water, drawing, painting, picking up small objects).
- Coordinate eye-hand movements (catching, throwing, woodworking, decorating the sidewalk with chalk).
- Improve balance (climbing, swinging, sliding, using the balance beam, using spring-rocking equipment, hopping, walking on different surfaces).

- Increase spatial awareness (swinging, climbing up, down, in, out, over, and under).

- Demonstrate persistence and endurance (playing group games, climbing on playground equipment or pumping on a swing for an extended period, banging nails into a tree stump).

These objectives are offered as examples of the many ways that outdoor play can promote children's learning and development. You can use them to help plan an outdoor program that will best suit the needs and interests of the children in your group.

II. Arranging the Outdoor Environment

Probably no other area of an early childhood learning environment varies as much in layout and appearance as does the outdoor area. Some programs have large outdoor areas complete with a playground structure designed for young children. Others have smaller areas with very little or no playground equipment. Whether your outdoor area is spacious or limited, you can provide children with many meaningful outdoor activities. In addition to arranging your own outdoor environment, you can enrich children's learning experiences by taking advantage of nearby public parks, playgrounds, and other spaces and by exploring the surrounding neighborhood.

Creating Space

In planning for outdoor play, a good way to start is to consider the variety of experiences you want to offer the children. There should be active and quiet areas as well as places for children to play together and to be alone. In assessing the space you have for outdoor play, you might ask yourself the following questions:

- Is the space large enough to accommodate all the children in the group? (Most experts recommend 80 to 100 square feet per child.)

- Will adults have an unobstructed view of the children at all times?

- Is there both sun and shade in the outdoor area?

- Is there enough equipment and materials so that children don't have to stand in line or fight for a place to play?

- Is there a variety of age-appropriate equipment and materials?

- Are there areas for active and group play as well as for quiet and individual play?

- Are there clear pathways for children to follow so that traffic patterns do not conflict?

- Is the outdoor area defined so that children know where the play area begins and ends?

- Is there adequate protection from vehicular traffic?

- Are water fountains and bathrooms easily accessible?

- Have drainage areas, electrical wires, and other hazardous equipment been covered?

- Is the area free of debris?

The outdoor area should be inviting for all children, no matter how varied their interests, physical abilities, or learning styles. Consider including the following activity areas:

- playground equipment,
- digging and pouring,
- riding,
- quiet play,
- pet play,
- gardening, and
- woodworking.

You can adapt the design of these areas to fit the constraints of your outdoor area. If space is limited, you may have to cut back or combine interest areas. For example, the riding area can be used for woodworking and the quiet area for art or group games.

The key to successful use of the outdoor area is safe, easy-to-follow traffic patterns. Children should have a clear idea of what activities are done where; signs illustrating activities can be posted. With clearly designated areas, it is possible to avoid accidents, confusion, and hurt feelings and to ensure learning and enjoyment.

Playground Equipment Area

Children of all ages love playing on playground equipment. They especially enjoy opportunities to climb, slide, swing, jump, chin, and hang. Children's developmental levels must be taken into account when selecting playground equipment. A play area can be both exciting and safe when playground equipment is challenging enough to invite use but not so challenging that it becomes dangerous.

As young children develop increasing strength, body coordination, and balance, they benefit from varied opportunities to develop and practice new skills on playground equipment. They also gain self-esteem and learn to share and cooperate. Playground equipment that children can safely enjoy includes the following:

- balance beams and log structures
- ramps
- short sliding poles
- chinning bars

- stairways and stepladders
- platforms
- net climbers
- tire climbers
- arch ladders
- suspension bridges
- tunnels
- conventional swings

- overhead horizontal ladders (note that many children under four can't safely negotiate upper-body devices)
- conventional swings
- tire swings
- slides
- spring rockers

Not all early childhood programs have their own outdoor area with playground equipment adjacent to the classroom. Many programs use nearby public parks and playgrounds for outdoor play. Even those programs with their own equipment sometimes go to a park for a change of pace and to provide children with more varied experiences. In considering the use of a public playground, you might ask yourself the following questions:

- Is the playground close enough so that children can walk there without becoming too tired to play?

- Is the playground well-maintained? Is equipment in good repair? Is the ground free of litter and debris?

- Is the equipment appropriate for the age of the children?

- Are there tables at the playground for quiet activities such as reading or drawing?

- Is there a water fountain? If so, is its size scaled for children?

- Does the playground have clearly defined boundaries so that children know where they can and cannot play?

Because children's rates of physical development vary greatly, playground equipment and activities must be designed to suit various skill levels. Different children will use the same equipment in different ways. Knowing children's individual abilities will enable you to help them pace themselves.

Digging and Pouring Area

The sandbox is a favorite area, particularly for younger preschoolers, and can be just as challenging for older children. A good sand area is large enough for several children to play either alone or together without feeling crowded. Locating this area close to a water supply such as outdoor faucets or water fountains allows children to experiment with both wet and dry sand. If this is not possible, consider making pails, pitchers, or spray bottles of water available for use in the sand area.

Here are some suggested additions to enhance digging, pouring, constructive, and dramatic play in this area:

- plastic and metal buckets, bowls, and pails with handles
- shovels, spoons, and scoops of all sizes
- funnels and sifters
- pots, pans, and molds
- plastic pitchers and jugs
- sand or water pumps and wheels

- small wheelbarrows
- old trucks, cars, fire engines, and trains
- plastic people and animals
- popsicle sticks
- small cardboard boxes and old or plastic blocks
- natural objects such as shells, sticks, stones, or leaves

Many children use the sand area as a setting for dramatic play. For example, children may begin "cooking," and poured sand then becomes cake batter or a cup of coffee. If children show interest in such activity, you might add cups and saucers, measuring spoons and cups, mixing bowls, and muffin tins. Prop boxes supporting farm or camping themes can also be brought to the sand area to promote children's pretend play.

In setting up the sandbox area, it's wise to consider sanitation concerns. Cats and other roaming animals are likely to regard the sandbox as a litter box if the area is unprotected. This problem can be solved by using a hinged top or plastic tarp to cover the sandbox when it's not in use.

Riding Area

Most children enjoy using tricycles, "big wheels," scooters, and wagons. These riding toys build large muscle strength while promoting balance and coordination.

The riding area needs a hard surface. Pulling and pushing wheeled toys and skills such as peddling, maintaining balance, starting, and stopping are all more easily mastered on a hard surface. Children who are well coordinated might also enjoy trying out roller skates.

You can enhance children's use of this area by adding signs, chalk road markers, directional arrows, and big orange cones to control traffic. Here too, prop boxes can extend play activities. A hospital prop box, for example, can turn bike riders into ambulance drivers. Children also enjoy using tricycles and the like in conjunction with fire, police, and mail delivery props. Similarly, you can introduce ideas or materials to support gas station or car wash experiences.

Along with riding toys, children will enjoy and can benefit from playing with jump ropes, Hula Hoops, and balls of many different shapes and sizes. Play with these materials, as well as some art activities, can take place on either an open grassy space or a hard surface area.

Quiet Play Area

As noted earlier, one important feature of an appropriate outdoor area is a place specifically designed for quiet activities. Although much of what takes place outdoors is lively and loud, children sometimes want to retreat from the bustle of climbing, riding, and shouting. They may need to take a step back from high-activity levels and relax with quiet, soothing activities.

Ideally, quiet outdoor areas should be located in the shade so that children can literally "cool off." The area might include places to sit—such as a blanket on a grass area or a picnic table near a tree— so that children can be comfortable. The quiet area can be equipped with materials that offer the child something to do, not just something to get away from. The following types of materials are suggested:

- crayons, chalk, and paper,
- books,
- a tape recorder and tapes,
- paints and easels,
- quiet board games with large pieces, and
- sawhorses and a blanket to make shade or a playhouse.

Another option for the quiet area is a small playhouse constructed of wood or a commercially bought plastic structure. A playhouse provides a retreat for children while also promoting dramatic play.

Garden Area

Learning from books how plants grow is one thing, but seeing this happen outdoors is quite another experience. When it comes to science, the outdoor environment is the perfect laboratory for learning.

A garden area offers a choice opportunity for combining enjoyment and learning. Depending on the availability of land, the garden area might be used to grow flowers or to plant a vegetable garden large enough to produce food for snacks. Most children are thrilled to see the seeds they have planted blossom into flowers and vegetables.

Suggested materials for the garden area include:

- several sets of garden tools,
- a wheelbarrow,
- seeds or plants,
- bags of dirt and fertilizer,

- access to water,
- watering cans and hoses, and
- string and wood to mark off the rows.

If possible, it's a good idea to locate the garden area away from more active outdoor areas and out of the way of heavy play traffic. One possibility is to use a different side of the building from those where other outdoor play takes place. For instance, flower beds can be planted near the front door; in this location, parents are likely to observe and enjoy their children's gardening activities. Another way of making gardening possible when space is limited is to plant your garden in a wheelbarrow, wagon, truck tires, or large pots. The advantage of using a wheelbarrow or wagon is that you can move them around to control the amount of sun your garden gets.

Pet Area

Having pets teaches children to care for animals and to be responsible for them. Rabbits, hamsters, gerbils, and guinea pigs are common pets in early childhood programs, although some programs have parrots, fish, lizards, and snakes. It is important to check licensing requirements before bringing in pets. Administrators, boards, and leasing agents should also be consulted ahead of time to ensure that there are no objections.

Cages for pets should be large enough for them to move around without getting hurt. They may have to be cleaned frequently. The location of the cage is important, as animals must be protected from weather and other animals if left out all night. In some cases, it may be best to take pets inside at night.

Even very young children can learn to care for pets. They may need your guidance in learning how to handle, hold, and pet animals without injuring them. Pets can get sick if given food that isn't in their diets. Labeled cans for pet food help children learn what their pets can eat.

Including pets in the outdoor area is an added responsibility for teachers. However, the lessons children learn from having pets are invaluable for social and emotional development. Having pets gives children a chance to work on responsibility, empathy, and caring. Children can observe growth, change, and the habits of a live animal. They can learn about birth, life styles, and sometimes death.

Woodworking Area

The outdoor area is an excellent location for woodworking. Activities with tools and wood can be as simple as banging nails into a large tree stump or as sophisticated as working at a workbench with tools, lumber, and assorted objects for decorating constructions.

Because children in this area are often intensely involved in what they are doing, it's helpful to locate the woodworking area in a place where children will not be disturbed. You will also want to have an unobstructed view of the woodworking area so that you can intervene at any moment in case an unsafe activity occurs.

If you have a workbench for your woodworking area, be sure it is sturdy and at an appropriate height for children—approximately waist level. If children will be sawing, the workbench should be equipped with C-clamps or vises to hold the wood securely.

Tools can be kept in a sturdy wooden box or hung on a pegboard with outlines to show where each tool belongs. It is important to protect tools, as many will rust if they get wet. A basic set of tools includes the following:

- claw hammers (11-13 oz.),
- cross-cut saws (12-16 oz.),
- assorted nails with large heads,
- hand drills,
- rulers,
- metal files and sand paper, and
- scraps of soft wood (pine) in assorted sizes.

Good sources for wood scraps may be parents, lumber yards, local carpenters, craftspeople, and furniture makers. Be sure to check all wood for splinters, broken-off nails, or other hazards before it is used by the children.

At first, children will enjoy experimenting with real tools and wood. Learning to use a saw, drill holes in wood, and hammer a nail into wood will be satisfying enough to maintain interest in the area for quite some time. As children gain skills, they will respond positively to the addition of new materials. Here are some suggestions:

- dowels
- popsicle sticks
- corks
- wire
- wooden spools
- Elmer's glue
- yarn and string
- styrofoam
- feathers
- bottle caps

Sometimes children like to paint the things they make at the workbench. Tempera paint from the art area can be brought outdoors, or the constructions can be brought inside for painting.

Storing Materials

Because most outside materials and equipment cannot be left unattended or exposed, many teachers wonder what to do about the problem of having to carry materials from inside to the outside area on a daily basis. One solution is to build a storage shed. Parents, senior citizen groups, or local industrial art classes can frequently be convinced to volunteer their services for a special building project. Alternatively, a shed can be purchased from a lumber yard and assembled as part of a class project. Depending on the shed's materials, its outer walls may make a wonderful mural area for children to paint.

Within the shed, the storage space can be organized into separate areas for various types of materials and supplies. For example, one section can be reserved for sand and water toys and another reserved for balls. Paint or tape can mark off areas on the floor for storing larger equipment such as signs and big orange cones used in the riding area. Hooks can be put up on the walls to hold Hula Hoops, jump ropes, and some gardening tools. Large, heavy-duty shelves can also help keep the storage shed more organized. Plastic milk crates are good for containing outdoor materials as they allow for drainage and air circulation. Children can easily carry an empty crate out to the digging and pouring area, for example, to collect the toys; they can then work together to carry the full crate back to the storage shed. Similarly, large laundry baskets (particularly tall ones) with holes for ventilation can be used to hold bigger outdoor materials such as balls.

Legal and Safety Concerns

Because many injuries occur outdoors, legal and safety concerns are especially important in this area. Most states have licensing laws and regulations that define minimum requirements for an outdoor play space. These laws usually set requirements for the number of square feet of area needed, access to the play area, fencing, basic safety regulations, and specifications for playground equipment. Counties often have additional requirements. All teachers and administrators should be familiar with both state and local laws and ensure that their outdoor play areas are in compliance.

Safety Is a Primary Concern

Because of the many different types of activities that take place outdoors and the variety of playground equipment in use, keeping children safe is no easy task. One factor to consider is the age-appropriateness of equipment and materials with respect to children's physical size as well as their cognitive and socio-emotional development. Injuries are less likely to occur when the design of equipment and materials matches children's sizes and skills.

It is essential to balance challenge and risk when planning outdoor play environment. The play area, including playground equipment, should present children with challenge—because challenges promote growth and learning. An optimal outdoor environment provides a series of graduated challenges so that children can progressively increase and test their skills. Adults must be careful, however, to ensure that the challenges are ones that children can perceive and choose to undertake. When an activity can lead to a hazardous outcome that children can't anticipate, a challenge becomes a risk. It is the role of adults to eliminate such hazards and unnecessary risks.

Why Young Children Get in Trouble on Playground Equipment

Although the playground equipment area is often referred to as "the most fun" by children, it is also the outdoor area in which most injuries occur. Young children are experimenters by nature; they're eager to explore the many ways in which playground equipment can provide fun and excitement. However, developmental factors beyond physical skill need to be considered in determining children's safety during this exploration. Some of these include the following:

- *A tendency to focus on only one aspect of a situation.* For example, intent on climbing to the top of a playground structure, a child is unlikely to see the danger he might be creating for other children (e.g., pushing another child out of the way).

- *Difficulty judging spatial relationships.* Young children may incorrectly estimate the height of a piece of equipment and injure themselves jumping.

- *Lack of attention to what is going on around them.* Young children may not notice a nearby moving swing or another child sliding their way.

These factors can lead young children unknowingly into dangerous situations. Careful adult supervision—including reminders of major hazards and rules for safe play—is essential in order to prevent accidents and injuries.

Using Protective Surfacing

Most equipment-related injuries involve falls to the surface below play equipment. Protective surfacing material is thus essential. Impact-absorbing surfaces can minimize both the frequency and severity of injuries. Asphalt and grass or soil do not provide adequate protection against falls.

The best surfacing materials to prevent injuries are wood mulch, sand, pea gravel, and shredded tire. Loose surfacing materials should be installed at a depth of at least six inches and regularly raked and leveled. (Details about impact-absorbing surfacing as well as other safety guidelines can be found in the Handbook for Public Playground Safety, available free from the U.S Consumer Product Safety Commission. Requests for publications must be in writing and sent to Publication Request, U.S. Consumer Product Safety Commission, Washington, D.C. 20207.)

Keeping Slides and Swings Safe

Slides and swings are a common cause of playground-related injuries among children under six. Slides are safer if they meet the following criteria:

- Platforms are large enough to accommodate several children.
- Handrails are positioned to give children support while moving from a standing to a sitting position.
- Slide chutes have sides at least four inches high along their entire length.
- The bottom of the slide is parallel to the ground to reduce a sliding child's speed and facilitate the transition from a sliding to a standing position.
- The exit end of the slide is located in a less congested section of the playground area.
- Metal slides are located in a shaded area. (Metal slides can get hot; adults should always check their temperature before children use them.)

For swings, check for the following safety features:

- Swing seats are made of lightweight, flexible materials such as rubber, canvas, or plastic to minimize the severity of any impact incidents.
- Swings for very young children provide equal support on all sides and are free of entrapment or strangulation hazards. (Bucket-style seats are one good option.)
- "S" hooks used to suspend swings are closed tightly so that children's clothes won't get caught in them.
- Structures that support swings are located away from other equipment and activities.
- Tire swings are separated from conventional swings.
- Animal swings, rope swings, trapeze bars, and swinging exercise rings should be avoided.

Inspecting and Maintaining Playground Equipment

Regular inspection and maintenance can prevent injuries. Some programs have their own systems for inspection and maintenance, including a checklist. Some of the questions to ask during routine inspections include the following:

- Is the area free of litter, broken glass, and debris?

- Is there any damage to equipment or other playground features caused either by wear or vandalism (e.g., broken or missing components)?

- Is there any deterioration of equipment, including rust, cracks, or splinters?

- Does all equipment have adequate protective surfacing?

- Are there any hazards (e.g., sharp edges, protrusions, pinch points, and clothing entanglement hazards, such as open "S" hooks)?

- Are children likely to trip on exposed footings on anchoring devices or on large rocks, roots, and other environmental obstacles?

- Is all hardware secure? Are connecting, covering, or fastening devices in good shape? Are moving parts, such as swing hanger mechanisms, worn out?

In addition to frequent general inspections, more detailed inspections are also warranted on a regular basis.

Weather Considerations

Unlike the indoor environment, the outdoors is constantly changing, and weather influences outdoor activities. It's important for children to be outside every day, but they should never be exposed to any danger. Dangerous conditions include lightning storms, weather-watch situations, intense heat or cold, and air-quality alerts.

The daily schedule can be changed to accommodate changes in weather. For example, on the first nice day of spring or after the first snowfall, you may wish to extend the time outdoors. On a chilly, windy day, you may wish to cut back on outdoor play time. Often, though, it is adults who find weather conditions bothersome—not children. If the weather isn't dangerous, children should have time outdoors every day.

When the temperature drops below freezing, you should take precautions if you have metal structures on your playground. Children have been injured by having their tongues frozen to metal structures. If they try to pull away, they lose the skin on their tongue, which is a very painful injury. Keep some warm water on the playground in these conditions and teach children the following rules:

- Never put your tongue on the equipment.
- If you do and it sticks, don't move! Call for help.

Keep the child still and pour water on the tongue so the child becomes unstuck.

In areas of the country where winters are severely cold, many of the activities suggested in this module can't be conducted outdoors. Try, however, to give children some fresh air and a place to use their large muscles every day. Even a few minutes to run around outside can be enough.

Assessing the Effectiveness of the Area

Children's use of the outdoor area will help you determine what changes to make and when these changes are needed. The outdoors is such an important part of your program that you will want to assess and enhance its effectiveness regularly. Here are some questions to consider:

- Are all areas used equally, or are some ignored?

- Are children able to stay involved in activities, or are they constantly distracted? If so, should areas be rearranged?

- Is there enough for children to do outdoors? Are some children wandering aimlessly?

- Are there any safety hazards that need attention?

- Are there sufficient challenges outdoors for the different skill levels of the children? Are some children ready for new challenges?

By constantly observing children's use of the outdoors, you can make adjustments and additions so that the outdoor environment is as challenging and inviting for children as the indoor environment.

III. Observing and Promoting Children's Learning

In the *Creative Curriculum*, teachers take time to observe what children are doing in the environment in order to design an appropriate program to meet the children's needs. The best way to learn about children's behavior in the outdoor environment is through direct observation.

How Children Use the Outdoor Area

Because children approach materials and activities incrementally and master skills one step at a time, a child's developmental level depends on a number of factors, including age, previous experiences, and individual abilities and interests. For each type of outdoor activity, however, children go through two basic stages: exploration and experimentation.

During the **exploration** stage, children find out as much as possible about the environment. They are asking themselves such questions as these: What is a sandbox for? How do swings work? Where do we climb? Children explore the properties of equipment and materials as well as possibilities for their use. If children have never played in a sandbox, they will sift the sand through their fingers, experiencing what it feels like, how it separates, and how it falls. They will sit in the sandbox, jump in it, and walk in it to learn what it can and can't do.

The second stage, **experimentation,** is an outgrowth of the first. Once children have acquired some experience with the materials, they will feel free to experiment and take risks. Children in the sandbox during this stage might add a pail of water to the sand to see what happens or dump a pail of sand upside down to see if a tower forms. New materials and time to explore lead children to make endless new discoveries outdoors.

Individual children are quite likely to be at different developmental levels for different activities. To illustrate, four-year-old Doug, who has well-developed large muscle skills, is likely to be in the second stage of development for climbing activities. His eye-hand coordination and fine motor skills are not as advanced, however, and Doug may only be in the exploration stage for woodworking activities. This means that the same child who will leap across the bars of a jungle gym may have difficulty hammering nails into wood. Teachers thus need to design their programs to meet not only the needs of individual children but also the differing developmental levels of each child in their care.

Observing Individual Children

Observing children outdoors demands concentration. Because so many activities are going on at once, it is easy to watch children without really seeing what is going on. It helps if you can focus your observations by knowing what you want to look for when observing children outdoors.

To learn about a child's use of the outdoors, you might ask yourself the following questions:

- What play areas and equipment does the child prefer?

- Are there play areas or equipment the child avoids? Should I encourage the child to try these activities?

- How long does the child play in each area?

- Does the child use the equipment area in creative ways?

- Does the child interact with others or play alone? Should I intervene?

- Does the child ask for help? Whom does the child ask (adults or children)?

- Does the child act differently (in terms of language, social, or physical skills) outdoors than indoors?

- What special interests does the child have, and how can I extend them?

Closely observing children outdoors lets you see how children use their skills in this unique environment. And by observing children both outdoors and indoors, you get a full picture of each child's strengths, needs, and preferences. You may see skills displayed outdoors that you never knew about, discover parts of the child's personality you've never seen before, and become aware of unexpected courage or fears.

Interacting with Children

Teachers who take time to observe children's use of the outdoor environment can use this information to promote their learning. Your attention and praise encourage children to keep trying new things.

In praising children for an accomplishment, be specific about what you are praising. If a child rides a trike by herself for the first time, you might say: "Tricia, I saw you ride the trike all by yourself! You rode a long way." If a child finally pets the bunny after being afraid to get too close, you can reinforce this accomplishment by saying "Darren, it was a little scary to pet the bunny, but you did it. How did the bunny feel?" A comment like this tells the child it is all right to be scared and offers him a chance to talk about it if he wants to.

In offering encouragement to children outdoors, the following guidelines are suggested:

- *Use the child's name* to make the child feel important and unique and also to assure the child that he or she is being addressed.

- *Be specific* about what the child has accomplished. If the child's climbing skills are noteworthy, mention this.

- *Avoid value-laden words* such as "good" and "great." Say instead, "You jumped high on the pogo stick."

- *Find something worthy* of encouragement for each child.

Children often seek reinforcement from their teachers. "Look at me!" or "Watch what I can do!" are often heard on the playground. Some children ask for acknowledgment many times during an outdoor session. As much as possible, try to return these requests with encouraging statements and to praise each child—even those who don't seek it. Climbing up one rung of the jungle gym may be as big an accomplishment for one child as climbing to the top is for another.

Intervening for Safety Reasons

Teachers must intervene whenever children's safety is jeopardized. If a child is standing dangerously close to a swing or if a child is using woodworking tools in a dangerous manner, a teacher needs to step in immediately.

When intervening for safety purposes, be sure to give clear, specific directions. Yelling, "Jared, be careful with the hammer!" doesn't tell Jared what he is doing incorrectly; it only interrupts his concentration. Jared needs to be told specifically what to do to correct the problem. For example, if he is pounding with the wrong end, you might say, "Jared, turn the hammer over and pound with the flat side." If this receives no response, you should show him how to do it. Similarly, yelling Sally's name if she is standing in front of the slide and another child is about to slide down and hit her may not have much of an effect. Sally is likely to stand there and look at you, but she will not necessarily move. She will, however, be likely to move if you say, "Sally, move out of the way. Jahmal is coming down the slide." This tells her what to do and why. After the incident is over, you can remind Sally of the rules for safe play and what could have happened.

For some children the physical challenges of the outdoor environment can be scary. It is therefore important to offer help as well as encouragement. Some children will want to feel your hand on their waist as they climb to the top of the slide or to have you catch them at the bottom. Others just want to know you are nearby. If you are unclear whether a child wants or needs help, just ask. "Do you want me to...?" will usually get an honest answer.

Sometimes a situation becomes too challenging. A child may cry or ask to be helped down or off a piece of equipment. In these instances, it helps if you acknowledge that the situation is scary, providing a way for the child to handle the frightening situation. Children need to hear the message that it is all right to be scared and to ask for help. "That was scary, being up so high. Not everyone likes being at the top." You can reinforce what a child has accomplished and suggest another activity. "You had a lot of fun yesterday on the swings. Do you want to try that next?"

As you observe children outdoors, you will have a clearer sense of what challenges a child is ready to tackle. This enables you to give each child the appropriate amount of encouragement to try new things or to practice old activities.

Using Teachable Moments

One of the great values of the outdoor environment is that it is often unpredictable. Events happen to promote children's learning. For example, you might talk to children about the birds flying overhead and ask, "Where do you think the birds are going?" A child may answer, "Home." You can expand on this answer: "They might be going home. Where else could they be going?" or "Does anyone know what we call a bird's home?" This could lead to the beginning of a science-related experience about birds and nests.

Interacting with children outdoors provides many opportunities for you to question children in order to help them to:

- recall experiences ("what did you see happening?"),

- predict cause and effect ("what do you think will happen if...?"),

- compare and classify ("which one is heavier?"), and

- create solutions to problems ("what are some ways to move the snow from here to the sandbox?").

A carefully arranged outdoor environment offers so many opportunities for learning that teachers can often simply observe activities that children initiate and react in ways that promote learning.

IV. Extending and Integrating Children's Learning

In addition to observing and responding to children's explorations outdoors, teachers can enliven time spent outdoors by planning special activities and by integrating outdoor activities with other curriculum areas.

Special Activities

Many of the materials you need for special activities are already available outdoors. Mud or snow, for example, can provide alternatives to sand and water play. All sorts of games can be enjoyed outdoors. And sometimes it's fun to plan a picnic on a nice day.

Mud Play

Many young children are delighted to play in the mud. Because mud is very different from sand in its coolness and texture, it offers new sensory experiences for children. Although most teachers won't want to make mud play a frequent activity, giving children this excitement from time to time is a good idea, especially in warm weather.

Mud is often naturally available after a warm rain. If there is a garden space that hasn't been planted yet, you can let children walk in it. They love to feel and watch the mud squish up between their toes and cover their feet. This type of exploration can also take place in a dirt hole. Mud pies and cakes are fun, too. Of course, making them is messy, and you may want to set up this activity on a summer day when the children are wearing their bathing suits and can be hosed off.

As an alternative to mud play, in which children literally get down in the dirt, you can put mud in a water table or in a wading pool set up on a low table. The mess will be reduced because children will primarily use their hands to play.

Mud play can be enhanced by the provision of props and materials similar to those used with sand and water.

Snow Play

Snow intrigues children. Few children can resist tasting a snowflake or lying down to make an imprint on a clean patch of snow. Creativity enters snow play when children use sticks or their hands to draw pictures. Water colors or food coloring can also be used to "paint" in the snow.

Similarly, building in the snow is exciting and challenging. Making snow people is always a favorite activity. Children will also enjoy digging in snow just as they do in sand. Together, snow and sand can be used to build tunnels, bridges, big buildings, and giant pizzas. Sand and snow structures can be watered down for children to witness the melting process. Conversely, bowls of water left in the sandbox can be watched for ice formation.

Games

Children love to play all kinds of games, and teachers can use games as an opportunity to encourage social skills. Most games can be modified to encourage children to work with each other rather than against each other. Parachute games, ball games, trust games, and group problem-solving games are examples of games in which everyone wins and no one loses.

Many indoor games can also be fun outdoors. For example, Kick the Can, hoop rolling, Ally Ally Over, Hokey-Pokey, Follow the Leader, Hide and Seek, and Simon Says are activities that children will enjoy both inside and out.

Games using balls, bats, croquet mallets, and horseshoes are all meant to be played outside. Most young children will enjoy any throwing games involving balls or frisbees. Running games are also popular, such as Red Rover and Red Light, Green Light. Treasure hunts and obstacle courses are particularly challenging outdoors.

Parents and grandparents are good sources for new games. Invite them to share games they remember from childhood. Children can also be encouraged to make up their own games. Most children like making up rules, challenging them, and negotiating new rules with others. The outdoor environment offers children both the space and the opportunity to play and enjoy games of all types.

Picnics

A planned picnic or a surprise snack outside are experiences both children and teachers enjoy. Planning ahead will make outdoor eating go more smoothly for everyone. The most important thing to remember is to serve easy-to-eat foods that won't spoil. Here are some suggestions:

- all types of fresh fruit;
- fresh vegetables (peas, carrots, celery, cauliflower);
- juices in individual containers;
- peanut butter and jelly sandwiches;
- hard-boiled eggs;
- pretzels, crackers, pita bread, bagels, and tortillas;
- nuts, seeds (pumpkin and sunflower), and dried fruit;
- olives and pickles; and
- tuna mixed with yogurt.

It is a good idea to plan foods that the children can be involved in fixing, such as ice cream, peanut butter, or a salad. If the classroom has a garden, it's thrilling for children to pull the carrots, wash them, and put them in their salads.

Picnics are also an opportunity to increase children's social contacts. You might invite parents, bus drivers, and other program staff to join in the event.

Integrating Outdoor Play with Other Curriculum Areas

As previously mentioned, most learning that takes place indoors can also happen outdoors. Teachers can integrate learning in both areas by providing some of the same materials and activities. The experiences children have will be different in the two environments, however, because the outdoors has so many special features.

Dramatic Play

Young children will engage in dramatic play regardless of the environment, but the outdoor area offers them some special opportunities. Playground equipment brings children's imaginations to life. There are places to climb, places to sit and watch others, and new things to explore. Equipment is often transformed into a boat, plane, a castle, a mountain, or a fort, and children then assume related roles.

Children need relatively few props to encourage dramatic play. Most of the typical outdoor materials used in the sand and riding area support this type of creativity. In the equipment area, a blanket can be spread over part of the structure to change its form. Crepe paper, scarves, or other objects can be given to children to add new dimensions to the structure. It's important to provide a mix of realistic props and more flexible materials that children can use symbolically.

Music and Movement

Music and movement inside is typically constrained by space and noise limits. Outdoors, children can often be as loud and move as freely as they like. Singing and dancing to lively music is therefore a different experience outside.

If possible, bring a tape recorder outside to provide music, and encourage children to move about freely. Children can dance on grassy or blacktop areas and even in the sandbox for a different and more challenging surface. Balance and coordination are both promoted through activities requiring large muscle movement. Streamers, big pieces of fabric, or scarves add a new dimension. Children will especially enjoy these materials in connection with music that calls for large, rhythmic motions.

Children can also have fun singing outdoors. Many outdoor group games include singing and don't require background music from records or tapes. Similarly, children can make their own music using outdoor materials. Most of the containers used for sand and water play make good drums. You could have a marching band parade around the outdoor area. Playground equipment and sticks can create a lot of interesting sounds. If children do some experimenting, they will find many ways to produce novel outdoor sounds—some of which may be quite musical.

Art Activities

Many fun, messy, large, and imaginative art activities can be undertaken in the outdoor environment. The large space, different textures and objects, and ease of cleaning up are all factors that contribute to the success of this activity.

Painting is an especially popular outdoor art activity. For easel painting, you might tape paper on a storage shed or use clothespins to attach it to a fence. Tables and the ground provide adequate and interesting surfaces for paper.

Outside painting should involve a variety of types and sizes of brushes and of paper. Or, brushes need not be used; foot and toe painting are also great fun. (Be sure to label young children's shoes!) The children can also walk on butcher paper or draw on it with their toes. Mixing the paint with liquid soap makes it easier to remove.

Finger painting is fun to do outside because children don't have to be as careful about making a mess. Another means of painting outside is to use squirt or spray bottles to decorate mural-size paper taped to the ground. Using house-painting brushes and water is enjoyable for children on a warm day; they can "paint" the building, shed, trees, or bus. Large projects such as these foster cooperation and teamwork.

Drawing with pens, pencils, markers, and crayons can be encouraged at picnic tables in an area for quiet activities. The sidewalk is a good surface for chalk drawings.

The many textures and natural objects found outdoors allow for unique art experiences. Children can collect small objects for collages or add grass and sand to glue paintings. In the fall, the changing leaves can provide great color for art creations. Texture rubbings can be made on trees and other outside surfaces.

Water Play

Most young children love playing with water. The outdoor environment allows for water play both similar to and different from that which occurs at an indoor water table.

A hose and sprinkler add laughter and coolness to almost any hot summer day. Young children can think about cause-and-effect relationships as they run through a sprinkler. When allowed to experiment with a trickling hose, they enjoy watering the grass as well as their feet and hands. They will also experiment with filling up various buckets and cups.

Water and bubbles are an especially winning combination. Bubble liquid can be formed by mixing water with liquid soap and a few drops of glycerine. Large bubbles can then be formed with rubber rings from canning jars, straws, pipe cleaners, thin wire, or other hollow objects. Plastic berry baskets will create multiple bubbles when dipped into bubble liquid.

Library

Outdoor play is usually associated with loud voices and boisterous activities, but the outdoor environment can also be quiet and relaxing. In fact, nature's softs sounds can be rather soothing and conducive to reading. Bringing library experiences outdoors fosters children's love of books and their notion of reading as a fun, relaxing activity.

Children can sit and enjoy books by themselves or with a friend. You may choose to take a particular story outside for a different experience. If there is a big tree close by, take the group to sit under its shade.

To enhance library experiences outdoors, select books that relate to children's outside play and learning. If gardening is a current activity, you might read a story in which children plant a garden. If children collected shells on a recent beach walk, you can read a story about a child's trip to the ocean.

Science and Math

The outdoors offers many opportunities to promote emergent scientific and mathematical thinking. Your observations about the changing seasons, the weather, or the shade from a tree can become the stimulus for children's creative thinking and problem solving. You might point out the water running in the gutter after a rain and ask children, "Where do you think the water comes from? Have you noticed it here before?" and then perhaps, "Why do you think it's moving fast?" In this way you invite children to be careful observers and to form theories. The outdoors also promotes respect for and curiosity about nature.

Digging and pouring with sand, water, snow, or mud allows for thinking about wet and dry, evaporation, and freezing. As children play with these materials, they explore change in size, shape, and texture. By introducing a variety of container sizes, children experiment with volume and mass.

Children can be encouraged to make collections of shells, stones, leaves, or bugs. These collections can be sorted, classified, and counted. If you have planted a garden, children will be interested in the different sizes of seeds and what they will grow into. Their questions offer you the chance to introduce a range of activities—from learning the names of flowers and vegetables to measuring the seeds and developing a graph so the children can measure the plants' growth and compare their present size to the original size of the seeds.

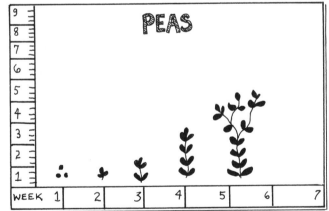

"Let's Look For" Walks

One way to help children build observation skills and increase their knowledge of the outdoors is to have a "Let's Look For" walk. On these walks, children look for specific things, and the discussion revolves around the chosen topic. Some targets of "Let's Look For" walks could be the following:

animals	things to measure
flower gardens	shadows
worms	vegetable gardens
signs	birds
wetness (after rain)	color
smells	tracks
trees	sounds
stores	trucks
water	trash

Planning ahead will make a "Let's Look For" walk a better and more exciting learning experience. Some objects that can enhance the experience include the following:

- magnifying glasses,
- binoculars,
- bags, cartons, and something to collect things in,
- measuring tape and rulers,
- a camera,
- paper and crayons, and
- a tape recorder.

Many of the objects collected on walks can be brought back to the classroom and displayed for closer examination.

As we've seen, there are many outdoor activities you can design to extend children's learning. The ideas presented here are intended to spur you to use your outdoor environment more creatively. For additional ideas, you might consult the resources listed in Appendix B.

V. Sharing Outdoor Play with Parents

Most parents recognize the importance of outdoor play and can appreciate the fact that spending some time outdoors every day is good for children's health. They know that fresh air is invigorating, that running and climbing help let off steam, and that playing with other children is good social experience. But not all parents are aware of the many opportunities for learning that exist outdoors.

Conducting Workshops on Outdoor Play

One way to help parents appreciate more directly the value of outdoor play is to hold a workshop on this topic or as part of an orientation to the program. You might start the workshop by asking parents to recall their own experiences, posing questions such as the following:

- What was your favorite outdoor activity when you were a young child?
- How did it make you feel?
- What did you learn from this activity?
- What do you like most about the outdoors today?

This technique promotes discussion of the the variety of outdoor activities and their benefits. It's also a good way to help parents remember the fun, freedom, and learning they experienced outdoors. You can use parents' experiences and ideas to explain what you do in your program.

Here are some other activities to include in a parent workshop:

- Distribute a list of interesting outdoor areas that families can visit, including nature preserves, gardens, fish hatcheries, public parks, and recreational areas.

- Talk about scheduled field trips, and invite parents to participate or suggest other possible trips.

- Discuss all the things that can be learned in one's own neighborhood or backyard.

- Inform parents about outdoor safety, including how to assess common playground equipment.

- Show the section on outdoor play in the videotape, *The Creative Curriculum,* and discuss the variety of activities presented.

Involving Parents in the Classroom

It's a good idea to invite parents to join the children for outdoor play. This gives you a chance to talk in an informal atmosphere. Grandparents and siblings can also be included.

You can also plan a "family workday" which can be an effective means of getting badly needed outdoor work done. Parents can be directly involved in their children's program while learning about specific values of the outdoor environment.

A workday needs to be well-planned if it is to go smoothly and accomplish its goals. Here are some suggestions:

- Inform parents of the date for the workday well in advance.

- Encourage parents to visit the program ahead of time so they can observe what their children do outdoors.

- Decide on a theme for the workday. Some suggestions are building a shed, tire swing, or climbing equipment; sanding; painting; and repairing equipment.

- Gather all the needed equipment and materials in advance so you're ready to go to work.

- Plan a picnic or potluck dinner to be held at the end of the day. During this time you can talk about the value of outdoor play for children's growth and development.

In addition to the ideas suggested here, you might also adapt and use the letter to parents which follows.

A Letter to Parents on Outdoor Play

What We Do and Why

Outdoor play is an important part of our curriculum. When the children are outdoors, they like to run, jump, swing, climb, and use all the large muscles in their bodies. They need space to work out and let off steam. They can race around, breathe the fresh air, look at the clouds, or catch a ball or a bug. They not only satisfy their physical needs for large muscle activity but also develop a sense of wonder about the miracles that take place in nature.

When we take the children outdoors at school, we talk about the things we can see, hear, touch, and feel so that the children become aware of changes in the weather and the seasons, the growth of plants, and animals. We help the children notice changes by asking them what is different about the trees, the caterpillars, or the sky. They lie on the ground and look up, or they climb the jungle gym and look down. We point out the many kinds of birds that fly overhead, butterflies, mosquitos, milkweed seeds, falling leaves, and rain as it begins. We wonder aloud where all these things come from.

By playing outdoors, your child can learn the following:

- to notice changes in nature;
- to discover what happens to people, animals, and plants when it is cold, hot, dark, or light, outside;
- to use his or her body in increasingly skillful ways; and
- to be a good observer.

When the children play outdoors, we encourage them to talk about what they are doing. For example, we might say:

- "What happened to the sun just now? I don't see it any more."
- "What is making the trees bend over the way they are today?"

We also ask questions that help children extend their thinking as they play outdoors. For example, we might say:

- "What happened to the water in this pan? It's hard now. What do we need to do to make it pour?"
- "If you keep digging your hole, how far down can you go?"

What You Can Do at Home

You can provide wooden boxes and boards for playhouses or an obstacle course; gardening tools to dig, plant, and cultivate a little garden; a big paintbrush and a pail of water to "paint" walls or fences; large balls to kick or throw; or old blankets or sheets to make a tent. You can take a walk around the block with your child and talk about all the different colors of cars that pass by. Your child will take great pleasure in collecting rocks, finding bugs, watching birds and airplanes in the sky, or pretending to go camping.

You can try some of these ideas with your child outdoors at home or on a trip to the park, the beach, the woods, or wherever you can find a place to run. Playing outdoors is fun for parents and children and enhances children's learning in many important ways.

APPENDICES

The *Creative Curriculum* Child Development and Learning Checklist

In the *Creative Curriculum* teachers develop plans to promote each child's socio-emotional, cognitive, and physical development by building on individual strengths and interests. To do so, teachers must know where each child is with respect to the goals and objectives of the curriculum.

The items on the Child Development and Learning Checklist assess children's progress with respect to the goals of the *Creative Curriculum*. We believe it is appropriate for assessment to be based on the goals of the curriculum. Too often an assessment instrument (such as a standardized test) shapes the curriculum. In our view the appropriate flow is like this:

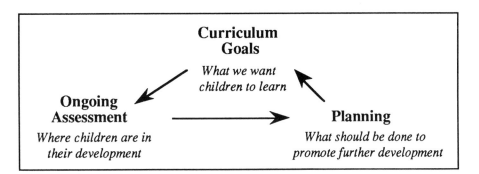

The *Creative Curriculum* Child Development and Learning Checklist is intended to be:

- a practical way of documenting each child's development from the beginning to the end of the year and

- a tool that you can use to develop a complete picture of every child in the program so that you can plan a program and design appropriate strategies to promote each child's growth and development.

This checklist is **not** intended to be:

- a means of comparing the progress of one child with that of another or

- a "benchmark" measure for assessing a child's readiness to enter a kindergarten or first-grade program. (It is not a list of skills that all children should have acquired by the end of the year before kindergarten or first grade, but a list of areas in which each child's ongoing development can be observed.)

When to Use This Checklist

We suggest that you complete the checklist at least twice during the year, once about a month after the child enters the program and again near the end of the year. It is not necessary to complete each item on the checklist in one observation period. Based on your daily observations of each child over a period of time, you will be able to complete many of the items on this checklist. If there are areas of special concern for certain children or if you find it helpful for planning purposes, you may want to make another copy of the checklist for each child in order to do an extra observation, perhaps at mid-year.

How to Use This Checklist

The Rating Scale. There are three categories for identifying where children are in their development with regard to each item on the checklist. "Not yet" means that you rarely or never see evidence of each skill. "Sometimes" means that you have seen some evidence of the skill. "Often" indicates that the skill or behavior is one that the child has mastered and demonstrates regularly.

Examples. The checklist includes skills and abilities that may show up in any area of the room and in a wide range of activities. The examples provided for each item are intended *only* **to suggest some of the kinds of behaviors** that might reflect a child's development in a given area.

For instance, under "Shows creativity and imagination," three examples are listed: "Finds new ways of moving body in a music activity," "Uses blocks to make a telephone," and "Makes up a different ending to a familiar story." These are just three of an infinite number of ways, verbal and nonverbal, in which a child might show creativity and imagination. The examples are intended only to suggest the range of places and kinds of behavior in which you might find evidence of a child's development.

Using the "Comments" Section. To continue with the foregoing example, assume that Nalini is very inventive in the block area but much less so with art materials. Noting such a discrepancy in the "Comments" section is useful for two reasons. First, you recognize that Nalini does show creativity and imagination (though you might have overlooked it if you had focused only on her drawings). Second, by noting that her creativity is showing up unevenly, you may be able to help her develop or unlock her creativity in art as well (maybe she is afraid of being "messy," and that's why she has avoided this interest area).

The checklist will be even more useful if you make notes about the specific contexts in which a child does and does not show the target skill or behavior. In the item "Participates in group discussions," for instance, you might observe that Timothy talks in small groups but not at circle time. Making this observation identifies an area where you need to do some thinking and planning to promote Timothy's comfort in larger groups.

The Developmental Continuum

From the time that a child is just barely three to the time when he or she is almost six, a vast amount of development takes place in the ability areas included on the checklist. Because development is continuous and uneven across areas, we have not attempted to provide different checklists for different ages. What we have tried to do, where appropriate, is to include among the examples a behavior characteristic of the **beginning stages** of development in that area (and to list it first), along with one or two that represent **more advanced stages** of the developing ability. The "Comments" section again will be useful in going beyond "Not Yet-Sometimes-Often" to describe the developmental level of the behavior observed.

We want to acknowledge the work of Samuel J. Meisels, Dorothy M. Steele, and Dorothea B. Marsden, who developed the *Early Childhood Developmental Checklist* (Field Trial Edition, Center for Human Growth and Development, University of Michigan, Ann Arbor, Michigan, 1991). This work was invaluable to us in creating our Child Development and Learning Checklist, which uses much the same approach but is specifically oriented to the goals and objectives of the *Creative Curriculum*.

THE *CREATIVE CURRICULUM* CHILD DEVELOPMENT AND LEARNING CHECKLIST

Child's Name: _____
Date of Birth: _____

Date Observations Were Completed:
Observation 1: _____
Observation 2: _____

I. SOCIO-EMOTIONAL DEVELOPMENT

SELF-ESTEEM	Obs. #	Not yet	Some-times	Often	Comments
Identifies self as a boy or girl, and a member of a specific family and cultural group Examples: Refers to self by name and as a girl or boy Talks about family members Draws picture of self, family members	1	☐	☐	☐	
	2	☐	☐	☐	
Shows pride in heritage and background Examples: Talks about a family holiday Shares songs and traditions from cultural group Shares recipe, shows how to eat a special food	1	☐	☐	☐	
	2	☐	☐	☐	
Demonstrates confidence in growing abilities Examples: Shows pleasure (smiles, claps) in practicing new skills Brings attention to what he/she has done (drawing, building, printout, completed puzzle) Comments on accomplishments and skills ("I did it all by myself")	1	☐	☐	☐	
	2	☐	☐	☐	
Demonstrates increasing independence Examples: Chooses and returns table toys independently Washes hands without assistance Climbs a stepladder or slides down slide unassisted Selects a tape and operates tape recorder independently	1	☐	☐	☐	
	2	☐	☐	☐	

SOCIO-EMOTIONAL DEVELOPMENT (cont'd.)

	Obs. #	Not yet	Some-times	Often	Comments
SELF-ESTEEM (cont'd.)					
Stands up for rights Examples: States that "it's my turn" when appropriate Tells peer not to knock down his/her block structure Defends self when challenged	1	☐	☐	☐	
	2	☐	☐	☐	
POSITIVE ATTITUDE					
Demonstrates trust in adults Examples: Asks for help in completing a new puzzle When appropriate, seeks adult help in dispute with peer Acts on teacher's suggestion for approaching a problem	1	☐	☐	☐	
	2	☐	☐	☐	
Shows ability to separate from parents Examples: Shows pleasure at seeing teacher and other children on arrival Says goodbye to parent without undue distress When parent has gone, gets involved in classroom activities	1	☐	☐	☐	
	2	☐	☐	☐	
Demonstrates interest and participates in classroom activities Examples: Gets involved with classroom materials without teacher prompting Participates in group activities such as singing Is willing to try new activities such as a new recipe or finger play	1	☐	☐	☐	
	2	☐	☐	☐	
Participates in routine activities easily Examples: Comes to circle time, snack time, nap, or other routine activities without much delay or protest Follows expectations, such as sitting in the circle and listening when someone is speaking	1	☐	☐	☐	
	2	☐	☐	☐	

SOCIO-EMOTIONAL DEVELOPMENT (cont'd.)

COOPERATIVE, PRO-SOCIAL BEHAVIOR	Obs. #	Not yet	Some-times	Often	Comments
Seeks out adults and children Examples: Joins other children playing in the activity area Starts conversation with teacher Asks another child to join in play	1	☐	☐	☐	
	2	☐	☐	☐	
Understands and respects differences Examples: Helps another child with a task Invites a child with a physical or mental disability to join in play Interested in how people in different cultures live	1	☐	☐	☐	
	2	☐	☐	☐	
Accepts responsibility for maintaining the classroom environment Examples: Puts materials back in their proper places Throws away trash after snack time Helps to take care of a classroom pet	1	☐	☐	☐	
	2	☐	☐	☐	
Helps others in need Examples: Gives a pat, friendly word, or toy to a distressed child Helps someone pick up something he/she has dropped Invites a child to play when other children have rejected him/her	1	☐	☐	☐	
	2	☐	☐	☐	
Shares; respects the rights of others Examples: Plays beside other children without taking their toys Allows others to finish their turns (on swings, tricycles) instead of crying or trying to get them off	1	☐	☐	☐	
	2	☐	☐	☐	

SOCIO-EMOTIONAL DEVELOPMENT (cont'd.)

COOPERATIVE, PRO-SOCIAL BEHAVIOR (cont'd.)

	Obs. #	Not yet	Some-times	Often	Comments
Works cooperatively with others on completing a task					
Examples: Pours water into bowl that another child holds / Works with other children in making a group mural	1	☐	☐	☐	
Joins a playmate in making a sand construction (one scooping the sand into a truck and one hauling it away)	2	☐	☐	☐	
Uses compromise and discussion to resolve conflicts					
Examples: Trades one toy for another	1	☐	☐	☐	
Asks teacher for help when dealing with others who are less able to resolve a conflict / When a playmate rejects being the baby, suggests a different role	2	☐	☐	☐	

II. COGNITIVE DEVELOPMENT

LEARNING AND PROBLEM-SOLVING SKILLS

	Obs. #	Not yet	Some-times	Often	Comments
Shows curiosity and desire to learn					
Examples: Notices and collects objects outdoors such as bugs or acorns	1	☐	☐	☐	
Explores new possibilities for using art materials / Asks questions about events in a story	2	☐	☐	☐	
Uses planning in approaching a task or activity					
Examples: Places a bowl below funnel before beginning to pour / Indicates what he/she plans to build or make	1	☐	☐	☐	
Collects several items for a task before starting	2	☐	☐	☐	

COGNITIVE DEVELOPMENT (cont'd.)

LEARNING AND PROBLEM-SOLVING SKILLS (cont'd.)	Obs. #	Not yet	Some-times	Often	Comments
Observes and makes discoveries Examples:					
Observes that apple cider is thicker at bottom of jar Notices that an empty bowl floats and a full one sinks	1	☐	☐	☐	
Discovers the source of a problem (e.g., that the blocks on a truck are too wide to go through the tunnel)	2	☐	☐	☐	
Finds more than one solution to a problem Examples:					
Goes over, around, and under a barrier Tries trading for a desired toy when asking for it doesn't work	1	☐	☐	☐	
Uses a shovel to tunnel under a sand hill and, when none is available, uses a cup or hand	2	☐	☐	☐	
Applies information or experience to a new context Examples:					
Piles up pillows to jump on ("It'll be softer, like with leaves") Having seen teacher tape a torn book, asks for tape to mend a torn drawing	1	☐	☐	☐	
Draws on knowledge and experience in dramatic play ("Don't touch the iron—it's hot")	2	☐	☐	☐	
Shows creativity and imagination Examples:					
Finds own ways of moving body in a music activity Uses blocks to make a train	1	☐	☐	☐	
Makes up a different ending to a familiar story	2	☐	☐	☐	
Shows persistence in approaching tasks Examples:					
Works for sustained periods of time, sometimes leaving and returning to a task Persists in a task even after encountering a difficulty or problem, such as a block bridge falling down	1	☐	☐	☐	
Finishes a puzzle or task once it is started	2	☐	☐	☐	

COGNITIVE DEVELOPMENT (cont'd.)

LOGICAL THINKING SKILLS	Obs. #	Not yet	Some-times	Often	Comments
Classifies objects by physical features Examples: Finds the one in a collection of things that does not belong Sorts objects according to common physical features Comments on similarities or differences among objects in shape, color, size, or texture	1	☐	☐	☐	
	2	☐	☐	☐	
Recognizes things that belong together conceptually (rather than by physical resemblance) Examples: From a pile of toys, selects food items to play grocery Points out a fish, boat, and duck as things that go in the water Makes a verbal comment about things going together ("kites and balloons go up in the air")	1	☐	☐	☐	
	2	☐	☐	☐	
Recalls the sequence of events Examples: Recalls the steps in a familiar routine (e.g., singing "Happy Birthday," blowing out candles, eating cake) Anticipates what comes next in a story Performs in proper sequence three steps in cooking	1	☐	☐	☐	
	2	☐	☐	☐	
Arranges things in a series Examples: Lines up measuring spoons from smallest to largest Makes three sizes of cookies for daddy, mommy, and baby Arranges several leaves from lightest to darkest	1	☐	☐	☐	
	2	☐	☐	☐	
Recognizes patterns and can repeat them Examples: Extends a row of blocks alternating in size (big-small-big-small) by placing another big and small Strings beads in a repeated pattern of colors Imitates the rhythm of a repeated series of claps	1	☐	☐	☐	
	2	☐	☐	☐	

COGNITIVE DEVELOPMENT (cont'd.)

LOGICAL THINKING SKILLS (cont'd.)	Obs. #	Not yet	Some-times	Often	Comments
Shows awareness of cause-effect relationships					
Examples:					
Observes what happens when red paint is added to blue	1	☐	☐	☐	
Notices that it is harder to pull a wagon with two children in it than one	2	☐	☐	☐	
Puts more rice in cans to produce different sounds					
CONCEPTS AND INFORMATION					
Shows an awareness of time concepts	1	☐	☐	☐	
Examples:					
Demonstrates awareness of sequence of the day's activities (e.g., being picked up after circle time)					
Can anticipate what will happen in the afternoon	2	☐	☐	☐	
Refers appropriately to doing something "yesterday" or "tomor-row"					
Identifies by name a wide range of objects and events	1	☐	☐	☐	
Examples:					
Points to objects, animals, body parts, etc., when label is given					
Names objects, body parts, etc., when asked, "What's this"	2	☐	☐	☐	
Uses correct names of objects and events in speech					
Makes comparisons	1	☐	☐	☐	
Examples:					
Says one ball is big and another little					
Describes one stick as longer than other					
Makes a three-way comparison ("You have a little juice, I have a lot, but she has the most")	2	☐	☐	☐	
Uses words to describe the characteristics of objects	1	☐	☐	☐	
Examples:					
Labels object "big"					
Describes characteristics more fully, such as "big, red, round, has ridges…"	2	☐	☐	☐	

COGNITIVE DEVELOPMENT (cont'd.)

CONCEPTS AND INFORMATION (cont'd.)	Obs. #	Not yet	Some-times	Often	Comments
Shows awareness of the roles people play in society Examples:					
Plays role demonstrating relevant behaviors, such as parent feeding baby or doctor giving shot	1	☐	☐	☐	
Describes what firefighters, grocery clerks, or other community members do	2	☐	☐	☐	
Shows understanding of different relationships of objects in space Examples:					
Follows a verbal direction, such as "Put the cup on the plate"	1	☐	☐	☐	
Describes spatial relationships correctly ("The ball is under the table")	2	☐	☐	☐	
Uses one-to-one correspondence Examples:					
Places one napkin for each cup at snack time Touches each object in a row and says each number in sequence	1	☐	☐	☐	
Knows that if there is one child for each chair, the number of children and chairs is the same	2	☐	☐	☐	
MAKE-BELIEVE PLAY					
Makes believe with objects Examples:					
Uses an object to represent another (e.g., a block as a car) Builds a sand castle and puts a shell on top for the "satellite dish"	1	☐	☐	☐	
Holds hand to ear and pretends to dial a phone	2	☐	☐	☐	
Takes on a pretend role Examples:					
Says "I'm a doctor" or "I'm the mommy"	1	☐	☐	☐	
Imitates actions and uses words of role ("You need to take your medicine")	2	☐	☐	☐	

COGNITIVE DEVELOPMENT (cont'd.)

MAKE-BELIEVE PLAY (cont'd.)	Obs. #	Not yet	Some- times	Often	Comments
Makes believe about situations Examples: Sits and rocks baby doll Pretends to go on picnic and involves others Suggests a play theme and discusses who will do what	1	☐	☐	☐	
	2	☐	☐	☐	

LANGUAGE AND EMERGING LITERACY SKILLS

	Obs. #	Not yet	Some- times	Often	Comments
Recalls words in a song or finger play (a younger child might remember a simple chorus, an older child the words to an entire song)	1	☐	☐	☐	
	2	☐	☐	☐	
Follows directions Examples: Puts napkin in trash when asked Follows two-step directions ("Put the doll in the stroller and push the stroller to the house corner") Carries out three-step directions ("Go to the block corner, get two blocks, and put them on the table")	1	☐	☐	☐	
	2	☐	☐	☐	
Uses words to communicate ideas and feelings Examples: Explains reason for action ("We're putting on boots because it's raining") States feelings with reasons for them ("I'm happy because it's my birthday") Says "I'm angry" or "I feel sad"	1	☐	☐	☐	
	2	☐	☐	☐	
Talks with other children during daily activities (younger children may pay little attention to each others' remarks; older children may engage in extensive dialogue)	1	☐	☐	☐	
	2	☐	☐	☐	

367

COGNITIVE DEVELOPMENT (cont'd.)

LANGUAGE AND EMERGING LITERACY SKILLS (cont'd.)	Obs. #	Not yet	Some-times	Often	Comments
Participates in group discussions Examples: Offers a word or phrase in response to teacher questions Presents an idea in sentences	1	☐	☐	☐	
	2	☐	☐	☐	
Shows enjoyment of books and stories Examples: Asks teacher to read book Makes comments about pictures and/or story Asks questions about aspects of story	1	☐	☐	☐	
	2	☐	☐	☐	
Tells a story in sequence, following the pictures in a book Examples: Talks about what's happening in pictures on each page Tells a connected narrative using pictures as cues	1	☐	☐	☐	
	2	☐	☐	☐	
Demonstrates knowledge of how to use a book Examples: Turns pages, looking at each Looks at book from front to back "Reads" pages from top to bottom and left to right	1	☐	☐	☐	
	2	☐	☐	☐	
Composes a story, letter, or song Examples: "Tells the story" to go with a picture or scribble Invents series of related actions/episodes in house corner Dictates a letter or story to teacher	1	☐	☐	☐	
	2	☐	☐	☐	

COGNITIVE DEVELOPMENT (cont'd.)

LANGUAGE AND EMERGING LITERACY SKILLS (cont'd.)	Obs. #	Not yet	Some- times	Often	Comments
Makes increasingly representational drawings Examples: Announces that a circle in painting is the sun Puts arms, legs, or facial features on person Makes a drawing with several people or objects	1	☐	☐	☐	
	2	☐	☐	☐	
Demonstrates an interest in using writing for a purpose Examples: Scribbles or dictates a sign to label something or state message Uses scribbles, letter-like shapes, or words to make list Creates some sort of written product and labels it a letter	1	☐	☐	☐	
	2	☐	☐	☐	

III. PHYSICAL DEVELOPMENT

GROSS MOTOR SKILLS	Obs. #	Not yet	Some- times	Often	Comments
Walks up and down steps	1	☐	☐	☐	
	2	☐	☐	☐	
Climbs up and down equipment without falling	1	☐	☐	☐	
	2	☐	☐	☐	
Throws an object in the intended direction	1	☐	☐	☐	
	2	☐	☐	☐	

PHYSICAL DEVELOPMENT (cont'd.)

GROSS MOTOR SKILLS (cont'd.)	Obs. #	Not yet	Some- times	Often	Comments
Catches a ball or beanbag	1	☐	☐	☐	
	2	☐	☐	☐	
Runs with control over direction and speed	1	☐	☐	☐	
	2	☐	☐	☐	
Jumps off low surfaces and over objects without falling	1	☐	☐	☐	
	2	☐	☐	☐	
Rides and steers a tricycle	1	☐	☐	☐	
	2	☐	☐	☐	
Shows balance in use of large muscles Examples: Walks along line or low beam Walks on tiptoe, on heels Balances on one foot	1	☐	☐	☐	
	2	☐	☐	☐	

PHYSICAL DEVELOPMENT (cont'd.)

FINE MOTOR SKILLS	Obs. #	Not yet	Some-times	Often	Comments
Coordinates eye and hand movements Examples: Puts pegs in pegboard Strings beads Moves the cursor to a desired place on computer screen	1	☐	☐	☐	
	2	☐	☐	☐	
Uses small muscles to complete tasks Examples: Cuts banana with a plastic knife Controls placement of blocks in building tower Glues seeds to make a design	1	☐	☐	☐	
	2	☐	☐	☐	
Uses small muscles for self-help skills Examples: Uses eating utensils competently Pours without spilling Zips and buttons clothing	1	☐	☐	☐	
	2	☐	☐	☐	
Uses writing and drawing tools with control and intention Examples: Makes a variety of lines and shapes in drawing Uses a crayon or marker with preferred hand and the other hand for keeping the paper in position Copies shapes from a model or letters of own name	1	☐	☐	☐	
	2	☐	☐	☐	

PHYSICAL DEVELOPMENT (cont'd.)

USE OF SENSES	Obs. #	Not yet	Some-times	Often	Comments
Demonstrates skills in discriminating sounds (e.g., pitch, volume, tone, rhythm) Examples: Lowers voice when teacher does Changes speed of dancing as musical tempo changes Stoops, stands, stretches on tiptoe with higher or lower notes	1	☐	☐	☐	
	2	☐	☐	☐	
Demonstrates visual discrimination skills Examples: Matches pictures in Lotto game Locates correct puzzle piece by examining the puzzle and pieces Finds an object or person in a complex illustration (such as Waldo in the *Where's Waldo?* books)	1	☐	☐	☐	
	2	☐	☐	☐	
Demonstrates ability to discriminate by taste and smell Examples: Comments on the taste of peanut butter in a cookie Notices that the outdoor area smells different after rain Distinguishes sunflower and pumpkin seeds by taste	1	☐	☐	☐	
	2	☐	☐	☐	
Demonstrates ability to discriminate by texture Examples: Distinguishes toys of different materials without seeing them Comments that a fabric is soft, scratchy, smooth, bumpy	1	☐	☐	☐	
	2	☐	☐	☐	

Dear Teacher,

The *Creative Curriculum* Child Development and Learning Checklist is a new addition to the revised curriculum. It was developed in response to a need expressed by many teachers for a developmentally appropriate way of assessing children's progress. The items in the checklist stem directly from the Curriculum's goals.

Because this instrument is new for us as well as for you, we'd very much appreciate getting some feedback from you on its usefulness and applicability. Please take a moment to fill out this questionnaire and return it to us at the address below at your convenience. Thank you.

Send to: Teaching Strategies, PO Box 42243, Washington, DC 20015

****

1. Grade/age group taught _____   No. of children in group _____

2. Number of children assessed using this checklist _____

3. Number of times checklist completed on each child _____

4. Do you have a need for a checklist such as this? Please explain.

    _____

    _____

5. How easy was the checklist to use? Would further explanation have been helpful?

    _____

    _____

6. How did you use the checklist (e.g., before parent conferences, as a planning tool, etc.)?

    _____

    _____

7. Were the examples appropriate? Were sufficient examples provided?

    _____

    _____

8. Does this instrument serve your program's needs for assessment? If not, what else is needed?

    _____

    _____

9. Any other comments you would like to provide about the checklist are welcomed.

    _____

    _____

    _____

Resources for Further Reading

Setting the Stage

Beaty, Janice J. *Observing Development of the Young Child.* Columbus, OH: Charles E. Merrill, 1986.

Bredekamp, Sue (ed.). *Developmentally Appropriate Practice in Programs Serving Children Birth Through Age 8.* Washington, DC: National Association for the Education of Young Children, 1987.

Cohen, Dorothy H., Virginia Stern and Nancy Balaban. *Observing and Recording the Behavior of Young Children, 3rd ed.* New York: Teachers College Press (Columbia University), 1983.

Derman-Sparks, Louise, and the A.B.C. Task Force. *Anti-Bias Curriculum: Tools for Empowering Young Children.* Washington, DC: National Association for the Education of Young Children, 1989.

Elkind, David. *Miseducation: Preschoolers at Risk.* New York: Knopf, 1987.

Elkind, David, *The Hurried Child: Growing Up Too Fast.* Reading, MA: Addison-Wesley, 1981.

Feeney, Stephanie, Doris Christensen, and Eva Moravcik. *Who Am I in the Lives of Children? An Introduction to Teaching Young Children, 4th ed.* Columbus, OH: Charles E. Merrill, 1991.

Greenman, Jim. *Caring Spaces, Learning Places: Environments That Work.* Redmond, WA: Exchange Press, 1988.

Katz, Lilian G., and Sylvia C. Chard. *Engaging Children's Minds: The Project Approach.* Norwood, NJ: Ablex, 1989.

Leeper, Sarah, D. Skipper, and R. Witherspoon. *Good Schools for Young Children, 5th ed.* New York: Macmillan, 1984.

Meisels, Samuel J. *Developmental Screening in Early Childhood: A Guide, 3rd ed.* Washington, DC: National Association for the Education of Young Children, 1989.

McKee, Judith Spitler, (ed.). *The Developing Kindergarten: Programs, Children, and Teachers.* East Lansing, MI: Michigan Association for the Education of Young Children, 1990.

Read, Katherine. *Early Childhood Programs: Human Relationships and Learning, 8th ed.* New York: Holt, Rinehart, 1987.

Seefeldt, Carol, and Nita Barbouer, *Early Childhood Education: An Introduction.* Columbus, OH: Charles E. Merrill, 1986.

Stone, Jeannette Galambos. *Teacher-Parent Relationships.* Washington, DC: National Association for the Education of Young Children, 1987.

Children with Disabilities

Chalfor, Ingrid, and Catherine Bell. *As I Am*. Ellsworth, ME: Action Opportunities (through a grant from the Head Start Bureau, U.S. Department of Health and Human Services), 1988.

Cook, Ruth, Annette Tessier, and Virginia Armbruster. *Adapting Early Childhood Curricula for Children with Special Needs*, 2nd ed. Columbus, OH: Charles E. Merrill, 1987.

Sourweine, Judith, Sheila Crimmins, and Carolyn Mazel. *Mainstreaming Ideas for Teaching Young Children*. Washington, DC: National Association for the Education of Young Children, 1981.

Safford, Philip L. *Integrated Teaching in Early Childhood: Starting in the Mainstream*. New York: Longman, 1989.

Blocks

Hirsch, Elizabeth S. (ed.). *The Block Book*. Washington, DC: National Association for the Education of Young Children, 1984.

Johnson, Harriet. *The Art of Block Building*. New York: Bank Street College of Education Publications, 1962.

Provenzo, Jr., Eugene F., and Arlene Brett. *The Complete Block Book*. Syracuse, NY: Syracuse University Press, 1983.

House Corner

Curry, Nancy E., and Sara Amaud (eds.). *Play: The Child Strives Toward Self-Realization*. Washington, DC: National Association for the Education of Young Children, 1971.

Hartley, Ruth, Lawrence Frank, and Robert Golderson. *Understanding Children's Play*. New York: Columbia University Press, 1952.

McKee, Judy (ed.). *Play: Working Partner of Growth*. Wheaton, MD: Association for Childhood Education International, 1986.

Smilansky, Sara, and Leah Shefatya. *Facilitating Play: A Medium for Promoting Cognitive, Socio-Emotional, and Academic Development in Young Children*. Gaithersburg, MD: Psychosocial & Educational Publications, 1990.

Table Toys

Baratta-Lorton, Mary. *Workjobs*. Menlo Park, CA: Addison-Wesley, 1972.

Bits and Pieces—Imaginative Uses for Children's Learning. Wheaton, MD: Association for Childhood Education International, 1967.

Charlesworth, Rosalind, and D.J. Radeloff. *Experiences in Mathematics for Young Children*. Albany, NY: Delmar, 1978.

Forman, George E., and D.S. Kuschner, *The Child's Construction of Knowledge: Piaget for Teaching Children*. Washington, DC: National Association for the Education of Young Children, 1983.

Kamii, C., and R. DeVries, *Group Games in Early Education: Implications of Piaget's Theory*. Washington, DC: National Association for the Education of Young Children, 1980.

Art

Bos, Beverly. *Please Don't Move the Muffin Tin: A Hands-Off Guide to Art for the Young Child*. Roseville, CA: Turn-the-Page Press, 1984.

Brashears, Deya. *Dribble-Drabble Art Experiences for Young Children*. Fort Collins, CO: DMC Publications, 1985.

Brittain, W. L. *Creativity, Art, and the Young Child*. New York: Macmillan, 1979.

Cherry, Clare. *Creative Art for the Developing Child: A Teacher's Handbook for Early Childhood Education*. Belmont, CA: Fearon, 1981.

Cole, Ann, Carolyn Haas, Faith Bushnell, and Betty Weinhergen. *I Saw a Purple Cow and 100 Other Recipes for Learning*. Boston: Little, Brown, 1972.

Cole, Natalie. *Children's Art from Deep Down Inside*. New York: John Day, 1966.

Croft, Doreen, and Robert D. Hess. *An Activities Handbook for Teachers of Young Children*. Boston: Houghton Mifflin, 1985.

Flemming, Bonnie, Darlene Mack, Softley Hamilton, and JoAnne Deal Hicks. *Resources for Creative Teaching in Early Childhood Education, 2nd ed.* New York: Harcourt Brace, 1990.

Kellogg, Rhoda. *Analyzing Children's Art*. Palo Alto, CA: National Press Books, 1970.

Kohl, Mary Ann. *Mudworks, Creative Clay, Dough, and Modeling Experiences*. Bellingham, WA: Bright Ring Publishing, 1989.

Lasky, Lila, and Rose Mukerji. *Art: Basic for Young Children*. Washington, DC: National Association for the Education of Young Children, 1980.

Pile, Naomi. *Art Experiences for Young Children*. New York: Macmillan, 1973.

Sand and Water

Hill, D.M. *Mud, Sand and Water*. Washington, DC: National Association for the Education of Young Children, 1977.

Rudolph, Marguerita. *From Hand to Hand: A Handbook for Teachers of Preschool Programs*. New York: Schocken, 1977.

Williams, Robert, Robert Rockwell, and Elizabeth Sherwood. *Mudpies to Magnets: A Preschool Science Curriculum*. Mount Rainier, MD: Gryphon House, 1987.

Library

Arbuthnot, Mary Hill, and Zena Sutherland. *Children and Books*. Glenview, IL: Scott, Foresman, 1986.

Bernstein, JoAnne. *Books to Help Children Cope with Separation and Loss*. New York: R.R. Bowker, 1977.

Huck, Charlotte. *Children's Literature in the Elementary School, 4th ed.* New York: Holt, Rinehart, 1987.

Jalongo, Mary Renck. *Young Children and Picture Book: Literature from Infancy to Six*. Washington, DC: National Association for the Education of Young Children, 1988.

Larrick, Nancy. A *Parent's Guide to Children's Reading, 5th ed..* New York: Bantam, 1983.

Raines, Shirley C. and Robert J. Canady. *Story S-t-r-e-t-c-h-e-r-s: Activities to Expand Children's Favorite Books* and *More Story S-t-r-e-t-c-h-e-r-s*. Mt. Rainier, MD: Gryphon House, 1989 and 1991.

Schickedanz, Judith A. *More Than ABCs: The Early Stages of Reading and Writing*. Washington, DC: National Association for the Education of Young Children, 1986.

Strickland, Dorothy S., and Lesley Mandell Morrow (eds.). *Emerging Literacy: Young Children Learn to Read and Write*. Newark, DE: International Reading Association, 1989.

Williams, Denise, and Elene Cooper. *A Guide to Non-Sexist Children's Books*. Orlando, FL: Academy Press, 1987.

Music and Movement (See Recommended Resources in the Music and Movement module.)

Curtis, Sandra. *The Joy of Movement in Early Childhood*. New York: Teachers College Press, 1982.

McDonald, Dorothy J. *Music in Our Lives*. Washington, DC: National Association for the Education of Young Children, 1991.

Painter, William. *Musical Story Hours: Using Music with Storytelling and Puppetry*. Hamden, CT: Library Professional Publications, 1989.

Sheehy, Emma. *Children Discover Music and Dance*. New York: Teachers College Press, 1968.

Sullivan, Molly. *Feeling Strong, Feeling Free: Movement Exploration for Young Children.* Washington, DC: National Association for the Education of Young Children, 1982.

Trelease, Jim. *The New Read-Aloud Handbook* (New York: Penguin, 1989). Chapter on poetry describes books that are particularly rich in sounds, rhythm, and other musical qualities of language.

Cooking

Cosgrove, Maryellen Smith. "Cooking in the Classroom: The Doorway to Nutrition," in *Young Children.* Washington, DC: National Association for the Education of Young Children, March 1991.

Goodwin, Mary, and Gerry Pollen. *Creative Food Experiences for Children.* Washington, DC: Center for Science in the Public Interest, 1980.

Greenberg, Polly. *How to Convert the Kids From What They Eat to What They Oughta.* New York: Ballantine, 1978.

Wanamaker, Nancy, Kristin Hearn, and Sherrill Richarz. *More Than Graham Crackers: Nutrition Education and Food Preparation with Young Children.* Washington, DC: National Association for the Education of Young Children, 1979.

U.S. Department of Agriculture. "What's to Eat and Other Questions Kids Ask About Food." Washington, DC: Government Printing Office, 1979.

Computers (See Recommended Software and Publishers in the Computers module.)

Baskin, Linda. *Teaching Early Childhood Educators and Other Adults How to Use Computers.* Urbana, IL: ERIC Clearinghouse on Elementary and Early Childhood Education, Univeristy of Illinois, 1985.

Campbell, Patricia F., and Greta Fein (eds.) *Young Children and Microcomputers.* Englewood Cliffs, NJ: Prentice-Hall, 1986.

Clements, Douglas A. "Computers and Young Children: A Review of the Research," in *Young Children.* Washington, DC: National Association for the Education of Young Children, November 1987.

Green, Peter, and Alan J. Brightman. *Independence Day: Developing Computer Solutions for Individuals with Disabilities.* Cupertino, CA: Apple Computers, 1990.

Haugland, Sue W., and Daniel D. Shade. "Developmentally Appropriate Software," in *Young Children.* Washington, DC: National Association for the Education of Young Children, April 1988.

Hohmann, Charles. *Young Children & Computers.* Ypsilanti, MI: High/Scope Press, 1990.

Papert, Seymour. *Mindstorms: Children, Computers, and Powerful Ideas.* New York: Basic Books, 1980.

Software Publishers Association. *Report on the Effectiveness of Microcomputers in Schools.* Washington, DC: SPA, 1990.

Swick, Kevin J. "Appropriate Use of Computers with Young Children," in *Educational Technology*, January 1989.

Outdoors

Ebsensen, Steen. *The Early Childhood Playground: An Outdoor Classroom.* Ypsilanti, MI: High/ Scope Press, 1987.

Frost, J.L. and B.L. Klein. *Children's Play and Playgrounds.* Austin, TX: Playground International, 1979.

Miller, Karen. *The Outside Play and Learning Book: Activities for Young Children.* Mt. Rainier, MD: Gryphon House, 1989.

Moore, R.C., S.M., Goltsman, and D.S. Iacofano. *Play for All Guidelines: Planning, Design and Management of Outdoor Play Setting for All Children.* Berkeley, CA: MIG Communications, 1987.

Williams, Robert A., Robert D. Rockwell, and Elizabeth A. Sherwood. *Hug a Tree and Other Things to Do Outdoors with Young Children.* Mt. Rainier, MD: Gryphon House, 1983.

NOTES